friend who has taught
me much about the
meaning of love.
With gratitude
Stephen F. Brett, SS

Enemies of Eros

ENEMIES
of
EROS

**How the
sexual revolution
is killing family,
marriage, and sex
and what we can do
about it**

MAGGIE GALLAGHER

Bonus Books, Inc., Chicago

93 92 91 90 89   5 4 3 2 1

Library of Congress Catalog Card Number: 89-61943

International Standard Book Number: 0-929387-00-7

Bonus Books, Inc.
160 East Illinois Street
Chicago, Illinois 60611

Composition by Point West Inc., Carol Stream, IL

Printed in the United States of America

To my father, William Walter Gallagher, Sr.,
a remarkable man

Contents

Acknowledgments / *ix*

Section I—Sex and Gender

1. Totem and Taboo in Manhattan / *3*
2. Sex Acts Phil Donahue Never Taught You / *23*
3. Baby Lust, Mother Love / *43*
4. The Devouring Housewife / *55*
5. Suffer the Little Children / *73*
6. Day Care and the Disposable Mother / *85*
7. The New Man Shortage / *108*
8. The Search for the Secret Self / *130*

Section II—Sex and Justice

9. The Curse of Contract / *157*
10. Baby M: The Art of the Deal / *165*
11. The Murder of Marriage / *191*
12. Abortion and the Children of Choice / *218*
13. Child Abuse and the Liberated Family / *235*

Section III—Just Sex

14. The Closing of the American Heart / *249*

Index / *275*

Acknowledgments

That I became a writer at all is due to an unusual circumstance, named Charles Bork, who in 1983 took me to Naples Pizza Parlor in New Haven, Connecticut, and asked "Want to write an article about Afghanistan?" Thanks, Charles.

My thanks also to Aaron Cohodes, publisher of Bonus Books, who took a gutsy risk on me with very little evidence which (I hope) paid off. The very intelligent suggestions of Ellen Slezak, my editor, were not only helpful but a pleasure.

The Richard Gilder Foundation provided financial support at a key time, without which the project might have foundered. Without Susan Vigilante's help of a different kind, New York City might have been cruel, rather than a productive place for me to be.

And what can I say about Richard Vigilante, who brought me to Manhattan, taught me to write, gave me unflagging advice and encouragement, and to cap it all placed his extraordinary editorial expertise at my service? Nothing, except that I appreciate his help more than I can now or will ever be able to express. His contributions to this book were both substantive and stylistic. Any errors or infelicities which remain are due entirely to my stubbornness and not his judgment.

My mother and father's remarkably steadfast support has made this and many other things possible. And I must thank my wonderful son Patrick Sean, who not only put up with several months of a crabby and distracted mother, but whose very existence provided much of the original research that (eventually) resulted in this book.

Section 1

SEX AND GENDER

1

Totem and Taboo in Manhattan

America today is one of the most sexually repressed societies in history.

If that assertion astonishes it is because as in all cases of successful sexual repression we are at best dimly aware of the psychological pressures created by our denial of our sexual nature. Our habits of thought are shaped by and in turn reflected in a dominant culture which denies the existence of sex.

I know, I know. Last night on the Morton Downey Jr. show three strippers and one porno actress described in intimate detail the pleasures of dancing naked. This morning when I turned on the TV, Sally Jesse Raphael was interviewing a man whose claim to fame is that he has had just one heck of a whole lot of sex. (His TV ID: Slept With

Countless Women.) Half-naked women hawk vials of perfume, hard-core pornography is available at the corner drugstore, television movies display adulterous lust and pregnant teens. Even *Sports Illustrated* devotes an issue to pictures of women that might have landed a publisher in jail in other days.

Sex is everywhere. We could hardly escape it even if we wanted to, and who wants to? And yet...

It was the *faux pas* of the season. At the elegant house of a movie mogul, ninety male power players, including two reporters for the *Washington Post*, gathered to celebrate the impending nuptials of one of their own. In midst of the party, something happened, the kind of thing that you read about in books or see in old movies but surely doesn't happen in this day and age: a naked girl jumped out of a cake. And do you know what the men did then? They slathered her with whip cream and then cleaned her off, they do say, *with their tongues*.

Back at the *Washington Post*, women reporters were reportedly shocked, simply shocked. These were the men they worked with, hung out with, maybe even slept with. By day their male colleagues had professed a commitment to gender equality and full faith in the personhood of women. And now, at night, here they were, licking whip cream off them. "I am really appalled," one D.C. media woman told the *New York Post*, "...Nobody has done anything like this in thirty years."[1] Ah, these modern Mrs. Grundys.

The cardinal rule of the new repression is simple: you must never, never allow yourself to suppose that men and women are different except, as a wit once remarked, for a few anatomical peculiarities "that don't matter except on special occasions." Even inside the bedroom, sexual difference has been conceptually reduced to a question of taste, a mere personal fetish one happens to have for the anatomical structure of a person of the opposite sex. Out of bed, we have become habituated to denying all the deeper manifestations of sexuality: the frailties and powers of either sex.

The women reporters at the *Washington Post* had every reason to be shocked at the behavior of their whip cream wielding colleagues. Like most younger, well-educated men, those reporters had made a verbal commitment to sexual equality. They supported government programs designed to eliminate the sexual stereotyping that, by creating gender differences, oppressed women and unfairly elevated men. They agreed when elite women asserted that sexual differences are a consequence of evil intentions, a will to dominate, reducing women to their bodies, something quite apart from mutually pleasurable sex which includes a deep respect for the personhood of women. And yet here were all those powerful young turks licking whip cream off the body of a young woman who they didn't know, and who didn't even have a graduate degree. Here she was, reduced to a mere toy for their pleasure— and they liked it that way.

Just what was it exactly that shocked these sexually-sophisticated women? Lust. The raw, undifferentiated desire for women, a woman, any woman to which almost all men are vulnerable at some point in their lives.

But not lust alone, it was lust with a gendered nature: lust of a sort almost unique to one of the sexes and therefore not only wrong, but by our current social standard of androgyny, officially incomprehensible. Indeed, officially non-existent. Men behaving like men when they had *promised* to behave like people. And behind that, the fact that in secret, away from the eyes of women, affluent, well-

5

educated, card-carrying members of the Democratic party, were not ashamed to behave this way in public, at least in the republic of men.

If sex in the sense of gender is merely a product of stereotyped ideas about men and women, then a commitment to sexual equality ought to change our sexual natures, to remake men into something better, higher, less frightening: into people. The really shocking thing about the whip cream incident is that it hints that sexual nature may not be merely a matter of ideology, and as such amenable to social control.

Of course, contrary to what the shocked Washington media women asserted, this kind of behavior on the part of men is not at all uncommon. Men have not ceased to behave in masculine ways, nor have women failed to act in feminine ways, despite intensive reeducation efforts. That educated, sophisticated women could be consciously unaware of sexual behavior in male members of their own class hints that culture is under the influence of a powerful taboo, a sexual taboo, which has the same texture of taboos that we recognize in other cultures and in our own culture in years past.

The recent history of sexuality in America has been the history of repression, of cutting off chunks and pieces of our sexual nature in the hopes that the remaining, deformed version of sex will be amenable to social control, to the manipulation of sexual liberationists or social reformers or visionary utopians. There is no denying that sexual repression ain't what it used to be. But the shift in content obscures a certain underlying continuity in form. The new prudishness, like the old, creates a series of sexual taboos for the purpose of maintaining social control, of shaping people's character and aspirations. And today, the chief casualties of this ambitious attempt to reshape our sexual landscape are women.

In Victorian America, the doctrine of "separate spheres" kept respectable women unaware of a large part of men's sex lives. In that era, separate spheres was both a moral metaphor and a physical fact. For example, many men's clubs served as discreet rendezvouz points for the married man with a wandering eye. If a lady wished to arrange a tryst, she sent an invitation to her intended's club where it arrived, as one social critic explained, "on a silver tray, butter side down; this was of course on the chance that the lady might be connected in some fashion with another member."[2]

The social life from which women were carefully segregated ranged from the sublime to the unsublimated. At the Tile Club, which boasted members such as noted architect and party animal Stanford White and the sculptor Augustus Saint-Gaudens, members often treated each other to sketching excursions, *sans* wives. On one typical occasion, they travelled up the Hudson river on a barge, dressed like Roman aristocrats and served by "models" wearing skimpy togas. At another party "every guest was supposedly given a naked girl after the guest of honor unfurled his nude companion from a broad red ribbon."[3] Red was then as now a very popular color for this sort of thing. Later parties at White's Madison Square Garden tower apartment featured a red velvet swing on which lovely young actresses were encouraged to swing high, wide, and free of all restraint, especially clothing. All this occurred at the same time as an intense public campaign to persuade young men to be chaste, so as to save their libidinous energy for building commercial empires. During the Gilded Age, the physical separation of men's and women's lives

7

fostered two moralities: one public and officially unisexual and one private and exclusively male.

Nowadays, of course, the sexes are flung at each other mercilessly. But the new sexual etiquette serves much the same function: segregating the sexual experiences of men and women, alienating women from their sexual nature and cordoning off a separate sex life for men (of which they remain somewhat ashamed), which shocks and surprises respectable women, such as *Washington Post* reporters. Even as the physical barriers between the sexes have been torn down, psychological defenses have been carefully constructed to protect the officially unisex public morality: the androgynous ideal of sexual equality.

Today, men and women are raised together, educated together, and work together in apparently interchangeable roles. Public institutions which once hinted at gender roles, from sex-based alimony to men's clubs, are undermined, or abolished, or made criminal offenses. In these and other ways, sexual androgyny is made the dominant cultural message. Oh yes, it is acknowledged, barriers to true sexual equality remain, but these are hangovers from an older era. The central message young, educated women hear is that sex differences are trivial, unnatural, or evil.

It begins in the schoolroom, where as Paul Vitz, a professor of Psychology at New York University discovered in a survey of over one hundred textbooks currently in use, not a single story or theme celebrates motherhood, while sex role reversals are common.[4] One major textbook publisher's code of guidelines warns authors, editors, and illustrators to avoid material that "reinforces any sense that girls and boys may have of being categorized as a sex group." Women are not to be characterized as "peace-loving" or "compassionate" or "nurturers."

Among the terms forbidden under this sex code are "suffragette," "co-ed," "housewife," and "career woman." Another publisher's editorial guidelines offers as examples of the kind of writing authors should use lines like "The boys are in the sewing class." "The girls learned karate," and "Her aunt scored a touchdown."[5]

Today as always, most women, including working mothers, continue to place their family's needs above career aspirations, and we pay a steadily higher price for doing so. But riffling through the pages of your daughters' school books, what you won't see (or your daughters either) is a single image celebrating the work women do as wives and mothers. That information, a whole area of sexual life, is carefully and systematically expunged from the official cultural record. Sexual equality is our culture's rationale for denying the existence of specifically female contributions, an excuse for withdrawing social approval and protection when women refuse to behave just like men.

We don't recognize the current sex taboos as taboos for much the same reason many respectable women of the genteel class remained unaware of their husbands numerous affairs: because we are not permitted to notice it. The current version of sexual equality acts as a screen, shielding out, as a matter of mental hygiene, the cultural information contained in gender roles. As a result, even the majority of young women who are not well versed in liberal feminist theory explicity, accept it implicitly. Gender roles are intellectually categorized as a kind of oppression, carefully inculcated through an illegitimate process of cultural conditioning.

I do not know that mainstream feminism is solely responsible for erecting the new sexual taboo, but a female elite is certainly its principle enforcer. The new prudishness, like the old, could not survive without its enforcers, social x-rays vigilantly chastising those who step outside the prescribed code of conduct. And, as always, the penalty for violating propriety falls heaviest on women.

Feminism, writes Betty Friedan, for example, is "the simple, driving need to *feel good* about being a woman. . ." Who would argue against that? And yet, just a few sentences away, here she is blasting the "cynically appeasing reactionary forces" who oppose abortion.[6]

How, I wonder, can this remarkable woman fail to see that with one rhetorical swoop she has depersonalized and dehumanized those women who happen to disagree with her? Instantly, millions of women, whose undesirable political views render them an embarrassment to the more enlightened of their sex are, through the wonder of linguistics, transformed into inanimate physical objects, tiny subatomic particles zinging this way and that about the political universe; an unavoidable force of nature operating on the body politic like the law of gravity on the bodies of aging baby boomers: undeniably powerful, yet without moral authority.

In this way, on this and many other sexual issues, women whose voices do not support the current wisdom are conceptually desexed and therefore silenced. The power to ostracize has always been one of the great bulwarks of sexual taboo.

Through this dual process of censoring sexual information and ostracizing sexual dissidents, young women are kept in a state of artificial ignorance of our own, and our partner's sexual natures. Indeed, women growing up today hardly know what to look for. And so we end up in much the same situation Edith Wharton depicts in *The Age of Innocence*, where relationships are "held together by ignorance on the one side and hypocrisy on the other . . . he had formed a wife so completely to his own convenience that, in the most conspicuous moments of his frequent love affairs with other men's wives she went about in smiling unconsciousness, saying that 'Lawrence was so frightfully strict.'"

Today a conspiracy still maintains sexual ignorance. This conspiracy is not so much, as in Edith Wharton's day, made up of "mothers and aunts and grandmothers and long-dead ancestresses," but instead of elite women, magazine editors, book publishers, screenwriters, advice columnists, and auteurs who are the moral guardians of the new generation, mentors to guide young women through the thickets of modernity into a sexual utopia that seems to be receding ever further into the horizon. From their perch atop the towers of Manhattan, they send their message out, carefully cultivating that hothouse product: the modern young woman, who knows how to make money and love with equal facility and who understands everything there is to know about missile throw-weights and humpback whales and nothing at all about men. Aren't men just like us? And vice versa, of course.

Sometimes of course men don't seem to be just like us. Sometimes they get together in a group and lick whip cream off a young lady's naked body. Sometimes they prefer a hotel room to a house in the suburbs, or beg us to exchange bodily fluids without ever exchanging phone numbers. Sometimes they do not seem to appreciate that making a baby is making a long-term commitment you cannot just walk out on when you're feeling unfulfilled. And sometimes your gentle little boy starts gang wars in the plastic animal kingdom (the plant eaters against the meat eaters mostly, with occasional bouts of reptiles versus mammals) while his girl buddies clamor for My Little Ponies with real rainbow-colored hair.

But there is a solution to all these problems. Any time your perfect faith in the androgynous ideal begins to waver, you simply close your eyes, click your heels three times and say, "cultural conditioning, cultural conditioning." Between the blinders of sexual etiquette and the power of this mantra, the thoroughly modern woman may venture through the world unmolested, her innocence intact.

In the books we read, in the movies we see, in the magazines that cater exclusively to us, the firmly entrenched ideal is androgyny. They stress that men and women are essentially the same. For society the goal is the elimination of gender stereotypes; for the individual, it is perfect sexual freedom. And, for the most part, we believe what we read, see, and hear.

So when gender differences erupt in a woman's life—when her husband leaves her for a younger woman and after a few months his willingness to support his children evaporates, or when she has a baby and discovers how difficult it is to reconcile the intensity of maternal love with a ruthless devotion to career achievement, or when her live-in boyfriend who says he loves her can never somehow make up his mind to marry—it comes as a surprise.

Mary Ann Mason is a divorce lawyer, a feminist, and a former labor historian. When she and her husband settled on a perfectly amiable divorce, she discovered that being the working mother of a young child is not necessarily an exercise in personal liberation. "Something has gone very wrong with the lives of women," she wrote in 1988. "Women are working much harder than they have worked in recent history, they are growing steadily poorer, and they are suffering the brutality of divorce at an unprece-

dented rate.... Feminists have sadly become prisoners of
their own political rhetoric, and this rhetoric is based on a
model of equality which is not suited to the lives of most
women. The young women I have known as students, as
friends, and, unfortunately, as clients in divorce actions,
are unprepared to deal with the reality they did not create
and do not understand."[7]

As a writer, I never intended to become preoccupied
primarily with "women's issues." I was going to be a celebrated journalist and write about Really Important Things,
like money and war. But as I began to work on gender issues and talked to more and more women about their situations, I could no longer make myself believe that the budget
deficit is the most desperate problem facing America.

Over and over again, among scores of women from all
social backgrounds I hear, as Mary Ann Mason did, a growing recognition that something has gone terribly wrong.
Working mothers face exhaustion, guilt, and (though now
the majority) a sense of social disapproval. Mothers at
home fear for their futures in a culture that no longer offers
them either social recognition or economic security in exchange for their work. Single mothers live in poverty, or on
its edge. Women without children wonder how they can
have a family without ruining their lives. A society in which
no social norms "oppress" us, it turns out, is a society in
which not just some women, but *all* women feel culturally
unsupported, isolated, and fundamentally alone.

Mainstream feminism, witnessing the outpouring of
pain from women and children, has responded by trying to
tailor the androgynous ideal to fit human beings who happen to get pregnant. Parental leave and federally-funded
day care have been added to the official list of women's issues, tinkering with the margins of a political agenda which

is fundamentally designed to persuade women to behave like men. If only day care were cheaper or better licensed, then, at last, the average woman would throw her energies into career success, instead of being trapped by petty family concerns. The androgynous ideal, in slightly altered form, remains the crucial social goal.

And, of course, sexual liberals have a final line of defense: whatever trauma has entered women's lives through the attempt to establish the androgynous society, the benefits to women have been worth the price.

Here are some of the changes of the last twenty years: women are more likely to be abandoned by their husbands, to have to raise their children alone, to slip into poverty and to experience all the consequent degradations, to live in crowded apartments in dangerous parts of the city, to experience bad health and poor medical care, to be beaten, stabbed, raped, and robbed. Domestic violence is on the rise. So is sexual abuse of children while the sexual abuse of women has become the social norm. Reversing historic trends, women today work longer and harder than their mothers did and, under the stress, are more likely to collapse in nervous breakdowns. Fewer women can find suitable marriage partners and many who do marry will never have the children for which they long.

So what is it that makes it appear that today is self-evidently better than yesterday? The answer, insistently repeated, is that today, "women have more choices than ever before."

Choice sanctifies every pain. Choice explains all suffering. Choice is the wand which magically produces justice in personal relationships. And choice, or the exaltation of choice as the highest human good, is the excuse society has given for institutionalizing the degradation of women.

Perfectly nice young men today think, as they have been taught, that there is no degree of danger or degradation into which you are not justified in drawing a loved one, so long as you get her permission first.

But whether choice is a great virtue or a nasty necessity depends a great deal on what your choices are. What the dominant culture attempts to deny is that in very many cases getting some choices precludes having others.

I had a conversation once with a man, a man that I loved. "I'm going to marry for life," I was saying, insistently and a little self-righteously, "I'll never get a divorce." He, a child of divorce, said only, "You could get divorced whether you want to or not, you know." An obvious truth, and under the circumstances a rather rude one.

I was stunned.

Amid all the pro-choice enthusiasm raging in the late seventies, which I largely shared, no one had ever pointed out to me one simple fact: I could never marry in the customary sense of the word. For *no one* today can choose to marry for better or for worse, until death do you part. Whether a person remains married or not is no longer under his or her control. No strong moral conviction, no upright behavior can innoculate against the divorce plague. Along with the many options we have gained, a whole generation has also lost something very precious: the right to marry.

A naive conception of individual choice is not the exclusive property of any part of the political spectrum. It grows out of the very core of American political traditions, which exalt the individual's power to shape his own destiny. What is more American than the self-made man? But the image of the self-sufficient individual, that part of the American heritage endlessly promoted by the right, is, of course, a myth. It is the sort of useful social myth that points to certain psychological truths and obscures others, including this: every individual choice, from property to marriage, requires a social structure to maintain and uphold it, to forge out of the chaos of nature a space in which human choices can be made.

When society fails to protect the family, it fails to protect women. Though motherhood is an increasingly dangerous proposition, women still want children and society still counts on us to bear and nurture the future generation. But regardless of whether our determined love for our children is a consequence of nature or nurture, it is very clear by now that men cannot be counted upon to share it. Why is it that the sexual freedom of the last twenty years hasn't produced hordes of impoverished single fathers? The answer is that in the absence of strong cultural pressures to the contrary, men as a group do not find it impossible to abandon their children when the task of supporting them becomes very difficult or very unpleasant. This comes as a particular shock to a generation of women raised by men who were dependable, at a time when reliable husbands and fathers were the norm.

A central fact in women's lives today is the capriciousness of men. You can see it in the myriad self-help books with names like *Smart Women/Foolish Choices* and *Women Who Love Too Much*. These authors, frequently psychologists, generally write as though the problem is *in* women: we make bad choices either because we are ignorant or have a perverse psychological desire to be abused. What that analysis fails to take into account is the way in which current male attitudes and behavior have been shaped by a culture which defines gender as oppression and sexual pleasure as inevitably liberating.

What do we get from this new kind of cultural conditioning? A lot of men like Tony. Tony is the guy Betty Friedan praises lavishly in *The Second Stage* for being one of the emerging class of New Men. Tony is not obsessed with career achievement. Tony wants to get in touch with his feelings. Tony left a $34,000 a year job as an airline pilot in order to find more meaningful work as a junior high school teacher. When the bell rings at three o'clock, Tony is out the door and onto the deck of the boat he built with his own hands, sailing towards the deep, blue sea: baby, the fish are jumping. His wife? She works in a florist shop during the day, and then as a waitress at night. But hey, as Tony says, "there are more important things in life than the dollar bill."

Or take Joe, who lived with Sheila in a most politically correct fashion for five years; they split chores and living expenses, and both retained their sexual freedom. When she hit the big thirty, Sheila realized she'd like to have children and asked Joe to make a bigger commitment. Joe promised he would think about it, and after spending a few weeks deep in thought, he moved in with another woman. Sheila spent the next six years looking for a family man, someone like her father and uncles, the kind of men she remembered having grown up around. So far, her search has been unsuccessful. Sheila, as Mary Ann Mason writes, "is still willing to blame herself and not face the fact that men have changed, and that there may not be many men like her father or her uncles anymore."[8]

The great difference between this generation of men and the previous is that by and large men no longer feel they need either a wife or children in order to be a successful man. Men are no longer recognized or rewarded by the culture or their peers for their own contributions to family.

And husbands and fathers do not appear to appreciate, understand, or even recognize the work women do for our families.

The contract model assumes two autonomous individuals ought freely to negotiate what they want from one another without undue "pressure" from legal or cultural mores. That is rather like asking a man to negotiate with the burglar who ran off with his Mustang convertible under a system in which car theft is not a crime. With what does the aggrieved property owner negotiate? When women's contributions to society and to the family are made culturally invisible, what do we have to bargain with when it comes time to negotiate the terms of our relationship with men?

Women encounter this difficulty in very concrete ways. Lynda, for example, worked through most of her two older children's lives. After several miscarriages, she became pregnant again in her late thirties, and she wanted to stay home with the baby. Guess who objected? Her husband. "That $10,000 a year was really important to him," she said, "He doesn't see the stress that I felt. I guess I handled things well enough that it wasn't bothering him."[8]

When society no longer values our work, women are too often left with the choice of either timidly expecting less and less of men in the vain hope that they will stick around and be a little useful to us and to our children, or retaining our pride and insisting on our own independence, which means letting our men off scot-free.

It's not that men are evil, exactly, just human. On the whole, if you tell them that men and women are going to be equal from now on, they will relieve themselves of all the burdens of gender and take what they can get of the pleasures. Compound these attitudes with powerful changes in the legal, social, and economic rules which once protected women in recognition of the essential nature of our work, and women's lives will be devastated, as they have been. To a very large extent, on the other hand, men will still get what they want from women because the truth is that we want to give it to them so much. Love, family, affection, commitment, children. It is only with great shock and under the unavoidable discipline of personal experience that women eventually recognize that the currency of our realm is no good any more. Neither the culture at large nor the men in our lives consider that to which we devote ourselves to be particularly valuable.

Sex is a more powerful force than can be contained in the cool calculus of choice, contract, and justice. Contract grew up to define and regulate relationships outside family or clan, relationships whose emotional power is trivial in comparison. It is an adolescent notion that these powers can be regulated or comprehended by contractual notions of justice which family relationships by their very nature contradict. What is any healthy marriage based on if not an unconscionable contract?

The old system, whatever its defects, had this singular advantage: it tied men to their families by their gonads. I do not mean only that for men, having sexual intercourse was made contingent on offering marriage (for premarital sex has been around for a long time), but more importantly, for men, achieving a successful sexual identity was dependent on successfully becoming a husband and father. The new system tries to get by with much weaker bonds—choice, contract, and the personal, i.e. private, morality of deal making. It is precisely because marketplace mores are not strong enough to hold families together that many men but few women experience the new ideology of choice and contract as a kind of liberation.

When a culture tries to sever the conceptual link between sex and family, both are left deformed, stunted and ultimately incomprehensible. When a culture encourages men and women to imagine that contract is the basis of kinship, families are left weak and vulnerable, which means that women are left weak and vulnerable. On the other hand, when society promotes a stunted conception of sex as an inconsequential lust for orgasm, the ordinary behavior of men and women becomes an inexplicable puzzle. For if there is one truth which all of the mating behavior of men and women conspires to prove it is that sexual desire is not a desire for pleasure. The energy which we focus into love, the risks we undertake in its pursuit, are not rationally related to the sensations of orgasm, which after all, one can attain in the privacy of one's own home without going to all that trouble in the first place.

The persistent attempt to reduce sex to pleasure is really an underhanded attempt to contain its psychological power so that sexual relations can be more comfortably fitted into the contract matrix. This effort to repress sexual information fundamentally distorts our perception of reality in potentially dangerous ways. When a whole culture fails to convey to individuals the larger dimensions of our sexual nature, the result is not personal liberation but personal disaster. Women are left ignorant about and therefore at the mercy of the sexual imperatives of men, who manage to convince themselves that there is nothing wrong with sexually using women, as long as they stay this side of actual rape.

As policymakers with this stunted conception of sex and family begin to institutionalize it in law, the personal disasters multiply into major social problems. When a society bases public policy on the assumption that sex is a simple appetite, and that families are created by legal contracts, we come up with answers to social problems that are simply ludicrous. We start up sex clinics in schools to discourage teen pregnancy and institutionalize surrogate motherhood to cure infertility. We solve the problems of divorce by encouraging young pregnant teens to become unwed mothers. We dispense contraceptives to prevent abortion and promote abortion to prevent child abuse. We facilitate no-fault divorce to cure the discomforts of marriage, and proffer taxpayer subsidies as a kind of consolation prize to women for the poverty into which male abandonment flings us and our children.

But troubles hardly begin or end in Washington. When a culture begins to promote false conceptions of sex, gender, and family, the reverberations are felt immediately, penetrating deep into the least public and most intimate of realms of our daily lives.

Endnotes—Chapter 1

1. "The Bachelor Party that Shook D.C." *New York Post*, June 30, 1988.

2. Carole Klein, *Grammercy Park, an American Bloomsbury* (Boston: Houghton Mifflin Company, 1987), p. 142.

3. *Ibid.*, p. 144.

4. Paul C. Vitz, "A Study of Religion and Traditional Values in Public School Textbooks." Paper presented at the conference, "Democracy and the Renewal of Public Education," November 18-19, 1985, New York, New York, sponsored by The Rockford Institute—New York, The Center on Religion and Society.

5. Nick Davidson, "Behind the Lace Curtain." Unpublished manuscript to appear in *National Review*.

6. Betty Friedan, *The Second Stage* (New York: Summit Books, 1982), pp. 86–87.

7. Mary Ann Mason, *The Equality Trap* (New York: Simon and Schuster, 1988), pp. 17 and 25.

8. *Ibid.*, pp. 26–27.

9. Barbara Ensor Cook, *A Mother's Choice: To Work or Not While Raising a Family* (White Hall, Virginia: Betterway Publications, 1988), p. 126.

2

Sex Acts Phil Donahue Never Taught You

Sex.
Love.
Romance.
Marriage.
Friendship.

Set out in black and white they appear so reassuringly solid, objective, but in the hearts of men and women these words like so many others take on different meanings.

Take Diane. She has been married to Bruce, a twenty-six-year-old electrician, for five years. This is her understanding of the sexual ground rules of their marriage. ''We've never spoken about cheating, but neither of us believe in it,'' she says. ''I don't think I'd ever forgive him.'' Bruce meanwhile is also confident they agree: ''Sure we have an understanding. It's: 'You do what you want. Never go back to the same one.'"

Cal and Alberta, on the other hand, had a frank discussion on the topic. They came away with a new understanding. Only trouble is, it isn't the same one. "...He knows I would never countenance such a thing, "says Alberta, a forty-year-old homemaker, "I trust him...I am sure we understand each other." Cal, a forty-one-year-old insurance executive, reports based on the same conversation, "I believe that if I was very discreet and didn't do anything serious, she could live through it. So it might be sometime that extreme discretion might allow an experiment."[1]

Men and women don't speak the same language. We go about talking to each other using the same words in the same syntactical structure and assume the message gets across. A dangerous assumption. A wealth of feminist research documents the influence that gender has in structuring and interpreting experience, especially interpersonal relationships. In *Women's Ways of Knowing,* four women scholars sum up recent findings: "Anecdotal reports as well as research on sex differences indicate that girls and women have more difficulty than boys and men in asserting their authority or considering themselves as authorities (Clance and Imes 1978; Cross 1968; Maccoby and Jacklin 1974; Piliavin 1976; West and Zimmerman 1983); in expressing themselves in public so that others will listen (Aries 1976; Eakins and Eakins 1976; Piliavin 1976; Sadker and Sadker 1982, 1985; Swacker 1976; Thorne 1979); in gaining respect of teachers for their minds and ideas (Hagen and Kahn 1975; Hall and Sandler 1982; Serbin, O'Leary, Kent, and Tonick 1973); and in fully utilizing their capabilities and training in the world of work (Gallese 1985;

Kanter 1977; Ruddick and Daniels 1977; Sassen 1980; Treichler and Kramarae 1983)."[2]

Recently, feminist scholars such as Carol Gilligan have begun to explore, with varying degrees of sympathy, differences between male and female's interpretation of similar events. Others, like Nancy Chodorow in *The Reproduction of Mothering*, have documented how resistant gender differences have been to current efforts at social manipulation.

Sex differences, however ubiquitous, can go unnoticed for long periods of time, however, because of the natural human tendency to assume that all people are alike. That is, like me.

One of the intriguing findings of the landmark survey *American Couples* was that although both husbands and wives are sexually possessive, women are a bit more possessive than men. The numbers aren't large, but the margins are impressive: 25 percent more husbands than wives (12 percent versus 9 percent) claim they wouldn't have a snit-fit if their spouse strayed once in a while.[3]

What *are* these men thinking about? Hasn't anyone told them that a real man is macho, territorial, ready to kill anyone who so much as looks at his wife?

Yet, "Many a man assured us that his relationship would survive an outside 'fling,'" report Pepper Schwartz and Phillip Blumstein. "Such men are so certain that they can enjoy sex without romantic entanglement, they assume that if the 'worst' happened and their partners were 'unfaithful,' they, too, could put sex in its proper perspective and not endanger the relationship. We think some men are less possessive than women, in part, because they do not really expect women to be nonmonogamous, [i.e. unfaithful] and they misjudge women's capacity for sex without love."[4] In other words, men project onto women their own sexual responses.

But men and women have vastly different tolerances for uncommitted sex. As one husband of nine years confesses: "For a man, sex is a physical thing and it can be as impersonal and as casual as shaking somebody's hand or eating a sandwich."[5] When asked by Blumstein and Schwartz "If you were involved in a relationship with someone, what would be your attitude toward having sex with someone you had just met and whom you could expect never to see again?" Only 20 percent of heterosexual women said okay, while 34 percent of heterosexual men said why not, and another 40 percent said, yes, but. Fifty-two percent of husbands, but only 37 percent of wives, approve of sex without love. (This is not only a moral but also a sensible response on our part, since the evidence suggests that, for many women, sex outside a committed relationship is not only emotionally empty but physically unsatisfying as well.)[6]

When "marriage partners" assume they are interchangeable units, they remain ignorant of each other's sexual nature, and frequently the state of their marriage as well. This may help explain why one study found unhappily married couples were more likely to *agree* rather than disagree on equal roles for husbands and wives.[7]

Many gender differences are less salacious and more subtle. Take communication, for example. Men are the chattering sex, outtalking females in intramural conversations by an average ratio of two to one. Men also interrupt more frequently; they listen more passively, while women frequently interject little verbal and nonverbal cues to indicate interest.[8]

We nod our heads, say "uh-uh," and ask little leading

questions to let the talker know we're really all ears. If you want to see an extreme form of this kind of male-female interaction, go to Tokyo. A Japanese woman is not inscrutable. As she listens to a Japanese man speak, she stares intently into his eyes, smiles incessantly, bobs her head up and down like a peculiarly graceful pigeon, and interjects a cooing *hai, hai* (yes, yes) about every other word. And it all looks perfectly sincere.

And you wonder why women frequently say their husbands don't listen, a complaint which leaves men utterly mystified. Here you are describing how your beloved childhood dachshund, Pistachio, happened upon the neighborhood pit bull and became canine chewing gum; there he is sitting perfectly quiet, staring into space. He undoubtedly thinks he's being as understanding as Dr. Joyce Brothers, but *you* have no idea whether he's really interested in what you're saying, listening with heroic resignation, or raptly contemplating the sixteen-year-old neighbor sunbathing in her itsy-bitsy-teeny-weeny on the lawn across the street.

The strength and persistence of gender differences has created a real problem for those committed to an androgynous vision of sexual equality. It is certainly true, as the prevailing wisdom says, that gender is socially constructed. Unlike the yellow-bellied sapsucker, humans don't come equipped with colorful courtship displays; we have to invent them. Scientists haven't yet uncovered a hormone that triggers an irresistible impulse to put on high heels and boogie.

To deny that gender is influenced by cultural mores would be absurd. Ideals of female attractiveness vary widely and change with breathtaking speed. In the fifties, fashionable women wore girdles to disguise their natural contours, and padded brassieres to enhance them. In the sixties, women tore off both girdles and bras and let it all hang out.

All which goes to show that human beings are not ants; we are not born with the software already inserted, precisely programmed with the intricate behavior patterns that will insure individual, or at least racial, survival. Call it free will or a paucity of innate behaviors, this universal flexibility, man's powerful ability to learn, accounts for the magnificent diversity in human customs and the tragic fragility of societal mores, the breathtaking rapidity with which the cultures that have survived a millennium can collapse. In human beings, sexual instincts, like all other natural impulses, are given distinctive shape by culture. And the artful form a biological urge assumes and is satisfied by, unquestionably varies widely over time and between societies.

Because gender *is*, in this sense, learned behavior, a culture which acknowledges sexual differences inevitably tends to reproduce them. Little girls and boys who encounter sex differences in the adults around them strive to acquire gender for themselves. Monkey see, monkey do. In this way gender differences are socially reproduced from one generation to the next. When gender itself comes to be experienced as oppressive, there is only one solution: Lie.

Purge sexual stereotypes from textbooks, movies, and other cultural images, denounce sexist language, tirelessly repeat that men and women are alike and if they aren't, it's because women have been oppressed, a temporary condition from which they (we) will soon recover because, after all, as Catharine Mackinnon asks, ''can you imagine elevating one half of a population and denigrating the other half and producing a population in which everyone is the same?''[9]

There's one problem with this formula. The androgynous ideal offers a disguised affront to women. Its promoters announce, in essence, that there is something wrong with female values, preferences, and desires, but not to worry: they can make us better than we were before. More ambitious, more powerful, less weak and above all, less dependent. (Independence has become something of a national obsession, the virtue par excellence. Even toddlers are now praised for learning to stand on their own two hands-and-feet.)

Sometimes, by way of evenhandedness, sexual liberals also remark in a desultory way that men should become more like women. But it's never a very convincing pitch. When have sugar and spice ever gotten anyone anything really nice, like a corporate vice-presidency? And if femininity has been degrading for women, what's it going to be like for *men*?

But for real women enmeshed in real lives, the myth of androgyny is not just insulting, it's dangerous. Even if sexual liberals were correct and by ceaselessly propagandizing the new generation a gender-free society can be created, in the short run, we, the new generation, get screwed.

Young women today experience the enormous stress of cognitive dissonance. A gaping canyon is opening up between the world as we've been taught to see it, and the world as we actually experience it in everyday life. As feminist lawyer Mary Ann Mason writes, ''Today's young women, as the inheritors of the egalitarian revolution, find the gap between their expectations and their everyday lives to be profoundly troubling.''[10]

Sex is a powerful force more easily repressed from

consciousness than actually transcended. Sexual ignorance isn't bliss. When women assume that we are just like men, or worse, that men are just like us, we court disaster.

Women haven't stopped behaving in feminine ways just because it's no longer chic to admit to it. Today, in fact, young women engage in what amounts to a painful parody of feminine behavior, catering to male sexual whims and desires to an extent unheard of in our mother's day; our mothers would have had more self-respect; they would have known, because they had been told, that an issue of self-respect was involved.

Brenda is a sales rep in her mid-twenties based in Oregon. Her boyfriend recently relocated to the East Coast and asked her to move with him. Like most educated women today, Brenda considers herself equal to any man. So why is she thinking of quitting her job and moving across a continent? She calls it, "taking a risk for love." I call it building your life around a man who has never promised to do anything of the kind for you.

The modern woman's new submissiveness is often disguised, even to herself, by the language of liberation. She's bold, she's brave, she's flouting convention, sexually "liberated" enough to do exactly what her man wants, no questions asked.

Modern reasoning goes something like this: if a woman insists on something from a man, like commitment, then she *needs* something from him, and if she needs something from a man then she is *dependent* on him, and if she's dependent on a man, well, that's a disgusting and degrading thing to be, isn't it? Consequently, women who stand up for their own needs frequently acquire a nasty set of labels: demanding, husband-hunting, dependent, hung-up, clinging.

Mademoiselle magazine is one of the most widely-read magazines for young women, with a circulation in 1988 of 1,121,336. It caters to single women who either are or want to be part of the female elite. Forty percent of its readers are either college graduates or currently attending college. Another 30 percent have had some college.

The September 1988 issue of *Mademoiselle* grappled with the growing phenomenon of the Almost-Husband— the man who looks like a husband, acts like a husband, gets all the benefits of being a husband, but just can't quite bring himself to make it official. "Women's lib, it seems, has thrown him for a loop. If his father suffered from the tunnel vision that dictated marriage as an entree into adult life, today's Almost-Husband finds that every desire—for sex, children, companionship—can be fulfilled without his moving toward the word 'commit.' " But traditional women don't necessarily get the guy, either, the magazine warns, "conventionally 'feminine' women seem like clinging vines."

Such a woman, according to the magazine, is Wendy, a twenty-eight-year-old graphics designer who started dating Bill, a good-looking investment banker, when they both were working in Raleigh, North Carolina. "She deferred to me on everything," exults Bill. Well, almost.

When Bill took a job in Boston, he made her a grand offer: she could move to Boston with him; they'd get engaged "later." When Wendy refused to leave her job and friends in Raleigh without a more definite commitment, like marriage, Bill was appalled. "She didn't trust me," he whines. Bill wasn't willing to wed, but he figured he could bring her around with an expensive pair of diamond earrings. That would reassure Wendy he was serious without tying him into anything definite. Five days before leaving, full of hope he knocked on Wendy's door. Wendy told him to take a long walk off a short pier.

Bill no longer knows if he wants a traditional girl. "The confusion is I want to be in charge but don't want all the responsibility," he candidly admits.

At this point in the article, I look up from the page and start cheering Wendy wildly; I'm flipping back and forth to see if maybe I skipped a paragraph or something: *this* woman is what *Mademoiselle* calls a clinging vine?

Sue, on the other hand, would never cling. Sue is a ballet dancer who has been living with Carl, a twenty-six-year-old Wall Street consultant (and part-time swimmer) for over a year now. The night before her twenty-seventh birthday, Sue brought up the dreaded M-word. "I told her we'd discuss it in a year," said Carl according to the magazine, "Swimming is such a burning desire that if I don't go for it now and give it my all, I'll always hate myself. Being honest, I like hearing that she's sure, that she wants to get married," Carl acknowledges, "But I don't want to admit that marriage is what I want in a year's time. There's a possibility that I might change my mind." Carl's need for space has lead him to look for a separate apartment. But Sue, being what *Mademoiselle* calls a liberated woman, is standing by her man anyhow.

Cohabitation is a good example of the way the prevailing ideology blinds us to the reality of unequal sexual transactions. Avant-garde in the sixties, living together has become routine in the eighties, a sign of love's flowering. When a man and a woman share an apartment, it appears they are each doing the same thing, each taking, or refusing to take, the same risks.

But the sexual lifespans of men and women aren't the same. For most people, male and female, marriage is a key to personal happiness—for men it may be a matter of life and death. (Single men die off at almost twice the rate of married men and three times as quickly as single women.)[11]

In the long run, both men and women benefit from marriage. The difference is that for women, the long run arrives a whole heck of a lot sooner. It's not true that men marry younger women; actually they marry young women. Only 10 percent of twenty-three and twenty-four-year-old men marry women five or more years younger. By contrast almost two-thirds of men age thirty and over select brides at least five years younger.[12]

As women age, our ability to marry declines. Of women who divorce under the age of twenty-five, 89 percent will eventually remarry. Of those who divorce between the ages of thirty and thirty-nine, 59 percent find new mates. But among women who divorce after age forty, only 31 percent can expect to marry.[13]

This is not my favorite fact. Many now deny this reality, which is easy to do. If you are an enterprising journalist, just ignore the low rates of marriage and remarriage for older women, and you can prove, as one journalist does, that there is a burgeoning market in younger men into which the middle-aged woman can tap: "According to the National Center for Health Statistics one-third of the women in the United States who married in 1983 chose younger men. In 6.2 percent of the marriages, there was more than a five year age difference."[14]

Or you can protest it vigorously and hope it goes away, as one woman did in a July 14, 1988, letter to the *New York Times*, opening up new vistas for rejected older women and impoverished divorce lawyers: "Maybe ten or twenty years from now a wife will be able to appeal to a court in a divorce and ask for damages based on sexual discrimination because her husband dropped her for a much younger woman.''

Ten years ago, according to Census Bureau statistics, 18 percent of New York women between the ages of thirty-five and forty-four were single. Today, the figure is 29 percent.[15] When a couple of college students live together, pregnancy aside, they are pretty much taking the same risk. When a twenty-eight-year-old professional woman lives with a man for five years, she has given up five of her most marriageable years to his comfort. Her equal bargain turns out to have been a very bad deal indeed.

Sexual ignorance is also part of the explanation for the rapid proliferation of another species of sexual exploitation: the mistress. The "other woman" used to be considered a strange and exotic bird, a fallen angel, part of a dangerous underworld. Now she is likely as not to be the girl next door.

Monogamy remains the cultural ideal. Three-quarters of married men (and an even higher proportion of married women) say they think it is important that they themselves are faithful.[16] Yet the ideal appears to be slipping further and further from our reach. In the 1980s, somewhere between 40 and 50 percent of married men report having had affairs; for those with incomes over sixty thousand dollars, the figure rises to 70 percent. Nearly 70 percent of married men under age forty expect that they will have at least one extramarital relationship.[17]

The vast majority of these men will sleep with single women. They get sexual release and emotional intimacy, no-strings-attached. What does the single woman get in exchange? A man who not only might not, but *cannot* be counted on. A man for whom she will have to wait patiently by the phone, trying to be available for the unpredictable moments when he can get free. A man who has proven his willingness to deceive at least one woman, his wife, in order to get what he wants. Yet in this day of the strong, independent, self-respecting, educated female, millions of perfectly nice girls will let themselves get involved with married men.

Why?

"The married man solution is thinkable, however, for large numbers of women only because the women's and sexual liberation movements have had a major impact on the consciousness of single women," according to Laurel Richardson, a feminist sociologist who conducted a survey of women involved with married men for her ground-breaking study, *The New Other Woman.*[18]

The new rush to adultery is part of a broader rethinking of sexuality that occurred over the last three decades. The feminist movement encouraged women to explore our sexuality. The sexual revolutionaries explained to us that our sexual desire is an appetite which, like hunger, has little moral significance yet must be satisfied. The two movements, in an unfortunate synergism, combined to create a new ethos in which it is considered more vital to satisfy one's sexual drive than one's sense of self-respect.

But most women do not coldly choose to violate another woman's marriage, or to suffer the indignities of being a man's second-best chick. For the most part, they slip into adulterous affairs unintentionally because they are unaware of the sexual dynamics of male-female relationships.

Sex influences most male-female interactions, but in different ways for men and women. A man feels good about himself when he is with a woman he believes finds him sexually attractive. A woman, on the other hand, experiences that kind of lift in the company of a man who respects her as a person, admires her achievements, values her intelligence.[19]

A man finds it very difficult to make a distinction between receiving social and sexual approval from women. To him, the idea that a friendly, attractive woman likes him as a person is highly improbable and vaguely insulting. Psychologist Frank Saal of Kansas State University asked two hundred students to watch a videotape of a typical professor/student interaction: a woman student approaches her professor after class, hoping for an extension on an assignment into which she has already put a great deal of work. He says he doesn't usually accept late work, but in view of her extra efforts, he will consider extending the deadline. See anything salacious about this exchange? Then you must be a man.

Saal and colleagues discovered that men saw more sexual innuendo in the conversation than women did. The male viewers rated both people in the videotape as more seductive and flirtatious, while women saw the exchange as friendly. In another experiment, researchers showed 163 people a videotape of a male store manager training a female cashier. Once again, the male viewers were much more likely to say the trainee was making sexual overtures to her boss, rather than merely friendly ones, as the women viewers thought. The men also tended to think the trainee wanted to date the manager, while women said she'd rather have him as a friend.[20]

Clearly something in the male sexual antenna is out of whack. Dr. Warren Farrell, who is evidently a very astute observer, calculates that a man risks an average of 150 rejections in order to get one sexual experience.[21] Men are, apparently, rather bad at determining when a woman is actually attracted to them.

I don't know how they can have failed to notice that, as a matter of hard empirical fact, not every woman who smiles at a man is signalling an uncontrollable desire to become his own sweet patootie. But from their point of view, it seems, men are constantly surrounded by lustful women who perversely refuse to sleep with them. (Lack of discrimination is a trait common to males of all species. As Fred Hapgood points out in *Why Males Exist*, male frogs and toads will inadvertently try to have sex with males, some insects court females of the wrong species, and a few particularly broadminded male flies have been spotted trying to mate with raisins.[22] But those were the sexual liberals.) What men are apparently doing is projecting their own sexual responses onto women. It's only natural, women do the same thing in the opposite direction.

One consequence is that women vastly underestimate the effect their sexuality has on men in relationships which they have defined as nonromantic. This emerged clearly in Richardson's landmark study of mistresses. "One of the primary reasons these relationships escalate is because men and women have different assessments of the situation. 'His' reality and 'Her' reality are not the same."[25] If forewarned is forearmed, women who believe in androgyny are ripe for the plucking.

And get plucked they do.

Nothing is more astonishing than the naiveté of the sophisticated woman. "We talked about it for several months," reports one other woman, "and I only saw him after work. I told him I wouldn't mind just being friends, purely platonic, but if he wanted a flesh relationship, forget it. Because he kept seeing me, I knew he wanted to be friends too.''

Another rising young executive still refuses to believe that when her boss started asking her to meet with him alone at the local disco, he was interested in raising anything but corporate profits. "He chose it," she said, "because he knew it was close to my apartment."[23]

Recognizing that men can be sexual predators means recognizing that sex, even consensual sex, can be exploitative. If men have always been mediocre at recognizing sexual attraction, women today seem unable to recognize sexual predation. Infidelity has always been with us, but one thing has changed: married men can now get perfectly nice girls to sleep with them. The great progress of the last century has consisted in this: formerly, men sexually exploited lower-class women; now, they get to exploit women of all classes.

Just as cohabitating women deny the inequality of the sexual bargain they have struck, women who have affairs with married men struggle to continue to believe the relationship is perfectly innocent even when it is patently obvious it is not. One woman insists that when a married man showed up at her doorstep late one evening with a bottle of champagne in tow, he was just making a thoughtful gesture of friendship. Another maintains that her boss called her at home every night because he was interested in advancing her career. Yet a third believes to this day that her supervisor's car really did break down, and that he ordered a single room (with two beds) at a nearby motel only because he wanted to save the company money.

What explains this sexual handicap? Innate gullibility? Were all of us pink-ribboned babies dropped on the head at birth?

Part of the explanation may lie in the observed tendency of women to defer to men in one-on-one interactions, a tendency exaggerated of course, when the man you are interacting with is, in fact, your boss.

But the heart of the problem is the collapse of cultural mores which helped protect women from exploitative advances, by creating a shared understanding of when an advance has taken place. Single women have been propositioned—or worse—by their supervisors since they began moving into the paid work force at the dawn of the Industrial Revolution. But I have a hard time believing that in any day but our own a woman could be asked to spend the night in a hotel room with her boss—and not even know he was putting the moves on her. A culture has to achieve a very high level of sexual sophistication before it can produce women so ignorant.

The chief disadvantage of having culturally-imposed sexual ideals is that, being general rules, they cannot be adapted to fit individual circumstances. This is also their chief advantage. Moral rules function as a reminder that really, despite all appearances to the contrary, you are just like everyone else. *Because* they are impersonal, cultural norms point to the profound connectedness of human beings. They say, yes, despite how uniquely personal this moment feels, his behavior really does mean what it would coming from anybody else.

Orthodox feminism is the only intellectually-respectable political movement that is essentially moral. It is theoretically preoccupied with what kind of people society ought to produce and how we go about producing them. In practice, it also offered women a simple moral rule-of-thumb. When in doubt, try to do what men have always done.

Applied to sex, this proved a disaster. Hey, we were told, now you too can go to bars, pick up men, and engage in a little carefree gratuitous friction. You too can contract genital warts and conceive blobs of protoplasm by somebody you just met and won't see again.

Okay, gee, that sounds great I guess, we all said: legions of women dutifully dropping our skirts in politically-prescribed liaisons. Until at last, a decade later under the cover of AIDS, we've agreed to end the sexual revolution, game called on account of pain. In the end, I don't know what we proved. Certainly not our worth as women. The reason women don't make notches in the bedpost is that getting a man to sleep with them can hardly be called a conquest. It's more like shooting ducks in a barrel. Unless terribly shy, unusually virtuous, or securely married, a man will sleep with virtually any attractive young woman. For men, sexual conquest is a dirty game. For women, it is a pathetic one. Imagine Ollie North proving his masculinity by challenging Dr. Ruth Westheimer to hand-to-hand combat. You get the general idea.

The function of cultural mores, including those of gender, is to provide signposts, to keep individuals from having, painfully, to learn all of life's lessons the hard way. At this point, even a few hints would be gratefully appreciated.

Denial of sexual difference is dangerous, especially for women. Differing sexual lifespans, the differing ability to separate sex from love, the gendered nature of even the most common communication—to the woman trying to construct a meaningful life, whether these gender differences are biologically based or culturally created is a whole lot less important than that they are real.

And we have not yet even considered the most obvious sex difference.

Endnotes—Chapter 2

1. Philip Blumstein and Pepper Schwartz, *American Couples* (New York: William Morrow and Company, 1983), pp. 286–87.

2. Mary Field Belenky, Blythe McVicker Clinchy, Nancy Rule Goldberger, and Jill Mattuck Tarule, *Women's Ways of Knowing: The Development of Self, Voice, and Mind* (New York: Basic Books, 1986), pp. 4–5.

3. Blumstein and Schwarz, *op. cit.*, p. 254. "Not possessive" in Schwarz and Blumstein's terminology; 79% of husbands and 84% of wives studied were judged "possessive," while the remainder in each category were classified as "neutral."

4. *Ibid.*, p. 257.

5. *Ibid.*, p. 257.

6. *Ibid.*, p. 586 and p. 255.

7. *New York Times Magazine*, March 6, 1988, p. 63.

8. See, for example, Sally Cline and Dale Spender, *Reflecting Men at Twice Their Natural Size* (New York: Seaver Books, Henry Holt and Company, 1987), p. 7-16.

9. Catharine A. Mackinnon, *Feminism Unmodified: Discourses on Life and Law* (Cambridge: Harvard University Press, 1987), p. 37.

10. Mason, *The Equality Trap, op. cit.*, p. 28.

11. George Gilder, *Men and Marriage* (Gretna: Pelican Publishing Company, 1987), p. 65. For statistical confirmation that marriage buys happiness see, for example, Gordon S. Black, "The Life Quality Index," *Public Opinion* (June/July 1985), and Kenneth F. Ferraro and Thomas T.H. Wan, "Marital Contributions to Well-being in Later Life," *American Behavioral Scientist* vol. 29, no. 4 (March/April 1986), p. 423ff.

12. James A. Sweet and Larry L. Bumpass, *American Families and Households* (New York: Russell Sage Foundation, 1987), p. 43.

13. Larry Bumpass, Teresa Castro, James Sweet, paper given before the American Sociological Association, reported in the *The New York Post*, August 29, 1988, p. 7.

14. Jann Mitchell, "Learning to Love Younger Men," *The Sunday Oregonian*, August 21, 1988, p. L6.

15. Jane Gross, "Single Women: Coping with a Void," *The New York Times*, April 28, 1987, p. B2.

16. Blumstein and Schwartz, *op. cit.*, p. 272.

17. Laurel Richardson, *The New Other Woman: Contemporary Single Women in Affairs with Married Men* (New York: The Free Press, 1985), p. 1.

18. *Ibid.*, p. 5.

19. *Ibid.*, p. 14.

20. Marjory Roberts, "Understanding Rita?" *Psychology Today* (December 1986), p. 14.

21. Warren Farrell, *Why Men Are The Way They Are* (New York: Berkley Publishing Group, 1988), p. 126. Farrell states that men must risk being told no. "Male Message 4: *If you don't initiate, women won't—and what little there is will go to those who ask for it. So be prepared to risk rejection about 150 times between eye contact and sexual contact.* Start all 150 over again with each girl."

22. Fred Hapgood, *Why Males Exist: An Inquiry into the Evolution of Sex* (New York: William Morrow and Company, 1979), p. 85.

23. Richardson, *op. cit.*, pp. 22–26.

3

Baby Lust,
Mother Love

In the spring of 1987, I took part in a panel on surrogate motherhood at Wellesley College. Four orthodox feminists plus me, the apostate, debated the new reproductive technology and the old, key issue: the status of motherhood in modern society.

In response to a student's query, the writer sitting to my right, a childfree woman, said rapidly and with great passion, "I don't want to say that a baby should always go to the mother in a custody suit, because someday, when you have a child, I don't want you to be told '*you have to stay with that baby*' just because you're the mother."

The girl nodded her head, impressed. I shook mine and thought, but didn't say, "Told by who?" Her grandmother, maybe?

The feminine mystique is a thing of the past, baby. If five years from now, that college student has a child her friends will probably tell her staying home will ruin her mind, the media will intimate she'll lose her sexual attractiveness, advice columnists will warn she is jeopardizing her career and economic security, and all her pediatrician will say is that it's *her* decision.

And if, against her best intentions and all societal pressure, if by chance she falls in love with that baby and longs to throw herself into that love—even for a little while, a few months, a few years—her husband may well inform her that the money she can earn is more important to the family than the feelings she has for their child. Because after all, hasn't he been told over and over again? "... all child care tasks but lactation can be done by people of either sex, and a child can learn from either parent (or from other people, for that matter)."[1] Maternal instinct is a sentimental fiction, but a new VCR lasts forever.

Who can blame him? Not the modern educated woman who has a hard time reconciling the unexpected intensity of maternal love with her prefab ideas of sexual equality. She has been disarmed by her own ideology. She can come up with no reason why her husband should support her when she has always maintained that financial dependence is a form of oppression. She must alienate herself from her own deepest feelings; they are irrelevant, or worse, treacherous. The attitudes of elite women toward mothering reverberate throughout the culture, disarming ordinary women, who do not have high-prestige jobs awaiting them, as well.

Growing up in the seventies, we envisioned being a working mother as a defiant act of personal courage. We would be brave new women overcoming the disapprobation of the world, and the fierce opposition of our own husbands

44

as well. Oh, a few reactionary voices maintained that bringing home the bacon was a service better performed by men for their wives and children. But by and large the consensus seemed to be that keeping women at home was men's way of maintaining power over them. Every fresh report that mothers of very young children were moving into the work force was treated as yet another sign we were emerging from male control, forging our own paths.

By the mid-eighties, I noticed a funny thing happening. The woman who lived next door to me in Beaverton, Oregon, had two children, the youngest just two years old. One day she told me her husband was pressuring her to go back to work. She did not want to leave her daughter, but she seemed to agree that supporting her while she took care of their toddler was too much to ask of her husband. So she went back to work—as a grocery clerk.

The signs are unmistakable. You do still hear tell of a few men frowning on their wife's employment—usually Italians or fundamentalists—but quite a number of men seem to have transcended encouraging their wives and now simply insist that they work. One sixteen-year study of college students suggests that while college women are increasingly interested in finding a mate who can support them, college men are now looking for a wife who can support herself.[2] "A lot of the single men I see are concerned about having to bear the whole burden of supporting a family," confirms Judith Sills, Ph.D., a clinical psychologist in Philadelphia. "They worry that even a woman who *looks* independent might one day 'revert' to depending on her husband."[3]

This does not mean that the average man wants a wife who has a high-powered career that requires more than full-time commitment and unexpected travel away from home. No, but few, it seems, object to a nice little job that brings home an extra ten grand a year. His wife may be doubling her effective work week to bring home that unthreatening amount, but never mind that. Nor, as researchers observing the behavior of the husbands of working wives have discovered, does he feel he ought to take on more of the household or child care chores in exchange. Being a breadwinner is very stressful, after all, and a man cannot be expected to do that all by his lonesome, can he?

That is what many women hear from their husbands these days and it only confirms what we've already heard from the culture at large. Take the *Washington Post* columnist who dished out some astonishing advice in the Sept. 4, 1986, issue to a woman who, after years of infertility, had just given birth to twins. "Now I find I don't want to return to work full time until my babies are older—preferably at least one year old," she writes, "But that would mean we'd be living off savings, as we cannot make ends meet on one salary... My husband wants me to go back to work now."

Here is a woman, with not one newborn, but *two*, who pleads for just a few months at home. Her impossible dream? To devote herself to her babies for one whole year. But don't expect sympathy for your irrational desires from a bastion of respectable opinion like the *Washington Post*.

"Just as you have a great need to nurture your children, so does your husband have a great need to provide for them," the columnist chides,... "From his point of view, you have a budget based on two incomes. He might feel quite put upon if you draw one of them from the family savings so you can stay home." And don't even *think* about asking him to accept a lower standard of living, or even take a second job, so you can indulge your stupid "nurturing needs." (Next column over on the page, as if by accident, another writer, feminist Florence King, editorializes, "I am sick of women's career versus marriage complaints, and most of all I am sick of their damn kids. The women 'n' children of the '80s are a corruption of the very meaning of feminism and I refuse to be tarred any longer with their grubby, sticky brush.")

Even men who kind of like the idea of a stay-at-home wife are not necessarily willing to assume the burden of paying for it. Theresa worked part-time as a computer analyst after her first child was born. She is currently on maternity leave with her second child and her husband's income is such that she now feels she can afford to stay home. Her husband does not like the idea of day care, either, but he thinks she should be able to work at home. After all, she doesn't have anything to do all day, does she? Theresa reports: "At first, he said, 'Well, you can get up in the morning early and work when they nap.' I just don't think men understand what goes on at home all day."

"Sometimes we have friction," Thesesa goes on. "He says, 'This isn't the 1950s you know. You cannot stay home and bake cookies all day.'...He wants to be supportive, but money is just the bottom line."[4]

In these women's lives, the rhetoric of choice disguises a new form of compulsion. When social norms dissolve, individuals are left to negotiate for satisfaction of various psychic needs all of which are, by definition, morally equivalent. Your need to feel responsible for and available to your children gets balanced against his need *not* to feel responsible.

Using this kind of normative analysis, you can, for example, agree with Dr. Warren Farrell who says that while women have a primary need for marriage and family, men have a primary need for sexual acceptance and adventure. Balancing these two needs, it becomes clear that one of our gravest social problems is that the really hot-looking women aren't willing to sleep with enough men. "Selling a body outright is called prostitution," says Farrell, "So euphemisms must be developed: 'I don't feel it's moral to have sex *until* I'm in love...I feel secure...feel a commitment...' For the male these become the conditions to which he feels he must adapt—since they are not his conditions... *When women are at the height of their beauty power and exercise it, we call it marriage. When men are at the height of their success power and exercise it, we call it a midlife crisis.*"[5] Ah, the injustice of it all. We all have psychic needs: You need support for raising a family; I need to sleep with my secretary. The Id has its reasons, which Reason knows not.

When social norms that support women's maternal impulses collapse, husbands and wives are reduced to endlessly mediating between each others subjective desires. And in that kind of contract negotiation, it is not surprising that women usually lose. In her much acclaimed study, *In a Different Voice*, Harvard Professor Carol Gilligan writes insightfully of the difficulty women frequently have asserting our right to what we desire. According to Gilligan this is not because women are insufficiently aggressive, but because we have a well-developed sense of the importance of relationship.

Consider Alison, a college student interviewed by Gilligan, who "considers responsibility to mean 'that you care about that other person...'" For Alison, notes Gilligan, "the experience of personal gratification compromises the morality of acts that would otherwise be considered responsible and good: 'Tutoring was an almost selfish thing because it made me feel good to do something for others and I enjoyed it.' . . .''[6]

Preoccupied with sustaining and expanding a network of relationships, women develop a profound sense of the duty to care. Consequently, we tend to view our own intense desires as morally suspect—even where it is a desire, as in this case, to take care of another.

When being a mother was defined as an act of self-sacrifice, women engaged in it without any moral scruples. In the modern world, where children are defined as objects of gratification, a woman feels unentitled to claim for herself the gratification of mothering if it comes at any cost to her husband's leisure time or peace of mind. Trying to judge between her own and her husband's wishes, bereft of any argument or social norm that would support her own desire, a woman is likely to yield to her husband. The very intensity of a woman's desire to care for her baby makes remaining at home a "selfish" act.

The rhetoric of androgyny may give women many reasons why they can ask their husbands to cook more, or take on a greater share of the child care. But blinding oneself to sex is not much use when a wife and husband sit down to negotiate whether or how soon she must return to work; neither of the parties has the language to describe why he should be willing to do what is necessary to support her while she cares for their baby. Feminine impulses remain and continue to shape both men and women's behavior and the structures of families. But because feminine desires have been rendered taboo, women are no longer permitted to recognize the nature of our desire or to insist on the social support necessary for its fulfillment.

In the name of maximizing choice, we are busily constructing a society in which young women have fewer options than ever before. Women are attracted to the ideal of sexual egalitarianism because of its promises of ease, wealth, power, and status, a multitude of happy choices in a multiple choice world. But because of the degree of self-deception the androgynous ideal induces in women, the choices we actually receive turn out to be somehow less glowing than advertised.

The only undisputed winners in the recent social revolution are childless professional women who want to stay that way. The trouble is almost all educated women start out as childless professionals and the rote answers of sexual orthodoxy look very appealing. Then, all too often, baby makes two and the real fun begins.

Today millions of younger women are trying to live with the system the sixties generation handed down, coping with the choices they fashioned for us. Let me tell you, choice is an overrated virtue. Sure, women today have more choices than ever before. Unfortunately, most of them stink. It comes down to this: we have the option to make sterile love, or to abort all surplus products of conception. We can do these things more or less freely; any other choice is damned expensive.

When women marry, we get to carry all of the traditional female burdens and part of the traditional masculine ones as well. Between 1959 and 1983 the number of hours women devoted to *Kinder* and *Küche* decreased by only 14 percent while the collective number of hours women worked outside the home nearly doubled. Meanwhile, men's combined work hours inside and outside the home actually fell by 8 percent.[7]

And these women, the exhausted, overworked, harried, but married mothers, are the lucky ones. For today, every woman with children is only a divorce away from welfare, and divorce can happen at any time for any reason or no reason at all.

For woman with children, the effects of male abandonment are immediate and disastrous. With all the new job opportunities for women that have opened up over the last forty years, single mothers are still six times more likely than married mothers to fall below the poverty line. In fact 54 percent of all single mothers live in poverty.[8]

Nature or nurture or just plain nuts, I don't know, but the fact that *any* women have babies under these conditions is *prima facie* evidence of strong maternal desires. The fact that most women want to have at least one, is *prima facie* evidence of insanity. For the sad truth is we've managed to restructure our social institutions so that for women, having a baby is an irrational act.

In her much cited 1974 classic, *The Future of Motherhood*, feminist sociologist Jessie Bernard argued that the then-prevailing institution of motherhood combined the worst of all worlds. "It is as though we had selected the worst features of the ways motherhood is structured around the world and combined them to produce our current design." Making caring for children a full-time commitment and giving women sole responsibility for them "seem in brief, to be incompatible with one another, even mutually exclusive." Bernard based this claim on cross-cultural research that found maternal stability and warmth were highest in societies in which family members relieved mothers of much child care responsibility. A child's older sister, occasionally a father or grandfather, or sometimes a co-wife offered women respite from the exclusive burden of mothering. "In view of these findings," notes Bernard, "it is sobering to note that in our society we seem to maximize this contradiction in the role so that mothers here have a significantly heavier burden (or joy) of baby care than the mothers in any other society.''[9]

What social conditions, according to Bernard, create bad mothers? ''Another study of forty-five cultures for which data were available found a relationship between a high incidence of mother-child households (as, for example, in polygamy) and the inflicting of pain on the child by the nurturant agent.''[10] Maternal warmth was lowered by either crowding or isolation. Maternal instability also increased ''If mothers have extensive economic or domestic chores, in addition to prolonged responsibility for children.'' Bernard concludes in essence that sole responsibility for children, combined with extensive economic and domestic chores in households that are either overcrowded or isolated makes for unhappy mothers and abused children.

Oddly, Bernard's work is often cited by writers who applaud recent changes in family structure. Oddly, because by Bernard's criteria the conditions for mothering over the last twenty years have radically deteriorated.

The most obvious case is the growing ranks of single parents, like myself. Under modern conditions, our lives have become both more isolated and more crowded at the same time. We lack adult companionship while at the same time we may be unable to afford simple, middle-class amenities—like a bedroom of one's own. More mothers and children are trapped in cramped apartments in lousy neighborhoods without the time or money for a social life. Not surprisingly, given Bernard's data on mother-child households, child-abuse rates have apparently soared.

Today even married mothers—in their roles as mothers—are more psychologically and physically isolated than ever before. If women stay home, they prowl through empty suburban streets, visiting with the nannies and *au pair* girls in the park to whose social status their odd proclivity for full-time motherhood seems to reduce them. If they work, women must carry extensive economic burdens along with the full weight of mothering and housekeeping when they return exhausted from a high-stress, usually low-prestige job. Today, all women, whether working or not, married or single, whether they have a family now or are only thinking about it in the future, suffer from the psychological effects of the devalued status of mothering in today's society.

Why is it that women haven't yet spoken up for our work, for our children, for our rights? The answer lies in the mysterious power of the new taboo.

Endnotes—Chapter 3

1. Paula J. Caplan, Ph.D., *Psychology Today* (October 1986), p. 71.
2. Willie Melton and Linda L. Lindsey, "Instrumental and Expressive Values in Mate Selection Among College Students Revisited: Feminism, Love and Economic Necessity." Paper presented at the Annual Meeting of the Midwest Sociological Society, April 1987, Chicago. "We have speculated that college women today would demonstrate a lower level of interest in the instrumental qualities of a prospective husband than college women fourteen years ago. The means on the instrumental index, in Table 5, clearly do not support our assertion. The mean for our contemporary women respondents (3.48) is larger than that of the earlier, 1972, female respondents (3.08). We also hypothesized that college males today, compared to those in the past would display a greater preference for instrumental qualities in a potential wife. The mean scores for male respondents indicates that they do..." pp. 6–7.
3. "Marrying For Money," *Self* (August 1988), pp. 134–35.
4. Cook, *A Mother's Choice*, op. cit. p. 118.
5. Farrell, *Why Men Are the Way They Are, op. cit.*, p. 105, emphasis in original.
6. Carol Gilligan, *In a Different Voice: Psychological Theory and Women's Development* (Cambridge: Harvard University Press, 1982), p. 139.
7. Mason, *The Equality Trap, op. cit.*, pp. 17–18.

8. *Ibid.*, pp. 20 and 211.

9. Jessie Bernard, *The Future of Motherhood* (New York: Penguin Books Inc., 1974), pp. 9–10.

10. *Ibid.*, p. 37.

4

The Devouring Housewife

The strains of combining work and mothering have become so obvious they cannot be ignored. But there is a boogey woman out in the woods, who, when we begin to doubt our gains, keeps us modern women in line. She has big, yellow, guilt-inducing eyes; her skin is hidden beneath a grotesque growth of polyester. She has the figure of a wounded penguin, and you can tell by her slightly-stooped posture, her hideously-thick waist: she has let herself go. She lives in a cage. A wall-to-wall orange-carpeted ranch house cage surrounded by little screaming demons who slobber and spit up and destroy, who use expensive silk blouses as halloween costumes and view red lipstick on Oriental rug as mixed media art. You know what I'm talking about; it's practically a new Jungian archetype. The Devouring Housewife. Levittown as the first circle of Hell. Your mother, and mine.

Oh no, anything but *that*.

You'll catch a glimpse of the frightening demon in mainstream women's magazines whenever an article reflects a little on the problems women face today. She is ritualistically held up and shaken at us, to frighten women from harboring the forbidden thought that, just maybe our lives today are not exactly as wonderful as we are being ever-more-insistently told. No matter how bad things are, at least we are not, *ugh*, Fifties Housewifes.

In orthodox feminist literature the boogey woman is ubiquitous. I sometimes wonder how a movement devoted to the personhood of women can fail to notice how it has dehumanized our mothers. A whole generation of women can now be compared to anything from rodents to Nazis without raising an eyebrow. Who protested, for example, when a *New York Times* book reviewer recently found in the celebrations of the achievements of homemakers an ominous parallel to the Third Reich?[1]

My mother, like most of my friend's mothers, was a full-time housewife, raising four children. This is how Dorothy Dinnerstein, whose *The Mermaid and the Minotaur* is a feminist classic on motherhood, characterizes her life's work. "The captive squirrel runs monotonously in his circular treadmill. The laboratory rat rigidly alternates between left and right pathways, both leading to the same reward, in a too familiar maze. My neighbor imprisoned in underdemanding housewifery waxes and rewaxes her intrinsically shiny vinyl floor."[2]

The prevailing ideology defines the psychic structure of femininity as a psychological disorder, an emotional handicap, a set of impulses that society must attempt to recondition, like worn-out sofas, rather than accommodate. Dinnerstein, for example, identifies the center of the current web of sexual pathology in this fact: women mother. If motherhood were genuinely free, she estimates, the average maternally-inclined woman would have three children at most and devote no more than six months a piece to their exclusive care. Motherhood, she estimates, should divert a woman from more important cultural achievement for no more than eighteen months out of a fifty-year career. And if women were freed from cultural pressures pushing us toward motherhood, she maintains, many more women would of course prefer to remain childless. Nancy Chodorow's fascinating work, *The Reproduction of Mothering*, is a variation on the same theme.

Conservatives who have noticed the disparity between married men and married women's behavior in the work force tend to think of it as a female deficiency: mothers are *less able* to put their kids out of their minds while they are on the jobs. Leaders of the liberal feminist movement, like Pat Schroeder, respond that if kids were just put in federally-licensed day care centers, women could wholeheartedly keep their minds on business. What both sides have in common is that they do not think women's ability to sustain this kind of connection to our children is particularly valuable.

There is a reason for this constant disparagement of mother's work. Many early influential works on motherhood assumed that women were coerced into having families, if not exactly against our will at least contrary to our true nature and our best interests. Betty Friedan discovered (in what she now confesses was overheated rhetoric) that homemaking women were prisoners in ''comfortable concentration camps.'' Jessie Bernard argued, ''The pressures exerted on girls to become mothers are enough to explain [the all-but-universal desire to have children]. Indeed, they are so great as to appear coercive to many women."[3]

Twenty years later, after an intense antinatalist campaign, it appears that this analysis was partially correct. Not all women are interested in having children. Just almost all. The idea that motherhood is a "trap" for women is justified to this extent: if women are given the choice to defer career gratifications and devote ourselves primarily to families, we overwhelmingly choose to do just that. The lie of androgyny was invented, as it were, to give a rationale for reshaping our social institutions so that women could not safely choose family over career. As Simone de Beauvoir commented with characteristically fearless honesty, "No women should be authorized to stay home to raise her children. Society should be totally different. Women should not have that choice precisely because if there is such a choice, too many women will make that one. It is a way of forcing women in a certain direction."[4]

Thus the economic and cultural pressures relentlessly pushing mothers of young children into the marketplace are viewed with equanimity by an elite gladdened that circumstances are forcing women to be free. Right now, we are setting about constructing society so that the woman who is not very maternal and intensely career-oriented will not feel odd or unusual or experience the teeniest bit of psychic discomfort that might deflect her from her goals. Somewhere along the way, in order that *she* may not be distracted, the rest of us have become socially invisible.

This coercive maneuver is justified on the grounds that what women might choose to do, given the option, is not what is actually best for us. The official interpreters of female opinion know us better than we know ourselves: *Arbeit Macht Frei*. Are they right?

If you rely on what women say about themselves, homemaking mothers are happier than working mothers. But homemakers also have higher rates of stress-induced illness, especially depression, which have lead many researchers to conclude these women are kidding themselves. (Of course the belief that one cannot be both stressed and happy is true only if you believe that man is most human in a sensory deprivation chamber.) From the sheer exhaustion of combining two roles, working mothers, however, are more subject to nervous breakdowns than their counterparts who work at home.[5]

Researchers at the Center for Research on Women at Wellesley College have divided components of happiness into two areas: feelings of pleasure or gratification, and feelings of mastery and achievement. Homemakers, they discovered, score low on the sense of mastery (they even have more doubts about their competence as mothers) and highest on personal gratification.[6]

Why don't women today experience motherhood as an achievement? A study of the gratifications of motherhood, cited by Jessie Bernard in *The Future of Motherhood*, found that for college-educated women, raising a child, as distinct from merely having a baby, *was* experienced as an achievement, "but this depended to a large extent on the feedback they got from others for their high-level child rearing."[7]

What kind of feedback do we get for our mothering today? We are told that professional child care workers do it better, that too much exposure to us may be harmful for our children, that all kids need from us is twenty minutes of quality time.

Mothering today is a very low-status occupation. The

constant barrage of contempt we experience creates vivid pain for many women, especially when it starts at home. In 1985, Louis Genevie, an assistant professor of psychiatry at Albert Einstein College of Medicine, and Eva Marolies, a New York psychologist, surveyed more than a thousand women to determine in depth their feelings about motherhood. Among the majority of women who say they do not receive adequate emotional support from their husbands, the authors noted, "particularly angry responses came from women who said their spouses undermined the value of mothering. It was one thing for a husband to refuse to do his fair share of the work at home, but the suggestion that motherhood was not all that important...struck at the very essence of many women's being." As one respondent described her husband's attitude, "He thinks I should resume my career and would if I were a hard worker. He doesn't value my mothering—he thinks a day care worker would be as good." "I think he feels that unless I'm earning money, I'm not very smart or something," wrote another. "When our first daughter was born, he pushed me back to work when she was six weeks old. That hurt to the deepest part of me. I wanted to be home with her so bad."[8]

Women with children who do not work for pay overwhelmingly report being made to feel intellectually and socially inferior. Dottie, twenty-eight, is a homemaker with two preschool children and a third on the way. She lives in Reston, Virginia, a suburb of Washington, D.C. "Society does not support my goals at all. [It perpetuates] the image of the housewife at home eating bon-bons and watching the soaps... The perfect 80s American woman certainly needs to work."[9]

Lisa, thirty-one, has temporarily left her career as a pediatric nurse to stay home with her daughters. "Society has not made it easy for women who stay home.... The women's liberation movement tried to make it easier for women to make a choice, to go back to work or to stay home. I think they made it harder for women at home. I don't think they intentionally wanted to do that, but they did."[10]

Women who must work also suffer from the great disjunction between the amount of praise and respect they receive for working outside the home, and the contempt society has for their work as mothers. For most of these women, children and not paid labor remains the central focus, but we know that is a sentiment that is not respectable to express at cocktail parties. *Ladies Home Journal* recently held a forum to celebrate the gains women have made over the last twenty years. In the midst of the celebration of choice, one audience member stood up and pointed out, "I stayed home for the first twenty years of my marriage, raised a large family, and then became a registered nurse and a writer. I published a small newspaper. I didn't get any support from society when I stayed home, and to this day, if something in me needs some praise, I tell people I'm a writer. I don't tell them I'm a nurse, because that's "women's work" so it's not valued, although I've never saved anyone's life as a writer...there are a lot of people who need praise who are doing lesser things in society's eyes, whether it's working in traditional women's jobs or being full-time mothers."[11]

Mothers today work because they have to. The truth behind that truism is a world of pain and coercion that the rhetoric of choice and the worship of androgyny tend to disguise. By returning to work a woman sustains the fantasies of the sexual-egalitarians. She goes to work part-time or full, most likely in a traditionally female job. Women's magazines, TV shows, network anchors will laud her decision to return to work; she is a modern-day heroine, a harbinger of the New Woman, an example of female progress. The jobs she takes won't be as prestigious as her husband's and won't make as much money. (If she makes more money at a higher-status job than her husband, both of them will probably be miserable.)[12]

This is what one might call the illusion of androgyny; the economic and social coercion of women recast as a liberating obliteration of sex roles. Despite outside pressures, women do not appear to have changed priorities much. Even if a mother returns to a job in a prestigious field such as law, or business, or medicine, she will probably continue to place meeting her family's needs above ever-spiralling career success. A 1980 Harris poll, for example, revealed that working women preferred part-time over full-time work by a 41 to 17 percent margin. Among professional, managerial and executive women, the margin was even higher. Female physicians, other research confirms, see 38 percent fewer patients per hour and work fewer hours than male physicians.[13] A 1986 *Newsweek* poll confirmed that most working mothers would prefer to work less than nine to five. Only 13 percent of all working mothers say they want to work full-time. A plurality of full-time working moms, (34 percent) prefer part-time work; 23 percent want flexible hours, 12 percent would like to make some extra money working at home and 16 percent of working mothers would like to be full-time housewives.[14]

Men and women maintain the illusion of sexual parity by grossly underestimating the importance of men's financial contributions to the marriage and grossly exaggerating the extent of his domestic and child rearing labor. At stake in opposing demeaning images of the Devouring Housewife

is more than just reclaiming the value of our mother's lives.
Today, millions of American women continue to work primarily or exclusively in the home. Among married women
with children under eighteen, only a minority of mothers
(39 percent) work full-time. Some 40 percent don't work
for pay at all.[15] In addition, one survey reports that *nearly a
quarter* (22 percent) of all full- and part-time women in the
paid labor force work out of their homes, many so that they
may remain close to their children.[16]

The family-centered woman is hardly extinct. She's
just culturally invisible. Her needs are considered unworthy
of public debate; her work, unworthy of public recognition.
If elite women fail to recognize female contributions to the
family (and, indeed, contemptuously deride them), you can
forget about persuading men to do so. Instead, politicians,
employers and spouses will increasingly assume that
women at home with children are frolicking on an extended
vacation at their husband's expense.

Sex roles are extremely stubborn. Women *have*
changed in response to the devaluation of motherhood.
We're having fewer babies, later in life and, in many cases,
returning to work a few weeks after they are born. What
hasn't changed is that for most mothers, even and especially those of us who work full-time, work comes second.

These family priorities are not confirmed to lower-class women, to the presumed brainwashed and brain dead
housewife with a high school diploma and few prospects.
Indeed, for college-educated women there is a direct, inverse relationship between the earnings of the husband and
the employment status of the wife. Even though educated
women are more likely to work than the average women,
the employment rates of married educated women decline
rapidly as the husband's income rises. Almost two-thirds of

college-educated women with husbands making less than
$20,000 work. When the husband's income rises to
$40,000 or more, the percentage of working wives plum-
mets to less than half.[17] In a similar vein, Jill Abramson and
Barbara Franklin's 1986 study of the women of Harvard
Law School's Class of '74, an unusually ambitious group,
found that fourteen of the thirty-eight mothers (nearly half
the seventy-one women were still childless) either stayed
home or worked part-time in order to devote themselves to
their children.[18]

These and other statistics suggest that when financial
circumstances permit (that is when their husbands are or
can be made supportive), women with children overwhelmingly choose to stay home, or to work part-time.

A new wave of social critics like Sylvia Ann Hewlett
say, on the contrary, the main reason women's work patterns are not the same as men's is that American women
don't have the kind of social welfare benefits that would allow women to compete successfully in the marketplace.
"The lack of any kind of mandated benefit around childbirth
is the biggest single reason for why women are doing so
badly in the workplace," according to Hewlett. "Unless
you support women in their role as mothers, you will never
get equality of opportunity."[19] If government only offered
women enough entitlements, we would shape up and act
like men.

Sweden has been pursuing that vision of equal opportunity for fifty years. In Sweden, usually pointed to as a
model state for women's rights, either parent can take up
to a year's child care leave at 90 percent pay. State-financed
day care accommodates 40 percent of all children under age
six. Eighty percent of Swedish women have jobs. But in
Sweden, when at home, mothers are still the ones that

clean the toilet and wipe the baby's nose. When at work, women still earn 62 percent of what the men do.[20]

What's going on here? If the work women do at home is really superfluous, how are all these women occupying their time? If caring for children is stultifying, why do we persist in structuring our lives around our families? Under the androgynous analysis, the answer must be that women are so brainwashed we continue to behave in feminine ways even when we receive no economic or social support for doing so. Are we really, as the orthodox analysis of women's behavior implies, the lazy or timid or unambitious sex?

I don't think so.

I think women remain family centered because we understand, even if the culture does not, that the work we do for our families is not superfluous at all. I think that the energy women put into their families is indispensable; the crime is that the work we do is so little acknowledged or respected, even among women. That, and the fact that caring for our families now exposes us to very grave financial risks in which our children share.

Because mothering has such low social status, women are encouraged to indulge in penis envy. Men have families *and* corporate vice-presidencies. Why can't we? This is another part of the great androgynous coverup. The answer is contained in an unmentionable sex difference: *Men do not have families the way women have families.*

All those (usually male) corporate vice-presidents with 1.8 children, even those who are very good fathers who love their children dearly and go to PTA meetings and coach Lassie League, do not have the kind of direct connection to their children that most mothers, working or not, manage to sustain. That kind of intimacy is no longer publicly esteemed, even for women. Instead women are actively encouraged to detach from our children temporarily if doing so will aid our careers.

When mothers return to work, we usually remain connected to our children in an extraordinarily intense way that fathers seldom, if ever, achieve. Our children, even when safely placed in wonderfully-licensed day care centers, or grown to an age in which they no longer require constant supervision, affect our work patterns in ways that they do not seem to affect men.

What exactly am I talking about? The experience of middle-aged women like Marie who returned to work when her three children became teenagers. After several years, she reports, ''I still have a difficult time detaching from their needs being more important than my work needs. I will usually put their needs before my own and when I get to work, I feel very rattled because I'm plugged into their needs so much.''[21] Another woman, who returned to work soon after her children were born, describes the essentially same transformation: ''When I went back to work after my first maternity leave, I found that things had changed: Emotionally, I was always at home even when I was working.''[22]

Today, this capacity for intimacy is everywhere desired and exploited, and yet everywhere disparaged. Men, we are told, have had the right idea all along: love your kids, but maintain enough emotional distance to be able to shove them out of your mind and concentrate on work.

In current debates over the status of motherhood, the value of parenting is usually described by all sides in extremely utilitarian terms; good parents produce children who produce money. The more money, the better parent. For example, working mothers are frequently described in scholarly literature as better for daughters than homemakers because daughters of working women tend to have higher educational and career aspirations—they want to make more money. It seems peculiarly insulting to describe a homemaking mother as a failure because her daughters aspire to be *like her.*

But strong families are not just an instrumental good, an utterly necessary building block to stable, productive communities. Being part of a close family is itself one of the great (if frequently irritating) goods a person can possess. Many women know this, not *"instinctively,"* but quite consciously.

"We have a very close and very happy family. And it doesn't just happen that way. I count it as *my* achievement. I made it happen. . .I don't think it's possible today," says Florence. She came to this conclusion by watching her daughters struggle in marriages where despite the fact they had paid jobs they were required to be "doormats" in a way Florence felt she had not been. Neither society nor husbands, she said, ever acknowledged the work her daughters had done to create harmonious family relationships.[23]

Why does anyone go to the trouble of having a family? Children are noisy, messy, time-consuming, and very expensive. Today, unlike through most of the rest of human history, they do not produce much of a return on the dollar. With social security and pensions, children are no longer even necessary to provide for one's old age. Indeed, modern grandparents are much more likely to report giving financial aid to their adult children than receiving it. Kids are no longer economic assets, just enormous, apparently never-ending headaches.

So why do we bother? Precisely out of the longing for the kind of emotional connection that is desperately sought and yet today, everywhere downgraded. Ideally, in today's culture, building relationships would be nobody's chief business and everybody's hobby. Women are supposed to stuff quality time into their children and spouses during those odd moments when we are not occupied with more important things, the paid labor for which we reserve our public applause.

In defining the oedipus complex, Freud proposed that toddlers long, with the intensity of adults, for what they cannot ever have: sexual union with their mothers. When I became a mother, it occurred to me that maybe Freud had it backwards. I wondered fleetingly whether oedipal strivings in the baby might be a projection of what the parent feels? Romantic love, the erotic longing for union, these are pale reflections of the intimacy that a woman actually experiences holding her baby in her arms. A separate being who is no stranger. Another who is not Other. What romantic love whisperingly promises, motherhood delivers.

That may be why, when asked to describe the best thing about being a woman today, 60 percent of women in one recent nationwide Roper poll picked motherhood. It swamped the second place choice, ''being a wife,'' by a margin of two to one. ''Taking advantage of women's increased opportunities'' came in a dismal fourth. Which is not to say necessarily that work is unimportant to women. Just that it does not compare.[24]

Antinatalist propaganda has been successful to this extent: women now say that it is not necessarily important for a woman to be a mother. But that's for ''other women'' (who we have been told are likely to be oppressed by motherhood). For most women, having children remains a crucial life goal, a primary form of self-identification.

The intensity of the maternal bond necessarily dwindles: children grow up, resist being known, struggle to break free. By contrast, in intact families, the emotional connection between children and fathers may very well swell as his knowledge, skills, and encouragement become more obviously necessary to them. The love between mother and child has a tragic dimension. Motherhood is planned obsolesence. The good mother is the one who learns to relinquish the most emotionally-satisfying relationship of her life.

Despite the intrinsic costs and despite intensive propaganda campaigns against femininity, women persist in behaving like women, and we are penalized for it though men are not penalized for behaving like men. They stay out of the kitchen, they throw themselves into their work, they abandon their children, they make their wives bring home the bacon and fry it up too—without incurring the least financial risk, or any significant social censure. Increasingly most men, the average good joes, are acting like the awful men our mothers warned us about. The lie of androgyny has made it socially acceptable to be a cad.

Women today are being punished, and the most horrifying part is that we are being punished *for our virtues*, for supplying what everyone wants and what society in fact needs us to provide: a strong, dependable love, an emotional commitment that children can count on. The harder we try to provide for our children, the more we are scorned, the more dangerous our position, the more vulnerable we are to male abuse.

But many prominent women today, from former Ambassador Jeanne Kirkpatrick, to Columbia Law School Dean Barbara Black, are testimony that caring for a family does not necessarily induce permanent brain damage in women. There does not seem to be any intrinsic contradiction for women between commitment to family and leading an interesting, productive existence.

Only when society decides to tear us from our children by punishing us for feminine desires does the contradiction emerge in the lives of countless mothers who, struggling for their own and their children's survival, find staying out of absolute poverty all the achievement they can muster for this lifetime.

None of the very real problems facing women today, from finding ways to combine fruitful work with a nurturing family life, to rescuing women from the economic disaster of divorce, can be resolved without abandoning the failed doctrine of sexual androgyny. That is, without firmly and quite unashamedly acknowledging the distinctive needs, desires, and contributions of women. Only once we drop the theory that women must act like men in order to be fully human persons, do a number of intriguing possibilities from sequencing to mommy tracks begin to open. Nor, if we continue to ignore women's achievements, will women be the only victims.

Endnotes—Chapter 4

1. "Consider the image of the 'total woman.' Having encountered it recently in our own society, we are more than a bit chilled to learn of its use by the Nazis...the problem for those of us who find such arrangements abhorrent is that they can hold considerable attraction for a large number of women and men. For various historical and cultural reasons, people who harbor deep fears of male-female equality can readily come to associate such equality with social and family disintegration." Robert Jay Lifton, *New York Times Book Review*, January 3, 1988, p. 16.

2. Dorothy Dinnerstein, *The Mermaid and the Minotaur: Sexual Arrangements and the Human Malaise* (New York: Perennial Library, Harper and Row, 1976), p. 19.

3. Bernard, *The Future of Motherhood, op. cit.*, p. 19.

4. "Sex, Society and the Female Dilemma: A Dialogue Between Simone de Beauvoir and Betty Freidan," *Saturday Review*, June 14, 1975, p. 18.

5. Friedan, *The Second Stage, op. cit.*, p. 77.

6. Grace Baruch, Rosalind Barnett, Caryl Rivers, *Lifeprints: New Patterns of Love and Work for Today's Women* (New York: McGraw-Hill, 1983), p. 1.

7. Bernard, *op. cit.*, p. 38.

8. Louis Genevie and Eva Margolies, *The Motherhood Report: How Women Feel About Being Mothers* (New York: McGraw-Hill, 1987), pp. 344–46.

9. Cook, *A Mother's Choice, op. cit.*, p. 95.

10. *Ibid.*, p. 160.

11. *Ladies Home Journal* (May 1988), p. 54.

12. See, for example, Blumstein and Schwarz, *op. cit.*, pp. 162–64. For evidence of a similar pattern among cohabiting couples see pp. 88–99.

13. George Gilder, "Women in the Work Force," *Atlantic* (September 1986), p. 22.

14. "How Women View Work, Motherhood and Feminism," *Newsweek*, March 31, 1986, p. 51. Interestingly enough, the editors played the results of this poll as evidence that "women want to work" when it clearly states that women with children want to work much less than they are doing now, and that, consequently, they want their husbands to assume more responsibility as breadwinners. Given the current low-prestige, isolated, and economically dangerous conditions being a full-time mother throws one into, it's surprising any women say they would like to remain home. If the conditions for full-time mothering were less punitive, even more women might prefer to remain at home, at least while their children are young.

15. Douglas J. Besharov, Michelle M. Dally, *Public Opinion* (Nov/Dec 1986), p. 48.

16. Thomas E. Miller, Link Resources Telework Group in New York, National Work-at-Home Survey, 1987. Reported in *Redbook* (May 1988), p. 114. (A spokesman for Link Resources Telework Group refused to confirm or deny the published figures, saying the survey is not in the public domain.)

17. Sweet, Bumpass, *American Families and Households, op. cit.*, p. 150.

18. Jill Abramson and Barbara Franklin, *Where They Are Now: The Story of the Women of Harvard Law 1974* (Garden City, New York: Doubleday, 1986), pp. 164–199.

19. *Newsweek*, March 31, 1986, p. 58.

20. Rita Kramer, "The Third Wave," *The Wilson Quarterly* (Autumn 1986), p. 129.

21. Cook, *op. cit.*, p. 81.

22. Lindsy Van Gelder, "Countdown to Motherhood," *Ms.* (December 1986), p. 38. The author ascribes her own "inability" to emotionally detach as

stemming from the lack of adequate day care in the seventies, but it echoes the experience of most women, even those (like myself) who find perfectly adequate day care arrangements.

23. Cline and Spender, *Reflecting Men op. cit.*, pp. 127–130.
24. *Ladies Home Journal* (March 1988), p. 70.

5

Suffer the Little Children

David Brom was a sixteen-year-old, clean-cut, all-American suburban kid. He went to church every Sunday and maintained a good record at Lourdes High, the local parochial school. On Feb. 18, 1988, according to an Associated Press report, David Brom did something rather unusual. He shaved the side of his head and fashioned his hair into punk spikes. He then picked up a twenty-eight-inch axe and chopped up his father, mother, brother, and sister.

Are you really that surprised? Neither am I.

It's easy to get used to the bizarre. Most American children are fine, healthy, normal youngsters, but occasionally one fine, healthy suburban teen decides to knock off his parents, or strangle his girlfriend, or rape a nun, or beat

up an old lady. It's a national peculiarity, like mud wres-
tling, and not even a seven-day wonder unless, like Robert
Chambers, you add a whiff of money and a healthy dose of
kinky sex to mere murder.

Sometimes, for entertainment, we go to the theater
and view reenactments of bloody deeds and cluck over the
childlike innocence of the criminals, as in *River's Edge*, or,
reenacting an even more primal scene, rejoice in the righteous slaughter of the wicked (sexually-abusive) father.

Other odd signs and bad augurs decorate the youth
culture. I am aware that parents have been loudly bemoan-
ing the decline of youth since Cain went off and did his own
thing. But still, even the paranoid have enemies. Yesterday
I went to the store and purchased a Teenage Mutant Ninja
Turtle for one of my six-year-old son's best friends. At a
somewhat older age many youths, making particularly effective use of black eyeliner and white powder, try very
hard to look dead. Millions of barely pubescent girls worship Billy Idol, a man clearly in need of reconstructive surgery. Michael Jackson, who has had it, is a folk hero. Think
about it.

Look, I don't know exactly what it means when school
children take reptiles as personal heroes, or when packs of
teenagers rove Manhattan looking for all the world like the
lost tribe of the Addams Family or when young intellectuals
at our nation's finest universities cheerfully admit (as a
friend of mine did) that there is no free will and they are nihilists. Maybe cheerful nihilists are nothing at all to be concerned about.

Oh, I admit these are mere anecdotes, vague personal
impressions, individual incidents. It may indeed be that the
symbolic violence of our youth is a mere prelude to a fundamental transformation in consciousness—the way station to

a new and higher form of being, uncluttered by ancient superstitions like free will and gender and clothing in colors other than black.

I might, that is, if hard statistics didn't paint a much grimmer picture: American children are doing very badly. It's not just money, though kids are following their single mothers into poverty at an appalling rate. Suddenly, inexplicably, American teens are dying off, or worse, taking their own lives, committing more crimes, having more illegitimate babies, dropping out of school, and performing poorly on standardized educational tests.

It's an astonishing phenomenon. This is America. Not only do we expect each generation to do better than the previous one, but, as Peter Uhlenberg and David Eggebeen point out, specific statistical indicators predicted that today's adolescents would be happier, healthier, better educated than teens in the sixties.

Take education, for example. Social scientists agree on a number of factors in a child's background which forecast trouble in school: poverty, parents with little or no education, and a large number of brothers and sisters. In each case, fewer teenagers today come from homes suffering from one or more of these handicaps.

In 1960, for example, 24.7 percent of sixteen and seventeen year olds lived in households with income below the poverty line. By 1980, only 9.9 percent did so. In 1960 over half of all teens came from households where either the mother or the father lacked a high school diploma. By 1980 only a quarter did so. And the number of teens who must split parental attention among four siblings or more dropped from 21 to 13.6 percent.

During the same period, per-pupil expenditures in

school jumped 99.6 percent (in 1980 dollars) while the average class size in high school dropped 17.9 percent.

Despite these favorable socioeconomic conditions, the proportion of eighteen year olds who are high school graduates, after climbing slowly five percentage points between 1960 and 1970 *actually declined* during the seventies so that today, roughly one-quarter of our teenagers drop out of high school.

Meanwhile the rate of juvenile delinquency in ten to seventeen year olds leaped 130 percent between 1960 and 1980. The illegitimate birth rate among girls aged fifteen to nineteen jumped 140 percent. In just a five year period between 1973 and 1979 the abortion rate among girls aged fifteen to nineteen also jumped 59 percent. Perhaps most troubling of all, the violent death rate for white teenagers skyrocketed between 1960 and 1980, the lone exception to a century-long trend toward better health and longer life for all age groups. The suicide rate among white teens shot up 139 percent in those twenty years. And teens' risk of being murdered jumped 231 percent.[1]

The cause and effect of social phenomena are very complex. Only the very daring or the very ignorant could pretend to isolate exactly which of the myriad social changes is responsible for the decline in our children's well-being. But what is certain and extremely ominous is that these statistical cries for help from the youngest generation emerge at the very time American culture is taking a historic turn away from children.

Ours is a nation which has a clear and unfolding history of increasing empathy for children's distinct emotional and psychological needs. And yet suddenly everywhere the voices of authority are telling parents that children must adapt to adult needs and fit into adult lifestyles rather than the other way around. The joyous clamor of the baby boomlet temporarily disguised the fact that there has been a fundamental change in the status of children in our society, a subtle decline which parallels the decline in the status of mothering.

It's a chicken and the egg problem. Which came first: Does the culture fail to praise women for nurturing children because it came to have contempt for our parenting skills? Or are our parenting skills disparaged because society no longer views children as the most important contribution most men and women make to the community? We have been told, by anthropologists, social scientists, and politicians that historic American child rearing practices, including an unusually close relationship between mothers and children, are unnecessary, even harmful to our own and our children's mental health. And at the same time we have been told that children, delightful little bundles of love that they may be, are harmful to our nation's future economic health.

Society no longer praises parents for creating the nation's future. That seems to us jingoistic, even coercive. In the interest of expanding an individual's right to choose, children have been transformed from a social *duty* to a personal *right*, and though the change has been welcome to indignant social reformers and harried parents, it has been rather unpleasant for the children concerned. This comes as a surprise to most social reformers who assume that when men and women carefully choose to have children for their own personal reasons, both parents and children will lead happier, healthier lives. It stands to reason, doesn't it? To both the left and the right, the idea that emphasizing "the choice to have children," results in a decline in the status of children seems counterintuitive. That is because we have rather lost sight of the fundamental truth that by and large human beings are a good deal more scrupulous about the performance of duties than the exercise of rights (which, being ours, we feel quite free to abuse as we wish).

Evidence of a new carelessness in our attitudes towards children abound. You can see it in the ongoing debate about day care. One women's magazine, for example, offered mothers advice on what to look for in a day care center. But if you can't find any really good day care centers, don't worry about it. "What if the child care you find isn't ideal?" asks educator Peggy Kaye. "Well, home life isn't ideal either." "If the place you found has a responsible staff and a safe, stimulating environment," the magazine rather cavalierly advises, "it's probably fine."[2]

You can see it in the rapidly growing ranks of single-parent families where women expect their children to substitute for the adult companionship they have lost. As women face greater stress, children are increasingly expected to adapt to and even fulfill parental needs—for time alone, for peace and quiet, for companionship, and for emotional succor during the storms of divorce.

And you can see it in popular propaganda about divorce, where despite the vast scientific evidence corroborating the instinct of a millenium—that disrupting families disrupts children—Americans are told, and tell each other that divorce is good for the children.

Even now, when evidence of the trauma divorce inflicts on children has become so great it is impossible to repress our awareness of it, we deny the implications of what we know. In the spring of 1989, Judith S. Wallerstein, a psychologist and executive director of the Center for the Family in Transition, published *Second Chances*, the results of a fifteen-year study of sixty families which divorced in the early seventies. The parents were, for the most part, white middle and upper-middle class individuals. The children selected for the study were all developmentally normal, doing well in school, and psychologically healthy. Her findings, though preliminary, are astonishing.

After five years, more than a third of the children were clinically depressed. Only one in ten children say they felt relieved when quarrelling parents divorced and these tended to be older children who had witnessed or endured physical violence. Of children whose mothers remarried, half said that they did not feel welcome in the new family. After ten years, 35 percent of the children had poor relationships with both parents and three-quarters felt rejected by their fathers. Two-thirds of the fathers who could afford to pay for their children's college education, refused to do so. Of all children over the age of eighteen at the ten-year mark, 60 percent are on a downward educational course compared with their fathers and 45 percent are on a similarly downward course compared with their mothers.

And yet the most astonishing thing about the study is Ms. Wallerstein's conclusion: despite her graphic and compassionate portrait of the pain divorce inflicts on children, Ms. Wallerstein firmly maintains: "To recognize that divorce is an arduous long-lasting family trauma is not to argue against it. Divorce is a useful and necessary social remedy."

Sometimes, that is undoubtedly what divorce is. But which times? The choice facing both parents and society as a whole is not between free and easy divorce and no divorce at all. The question is under what circumstances are we justified in inflicting this trauma upon our children? And Ms. Wallerstein's answer, echoing that of her reviewers and the general culture, is simple: parents should divorce whenever a married individual strongly feels his or her well-being depends upon it. When couples ask Ms. Wallerstein if they should stay together "for the sake of the children" she always replies, "Of course not."[3]

If you want to pinpoint the year children lost their time-honored status as custodians of the future, the most important contribution men and women make to the community, pick 1971. That's as good a year as any to describe the moment three social movements converged: the sexual revolution, which viewed children as an unwelcome side effect of orgasm; feminism, which in its virulent early form denounced children as an impediment to female power; and the population police who, just as birthrates tumbled, successfully promoted the view that children (especially children of the poor) are a menace to adults' survival. The toothless mouth and the undiapered bottom—that was how the end would come. It was an alternate apocalyptic vision to the one proffered by anti-nuclear activists. Not with a bang, but a whimper.

Sex and power were the carrots, poverty and annihilation were the sticks used to prod Americans into discarding the view that children are a national resource and that undertaking the responsibilities of raising a family is an important part of becoming a contributing member of society.

Today, children have been demoted from a public good to a private pleasure. In the process, women's work has been transformed into a play activity, a hobby, like collecting model trains. Kids are supposed to be weird objects of gratification to parents, a bothersome nuisance to everyone else. You prefer to spend your money on your (noisy, smelly) kids. Me? I prefer a Ferrari.

The devaluation of children combined with the devaluation of mothers has had a devastating effect on the welfare of both. There is synergism here. When children are devalued, family-centered women become declassé. When women are encouraged to invest less emotional energy in our families, children experience a decline in both status and well being. American society must answer a central question: When most women (including working women) defer career ambitions to devote time to family, are we performing an utterly essential service to our children and to the community, or are we merely indulging ourselves in an interesting pastime? At the most basic level are children— are *people*—resources or liabilities?

There is no doubt where some of the early mothers of the current wave of orthodox feminism stand. The overpopulation panic which swept the country between 1967 and 1971 was seized on by an elite who felt, in any case, that motherhood strangles women's career prospects. Twenty years later, the pervasive fascination with overpopulation and eugenics which pervades many early feminist works on reproductive rights seems grotesque, frightening, and overwhelmingly patronizing. All those little women happily, instinctively, stupidly breeding us into extinction. Someone must refine their sensibilities, elevate their tastes, unplug those goddam baby machines.

"It is increasingly recognized," wrote feminist sociologist Jessie Bernard in 1974, "that the future is sure to call for only very modest indulgence in childbearing and that we can no longer persist in our pronatalist attitudes." She continues:

> A variety of ways have been suggested for reducing [women's] desire for babies. One commonly suggested proposal to achieve this goal is greater encouragement of labor-force participation by women. More esoteric ideas have to do

with the possibility that we could "androgenize" women, that is, give them the hormone androgen, for androgenized women apparently tend to be less interested in motherhood than other women. No one has yet suggested Skinnerian behavior modification by means of "aversive conditioning." But someone doubtless will in time. Girls will be given an electric shock whenever they see a picture of an adorable baby until the very thought of motherhood becomes anathema to them...[4]

The devaluation of children and therefore mothering (and vice versa) has slowed since the early seventies when a prominent intellectual could, without apparent embarrassment, talk of hormonally reeducating baby-prone women. Slowed, but not died.

Recently the *New York Times* editorial page found fit to print a long letter from a group called Negative Population Growth, Inc., urging a reduction in the world population from five billion to two billion, as well as eliminating about one hundred million excess Americans, warning, "The great lesson of the Industrial Revolution, virtually ignored until now, is that vast numbers of people are simply incompatible with an industrial society."[5]

America's fertility rate has now fallen to about 1.8 births per woman, well below the 2.1 replacement level. On Jan. 31, 1989, the Census Bureau projected that the U.S. population will peak in 2038, and decline thereafter. My son, currently six, may well live to see a rapidly depopulated United States. If you have ever lived in an area with a declining population, you know that is not a pleasant prospect.

In the *Birth Dearth*, Ben Wattenberg elegantly sketches the likely effect the missing generation of children will have on America's economy and on the future of the whole West. America will begin to feel the effects soon, when the children who failed to be born in the late sixties and early seventies, fail to mature in the mid-nineties, precipitating both a labor, and eventually a consumer shortage. In West Germany, where one study found that only 10 percent of post-war married couples believe that children are more important than consumer goods or careers, the military has already been forced by the shortage of young adults to begin drafting married men.[6] By the end of the next century, if current trends continue, West Germany's population will dwindle from 61 million to 20 million; achieving, at last, a ghostly *Lebensraum*.[7]

Explicit denunciations of children are rarer now, and celebrations of anonymous intercourse have just about died out. But the downward slide in the status of mothering, fed by economic necessity and ideological fervor, is by no means over. Mothers must work today, and a whole industry has sprung up to reassure us that our children do not need us hanging over them all the time. An exclusive mother-child bond is only one way, the experts tell us, and by no means the best way, of ordering our family relationships.

In its nicest form, the devaluation of mothering is merely an attempt to relieve the awful burden of guilt women who must work carry when we leave our children at the day care center. But it is dangerous to belittle the work women do raising children. Dangerous to the majority of women (who receive the message that our primary occupation isn't important), and also dangerous to our children.

For perhaps children do not grow up the same no matter how they are raised. The recent dramatic decline in our adolescent's well being ought, at the very least, to make us ponder that possibility.

Endnotes—Chapter 5

1. Peter Uhlenberg and David Eggebeen, "The Declining Well-Being of American Adolescents," *The Public Interest* (Winter 1986), p. 25ff.

2. Nancy Hathaway, "Working Mothers Does Your Child Need You Now?" *Harper's Bazaar* (July 1988), p. 143.

3. Judith S. Wallerstein and Sandra Blakeslee, *Second Chances: Men Women and Children a Decade After Divorce* (New York: Ticknor & Fields, 1989), pp. 16 and 305.

4. Bernard, *The Future of Motherhood, op. cit.*, pp. 39–40.

5. "Population Size Can't Be Overlooked as an Environmental Danger," *New York Times*, October 31, 1988, p. A18.

6. William Drozdiak, "West German Birth Rate Dropping," *The Washington Post*, January 10, 1984, p. A10.

7. Ben J. Wattenberg, *The Birth Dearth* (New York: Pharos Books, A Scripps Howard Company, 1987), p. 178.

6

Day Care and the Disposable Mother

If you survey recent social science literature, you will get the distinct impression that the mother-child bond is a modern invention. It is something American culture dreamed up to trap women within the home, which can easily be dispensed with, or broadened to include men, other relatives, and the local day care teacher.

Everything we know about parenting suggests that the strong emotional bond that generally exists between mothers and children is a key to raising psychologically healthy children. And yet it is precisely the mother-child bond which, because it tends to deflect women from aggressively pursuing career success, has become the target of a sustained intellectual and cultural attack.

Anthropologists survey the vast panorama of child

rearing practices among !Kung Bushmen, Apache tribes-women, Afghan nomads. Social historians pour over 18th century child rearing manuals and successive editions of Spock and underline in Day-Glo yellow the dizzying revolutions in expert advice that have taken place over the years.

In her widely acclaimed book, *Mothers and Such*, for example, anthropologist Maxine Margolis surveys the advice American parents received from the 17th century to the present. Child care manuals addressed specifically to women only appeared in the early 19th century, she maintains, and prior to that time, men and women appear to have parented interchangeably. "During the colonial era the advice of the clergy—the major prescriptive voices of the day—minimized differences in parental roles and duties . . . parenting was not a specialized function within the ken of one sex or the other. Nor was there any indication that a special tie existed between mother and child."[1] Of course, in 1700 when only 20 percent of American women were literate,[2] it would have been difficult for publishers to find an audience for books addressed chiefly to women. I am not at all surprised that books addressed to men did not highlight the importance of women's work in the home or with children. (The publishing climate of the 18th century is a reversal of the current situation where many books on child rearing—whose market is chiefly among women—are nonetheless addressed to ''parents.'' A future cultural historian, surveying the newly-emergent literature may someday conclude that there are few if any distinctions between maternal or paternal roles.)

Social scientists like Margolis emphasize that at different times in different places, children have been raised in a startling variety of ways. Customs differ. Who are we to say that they are wrong?

A broad historical and cross-cultural perspective of the mother role highlights the degree to which social scientists and other advice givers are bound by time and space. The long emphasis in the United States on the need for an exclusive mother-child arrangement is a good example...if such [an intense mother-child] relationship were in fact essential, we would have to conclude that prior to the nineteenth century and in many cultures past and present its absence produced damaged children and damaged adults. We would have to believe that mothers throughout the ages have failed their offspring and that only within the last 150 years in the United States and other western industrialized societies have the psychological needs of children been met.[3]

What social scientists such as Margolis fail to consider is this: All the varying ways of raising kids may well be, in the narrow anthropological sense, equally *natural*. That doesn't mean they are equally enjoyable for children or produce adults with the same emotional and mental capabilities. Kalahari bushparents are very adept at producing children who fit into a foraging, seminomadic illiterate culture. It is not clear that their child rearing practices would be equally adapted to raising children who can read and write, hold down a nine to five job, respect authority and yet retain a healthy commitment to individual rights and political democracy.

Nor does the noble-savage allure of preindustrial child rearing techniques always hold up under close inspection. Apache mothers, for example, would score high on Jessie Bernard's scale, which considers displays of maternal warmth to be the key index of quality of mothering. Apache women are not burdened with "excessive domestic or economic chores," which tends to depress displays of maternal warmth. The women have plenty of free time to gossip, shop, gamble, drink, and flirt, and they frequently drop their children off with an obliging relative in order to do so. There's no question that under these circumstances Apache women display the emotional expressiveness Jessie Bernard approves of in cultures where women aren't (as we are in our culture) overburdened with excessive maternal duties: They nurse their children frequently, smother them with hugs and kisses, smiles, and nuzzles.

But perhaps displays of emotion are not the best index of dependable maternal love. For, unfortunately, it seems, Apache mothers also have the discomfiting habit of losing their babies like a misplaced hat. According to one researcher, "A great many [Apache] mothers abandon or give away children—babies they had been nursing lovingly only a week before...Not only do they feel scant conscious guilt for this behavior, but at times they are overtly delighted to have been able to rid themselves of the burden. In some instances, mothers who have given children away, 'forget they ever had them.'"[4] It happens often enough that the Apaches even have a term for it: throwing-the-baby-away.

The Apache mother may be an extreme example, but institutionalized child abandonment (or worse) is by no means a historically unusual practice. As Lloyd DeMause, Director of the Institute for Psychohistory in New York City writes, "The history of childhood is a nightmare from which we have only recently begun to awaken. The further back in history one goes, the lower the level of child care, and the more likely children are to be killed, abandoned, beaten, terrorized, and sexually abused."[5] The evidence of child rearing practices in Western history is sketchy and incomplete, but what we have suggests the average level of parenting even two hundred years ago would today be considered child abuse.

Mothers, as Margolis points out, have not always spent a great deal of time and energy supervising young children. That is quite true. But when prestigious academics say that an intense mother-child bond is a recent invention and easily dispensed with, they do not usually tell you how children fared in the good old days when women were preoccupied with household production rather than child care. In America, before the emergence of the oppressive Victorian ''motherhood cult,'' children under five were routinely left alone and just as routinely drowned at the bottom of wells or burned to death in the family fireplace. Working class parents who wanted peace and quiet drugged their children with opium and trotted off to the neighborhood pub.[6]

Nor did even babies receive excessive coddling, and women were not expected to take on the exhausting chore of being constantly attentive and emotionally available toward their newborns. Babies who were too demanding, it seems, were often simply beaten. One 19th century mother wrote without selfconsciousness of her first battle with her son: ''I whipped him til he was actually black and blue, and until I could not whip him any more, and he never gave up one single inch.''[7] Her son, at the time, was four months old.

For centuries in Europe, infants were expected to remain quiet and immobile. Swaddling, the practice of tightly wrapping the arms, legs, and head of a newborn so that it could not move, was the norm. These mummified infants were left to themselves for long periods, or occasionally tossed from one side of the room to the other as sport for gentleman or frustrated nursemaids. A baby who cried too often might even be called a changeling and killed.

Indeed, although the law first began to recognize in 374 A.D. that killing a baby was murder, snuffing out legitimate babies (mostly girls) remained a relatively common practice probably until at least the 17th century. Thomas Coran opened the first foundling hospital in London in 1741 because he could not stand to see the dying babies slowly rotting in the gutters, but as late as the 1890s dead babies were still a common sight in London streets.

Perhaps most telling of all, in Europe, infants were routinely sent away from their mothers to wet nurses for periods of two or three years and then returned to their mothers. "When a child is given to another and removed from its mother's sight, the strength of maternal ardour is gradually and little by little extinguished," Aulus Gellius noticed long ago, "...and it is almost as completely forgotten as if it had been lost by death"[8] Under such conditions, indeed, women did not develop the strong maternal bonds that so oppress us today.

In America parent-child relations appear to have always been more attentive and affectionate than those in Europe, perhaps because Americans, with a vast continent to explore and a boundless faith in the future, had always tended to portray children as a public boon, rather than a drain on the treasury. (For instance, the *New York Mercury* on Nov. 12, 1739, published an announcement of a birth of triplets and predicted discontent among married women "that their husbands cannot perform the same piece of manhood.")

As one scholar put it, "The evidence suggests that the American mother of the eighteenth century was in closer and more constant contact with her children, and interacted more often and more deeply than her counterpart in Europe."[9] But the Marquis de Chastellux, travelling through North America in the early 19th century, claimed that American women did little more than take care of their children and clean house, hardly enough, he comments with archetypically male disdain, to keep a woman busy. (This at a time when that average American woman had six children!)

In the early 19th century, Tocqueville, observing the universal energy and vigor of American life, gave much of the credit to the quality of American women. Modern scholars tend to dismiss Tocqueville's observation as misplaced gallantry, the kind of sentimental sop routinely tossed to women who were otherwise excluded from the important business of life.

I suspect he was on to something.

Perhaps, amid the cluster of ideological and material factors commonly said to cause the Industrial Revolution, it is no historical accident that the Industrial Revolution was the brainchild of England, a nation which had much more enlightened child rearing practices than the continent. Nor that England, in turn, was soon surpassed by America, where parents invested even more emotional energy in children. In an industrial society, human capital is the major asset. Perhaps it's mere coincidence that the explosion of entreprenuership, invention, and economic growth in the 19th century came just as more American women were rapidly educating themselves and just as intently turning their attention to the care and education of their children.

Child rearing practices deserve more than the footnote they generally receive in history. If human character is shaped by culture, that culture is always passed from parent to child "...because psychic structure must always be passed from generation to generation through the narrow funnel of childhood, a society's child rearing practices are not just one item on a list of culture traits. They...place definite limits on what can be achieved in all other spheres of history. Specific childhood experiences must occur to sustain specific cultural traits, and once these experiences no longer occur the trait disappears."[10]

But whether or not the creation of a specifically female domestic sphere is the proximate cause of economic growth, the new emphasis on the maternal bond so sappily, happily celebrated in Victorian literature certainly coincided with an enormous increase in the welfare of children, especially girls.

The opportunity for an intense mother-child bond is a cultural achievement which, like all achievements, can be destroyed. A child-centered household is an enormous amount of work, demanding a great willingness to delay gratification, and to endure frustration. It requires adults have sufficient psychological development to intuit correctly a child's needs and the emotional maturity to be willing to fulfill them. Instinct is not enough. If culture fails to reaffirm and to support structural conditions necessary for mother-child bonding, it can be severely damaged if not entirely erased.

As Simone de Beauvoir pointed out in *The Second Sex*, "...The close bond between mother and child will be for her a source of dignity or indignity according to the value placed upon the child—which is highly variable—and this very bond, as we have seen, will be recognized or not according to the presumption of the society concerned."[11]

Given the importance of culture, it is particularly disturbing that the many voices in current public debate about family issues display a cavalier disregard for the welfare of children and supreme indifference to the value of women's work.

One would expect proponents of parental leave, which (since men almost never take it) is the current polite euphemism for maternal leave, to emphasize that mothers are important for babies. Among a number of pediatricians and child-development experts, that's correct. But among political advocates (including, sadly, many feminists) much more energy these days is invested in unshackling women from intense maternal bonds.

A *Glamour* magazine article on parental leave actually warns mothers to hustle back to work before six months lest they (gasp) fall in love with their babies: "Babies are hard to resist once they're at this stage, and mothers can sometimes find it difficult to 'break away' if they delay too long." *Glamour* applauds the attitude of one allegedly guilt-free Washington, D.C., newscaster who left her newborn: "On the first day back, my sitter brought the baby in so I could nurse him. I was working and saw a stroller out of the corner of my eye. I thought, 'Who's that baby? I was so into a work mode that I forgot for four hours that I had a baby.'" The bottom line, according to *Glamour*, is that whenever you decide to go back to work, "there's no evidence that exclusive mothering is good for babies," so you might as well get back on the fast track pronto.[12]

Women are repeatedly told that caring for babies is not only unnecessary, but may actually be harmful to the child. Consider the message of Sirgay Sanger, M.D., coauthor of *The Woman Who Works, The Parent Who Cares*, who is quoted in a popular women's magazine as saying: "Studies show that laundry, shopping, preparing dinner—all the routine chores that fill up the at-home mother's day—so occupy her hours that she spends no more time in direct one-to-one exchanges with her child than you spend with yours." Indeed, the magazine cheerfully points out, "Research suggests that children in quality child care socialize more effectively, are more self-reliant, do better in school later on, commit fewer crimes, and are more likely to graduate from high school and continue their education than those whose mothers stayed home with them all day."[13]

If this condescending attitude toward women were confined to the pages of fashion magazines, it would be merely a disturbing blip on the cultural horizon. But in 1988 it became official. In that year, the House of Representatives voted to table George Bush's proposal to offer a tax credit to all low-income families which could be used to pay for all forms of child care: to pay a relative, a family day care provider, a day care center, or even to allow the mother to remain at home. Instead, for the first time, the House voted to approve a taxpayer subsidy that bypasses family choice and goes only to women who put their kids in day care centers.

With that vote, the most democratic branch of the federal government came down squarely against maternal care of children. The insult to women is hard to miss: your baby is better off without you than with you. Get off your behind and do something useful. Let the experts do what they do best.

From a public health standpoint alone, one would think that government would try to maximize care by mothers, relatives, or even smaller family day care over large day care centers. Researchers at the University of Arizona, for example, surveyed six thousand pediatricians; two-thirds said children in day care develop more acute infections than children in home care.[14] The best summary of the potential health hazards of day care was compiled by Dr. Bryce Christensen and published in the November 1987 issue of *Family in America*, a publication of the Rockford Institute.

According to the American Academy of Pediatrics, "outbreaks of gastroenteritis caused by bacteria, viruses, and parasites; bacterial meningitis [or] hepatitis A, have been documented in day care groups." A 1984 study of hemophilus influenzae type B (which can lead to childhood meningitis and epiglottitis) concluded that day care children were twelve times as likely to catch the disease than children cared for by their mothers. Another study by the Center for Disease Control found rates of infection for giardiasis were fifteen to twenty times higher among day care children. Health Department officials in Phoenix have concluded that "day care centers may represent the major source of hepatitis A cases of uncertain origins" (up to 60 percent of the total). And *The New England Journal of Medicine* (May 28, 1987) reports that pregnant women run "an increased risk" of contracting the potentially-dangerous cytomegalovirus (CMV) if they have children in day care.

Dr. Stanley Schuman of the Medical University of South Carolina maintains day care centers are responsible for recent "outbreaks of enteric illness-diarrhea, dysentery, giardiasis, and epidemic jaundice—reminiscent of the presanitation days of the 17th century." He says day care centers can take measures to reduce the incidence of hepatitis A and some forms of diarrhea, but that, for most day care diseases, "there seem to be few specific actions to be taken."

Babies and toddlers wear diapers. They suck their fingers, slobber on toys, and joyfully spit up food. From time to time, they take one of those brightly colored educationally-approved wooden blocks and stick it in their wet little mouths, and then pass it on to a friend. They do these things regardless of how caring the personnel, or how strictly licensed the facility.

And as long as babes will be babes, putting two dozen or so toddlers in one room will facilitate the spread of disease. In fact, as Dr. Schuman points out, the average toddler will put "a hand or object in the mouth every three minutes."[15]

Despite this obvious fact, the prevailing view now, solemnly endorsed by experts, ratified by at least one branch of the national legislature, and promoted in the popular press, is that large day care centers are beneficial for children—the unspoken corollary, that women's excessive attention to children is a waste of time.

In coming to this conclusion, creative labelling helps. When studies reveal day care children are more aggressive, researchers say they are merely outgoing and assertive. Astonishing new virtues, like "independence" are created, so that home reared children may be rated "less secure" than day care children which does not mean of course, less securely attached to their mothers, but just the opposite: as children, they are more reluctant to leave their mothers, more timid in the company of their peers. How they function as adults is a different matter.

Those studies that report day care is beneficial are overwhelmingly conducted on children in poverty, which doesn't prevent magazines catering to middle and upper-middle class women from using the results to suggest their children, too, are better off in day care. That, as Connie Marshner puts it, is rather like saying, "If hospitalization helps sick kids, think how much good it will do healthy children."[16]

A careful survey of the evidence suggests that ghetto children (whose frequently single mothers are less likely to offer them consistent, quality care) may benefit from high-quality day care. But even for ghetto children, day care in the real world is very different from the research fantasies in ways that no federal funding is likely to change.

Take a poor child. Give him a couple of very motivated caretakers who signed on to a research day care center for the duration of the scientific experiment, and research will probably find that he is, on average, better off than if he had remained confined in his ghetto household. In the imperfect real world, a child unlucky enough to enter day care will spend his infant and preschool years being cared for by a rapidly changing succession of kind, considerate, emotionally-uninvolved people.

A number of child-development experts have recently emerged who challenge the conclusion that day care is harmless, or even, advantageous experience. During at least the first three years, as one child psychologist maintains, children need "quantity times, so that the mother is on hand to fulfill a need at the moment it is necessary."[17] These voices are being raised despite the fact that even tepid criticism of day care has become politically unacceptable in the academic community. (One prominent child-development expert recently noted, "There are a lot of people out there [in academia] who won't open their mouths because they know how vehement the reaction can be.")[18]

Research data suggests day care children may have weaker attachments to their mothers, especially (as the examples from *Glamour* suggest) when they are put in day care full-time as infants. One study, for example, found that day care children commit fifteen times more aggressive acts than children cared for by mothers. Dale Farran, a senior researcher at the Frank Porter Graham Development Center, concludes that, "Along with greater aggression, children who have been in day care since infancy have also been rated as more active, more easily frustrated, less cooperative with adults, more oriented to children than adults, more distractible, and less task-oriented."[19]

In a 1978 article in *Child Development*, Jay Belsky and Lawrence D. Steinberg reviewed all the literature on day care and concluded that "on the basis of available evidence, high-quality center-based day care has neither salutary nor deleterious effects upon the intellectual development of the child." The authors warned, however that there was "shockingly little" research on the long-term effects of day care.[20]

In 1985 in an article published in *Advances in Developmental and Behavioral Pediatrics*, Belsky reviewed the latest scientific research, and stepped up his warning against full-time day care for infants, saying day care infants later become "more aggressive both physically and verbally with adults and peers, less cooperative with grown-ups."[21]

As Belsky pointed out, widespread use of day care has not been around long enough for there to be a great deal of evidence of its long-term effects. What there is though, is disturbing. One of the few longitudinal studies of the effects of day care was conducted in England by Terrence Moore. He concludes in psychoanalese, "instability of regime [a succession of caretakers] introduced cumulative stresses that are likely to be detrimental to personality development." When a child enjoys maternal care to the age of five, however, "the child tends early to internalized adult standards of behavior, notably self-control and intellectual achievement, relative to other children of equivalent intelligence and social class."[22]

The work of a number of economists confirms Moore's conclusion. Unlike child psychologists, economists interested in the development of human capital have made many attempts to measure the long-term effect of maternal care on the quality of children. Belton Fleischer for example, used the Department of Labor's National Longitudinal Survey to construct a measure of how much time children spend under maternal care. His index calculated the number of years during which the mother worked less than six months of the year while her child was fifteen years or younger. Taking into account other variables, including schooling, earnings, and IQ, he found that the earnings payoff resulting from each year of formal school for a child was positively related to the index of mother's child care time. In other words, if you take two children with identical education and intelligence, the child whose mother devoted fewer full-time years to the workforce will, on average, be more successful.[23]

In *A Mother's Work*, Deborah Fallows went to hundreds of day care centers and saw what hundreds of social scientists refused to: the pain, loneliness, confusion, and boredom of many toddlers in group day care. I have put my own son in four different day care centers in three different states, and I cannot disagree with her.

Nor apparently, do many other working mothers. Indeed, when asked "what worries you most about raising children?", 29 percent of women in a recent Roper poll said, "Working and not being home full-time." When you consider that about a third of mothers *are* home full-time, that suggests that about half of working mothers are experiencing a great deal of anxiety about the fact.[24]

This is particularly disturbing because one fairly consistent research finding is that when mothers are unhappy about being in the work force, the negative effects of day care are likely to be exacerbated. (Researchers frequently then attribute the child's trouble to "family stress" not day care.) So why are we busily constructing a society in which women have no other option?

Day care as a choice for women who want to work is a very different matter than institutionalizing socialized motherhood, as we are now doing. The structural pressures now pushing mothers of young children into the work force guarantee that day care will be a harmful experience for many more children than when it is voluntarily chosen by women who have the option to withdraw if their children are suffering because of it. When women work because we "have to," children are stuck in day care, whether they respond well to it or not. That does not bode well for the future well being of adolescents.

Take for example one survey which found that 71 percent of working mothers in Washington, D.C., reported no discipline problems with their children related to the time they spent away from them.[25] That according to the *Washington Post Magazine,* indicates day care is perfectly harmless. And indeed, it sounds reassuring until you think about that 29 percent of children who *are* becoming discipline problems. Even a minority of aggressive, impulse driven adults can make life miserable for the rest of the neighborhood.

The political elite's enthusiasm for day care is particularly odd in that very few parents share it. One of the most obvious and least noted facts about substitute child care is that most of it is provided by relatives. As of 1985, almost half the preschool children of working mothers are cared for by relatives. Only 23 percent are in formal day care centers and about the same proportion are in family day care.[26]

The longer this remains true, the better off children are likely to be. To a child, an aunt or a grandmother is a permanent fixture in his universe. Unlike a babysitter or a day care "teacher," wherever he goes, however far away from him his relatives might move in this mobile society, they will always exist for him, in relation to him. And of course vice versa: The emotional energy one pours into the niece or grandson is never so wholly lost, so generously gratuitous, as it is when one babysits an unrelated child.

The majority of mothers who put their children in the care of relatives are recreating an age old pattern that may well enrich children's lives: creating stronger attachments to grandparents or aunts and uncles or, occasionally, the father (though what the next generation is going to do, with hardly any siblings, and mothers, aunts and grandmothers all working full-time is anyone's guess).

But, as the House's vote on day care indicated, there is currently no effort being made to encourage or sustain this joint family approach to child care. Federal subsidies to day care chains (a big business rapidly expanding) will not help women who hire a relative or a neighbor to care for their children, or encourage those who do the even more politically correct step of getting their husbands to take on child care while they work. Yet a federal subsidy for day care operators is the darling of intelligentsia, especially among women wealthy enough to hire nannies and au pair girls for their own kids.

In a more or less forgotten novel of Harriet Beecher Stowe, a group of elite, educated ladies are discussing the European practice of sending babies out to nurse until they are two or three "...so the leisure of parent for literature, art, and society is preserved."

> "It seems to me the most perfectly dreary, dreadful way of living I ever heard of," replies her mother, "...if that's what's called organizing society I hope our society in America never will be organized. It cannot be that children are well taken care of on that system. I always attended to every thing for my babies *myself*, because I felt God had put them into my hand perfectly helpless; and, if there is

any thing difficult or disagreeable in the case, how can I expect to hire a woman for money to be faithful in what I cannot do for love?''[27]

This is a perfectly obvious question and yet it is one we seldom ask. Where are the warmhearted substitute caregivers going to come from in a society which increasingly declines to celebrate children, child rearing, and mothering? Values are funny things. We cannot insistently warn women that childbearing is a potential trap and childraising a degrading preoccupation, and then expect the day care industry to be flooded with eager, committed, emotionally-giving workers.

What makes a good substitute caregiver? Child development experts say that substitute care *must be consistent*. To become a psychologically healthy adult, the young child must feel it is safe to love the adult(s) who care for him. That is just what the average day care center is unable to provide. The turnover among ''substitute caregivers'' is truly extraordinary. Among family day care providers, it is estimated at 60 percent and among day care centers about 40 percent.[28]

This is as true in licensed facilities that charge five thousand dollars a year as it is in any other kind of facility. For fundamentally, the problem is not economics so much as it is culture. If the culture recognizes and rewards child nurturing, then there will probably be both more full-time mothers and more emotionally nurturing day care workers available. But when women are actively discouraged from caring for their own children, the supply of day care workers is likely to be overwhelmed by the demand. Child care is a labor intensive industry with few economies of scale; babysitting children is never going to make anybody rich. When women are encouraged to view caring for children as intellectually stultifying and demeaning, where are all these millions of nurturing, devoted, consistent substitute care-givers going to come from?

The answer, temporarily, is Jamaica.

But that's a solution only for those wealthy enough to import a full-time babysitter. There is always a tragic dimension to this kind of personal solution. British aristocratic mothers obtained their devoted nannies because lower-class women had few other job opportunities and without dowries or prospects were unlikely to marry. The mothering of the rich was purchased by denying families to the poor. In today's version, the poor immigrant mothers in Brooklyn leave their own children alone and uncared for, so the well-to-do Manhattan women can go to work with the warm glow of knowing little Jessica is in capable, maternal hands.

I am certainly not arguing that day care is always and everywhere destructive. But there is a world of difference between reassuring mothers that many children do fine in day care, and trying to make day care the dominant form of child rearing in America. A number of problems emerge when the latter happens, from unhappy children forced into situations which do not suit their temperments, to worried and anxious women compelled to put their children in day care against their best judgment, to a sudden and drastic decline in the quality of substitute care, as the demand for nurturing women swamps the supply.

There are women (and a few men) who make wonderful caregivers; there are day care centers where long-time employees make their young charges feel secure and loved. But providing high quality child care in this sense is not a job, it is a vocation. It means allowing yourself to be seduced into falling at least a little in love with a youngster who will certainly abandon you more completely and finally than any child ever abandons his parents. Such women are rare and, in a society which increasingly declines to praise such attributes in women, are growing rarer.

These cultural contradictions are beginning to be noticed. A *New York Times* article notes, "To the well-documented strains associated with day care, add another: as more women leave home for work and careers, fewer are available to take care of other people's children..." About a quarter of the nations preschool children whose mothers work are placed in an informal day care center run out of a neighborhood woman's home, a form of child care generally termed "family day care." But in many cities, that warm motherly neighbor who takes in kids part-time is an endangered species: "Those neighbors and aunts and grandmothers who have been going out and getting jobs are the very same women who would have been taking care of kids in the days when women stayed home," said Ellen Galinsky, director of Work and Family Life Studies at Bank Street College of Education. "It's a nightmare," confirms Dr. Michael Rothenber, who coauthored the latest edition of *Dr. Spock's Baby and Child Care.* "We all know that by 1990, 80 percent of the mothers with children under one will be working and looking for child care, and where the hell are they going to find it?"[29]

Creating close family relationships, as women do, is (as I have said) a good in itself. But it is also instrumental to producing a new generation of adults who can carry America into the increasingly complex, competitive world of the future. Our children today are troubled. The causes are complex; the solutions are long term and difficult. But solutions won't be found in a society which increasingly insists that children exist to give pleasure to the adults who raise them, and that women have more important things to do than take care of babies.

When women risk economic disaster and get nothing from society in return for nurturing the next generation, we will inevitably have to invest less in our children's welfare. That is, in fact, the agenda of an ideological elite which fails to appreciate the value of women's work. They will probably not succeed in making women as work-centered as most men are. They may well succeed in making the conditions for mothering so punitive, that our own and our children's well being will continue to decline.

The cultural anthropologists and social historians have hit the nail on the head: a child-centered household is not a historical inevitability; it is the invention of an affluent society, in which educating children to perform in the high-stress adult world takes a great deal more time and effort that it used to. It is simply a lot less difficult to raise your children to be successful peasants or country squires, than successful doctors, lawyers, engineers, accountants, and computer technicians.

If women are being pulled by economics, by ideology, and by male abandonment away from nurturing our children, there is no guarantee that a host of loving child care workers or fathers will spring up to fill the gap. The close bond between mothers and children *is* a cultural artifact in this sense: If women opt out of family nurturing, no natural law says *anyone* in a culture must care very much about what children need. Certainly not, as we shall see, men.

Endnotes—Chapter 6

1. Maxine L. Margolis, *Mothers and Such: Views of American Women and Why They Changed* (Berkley: University of California Press, 1984), p. 60.

2. Steven Mintz and Susan Kellogg, *Domestic Revolutions: A Social History of American Family Life* (New York: The Free Press, Macmillan, 1988), p. 56.

3. Margolis, *op. cit.*, pp. 104–05.

4. L. Bryce Boyer, "Psychological Problems of a Group of Apaches: Alcoholic Hallucinosis and Latent Homosexuality Among Typical Men," *The Psychoanalytic Study of Society*, vol 3 (1964), p. 225.

5. Lloyd de Mause, "The Evolution of Childhood," in *The History of Childhood: The Untold Story of Child Abuse*, Lloyd de Mause, ed. (New York: Peter Bedrick Books, 1974), p. 1.

6. "Textile families in Lille were known in the 1830s for their habit of doping the children with laudanum, a working-class babysitter, so that the parents could go off to the neighborhood bar." Peter N. Stearns, *Be a Man! Males in Modern Society* (New York: Holmes & Meier, 1979), p. 75.

7. de Mause, *op. cit.*, p. 41.

8. John F. Walzer, "A Period of Ambivalence: Eighteenth-Century American Childhood," *History of Childhood, op. cit.*, p. 358.

9. *Ibid*, p. 358.

10. de Mause, *op. cit.*, p. 3.

11. Simone de Beauvoir, *The Second Sex*. Translated and edited by H.M. Parshley, (New York: Vintage Books, 1974), p. 41.

12. Andrea Boroff Eagan, "Long vs. Short Maternity Leaves," *Glamour* (March 1986), p. 214ff.

13. Hathaway, "Working Mother Does Your Child Need You Now," *op. cit.*, p. 108.

14. Cook, *A Mother's Choice, op. cit.*, p. 100.

15. Bryce J. Christensen, "Day Care: Thalidomide of the Eighties?" *The Family in America*, vol 1 no 9 (November 1987).

16. Connaught Marshner, "Socialized Motherhood, As Eash as ABC," *National Review*, May 13, 1988, p. 30.

17. Eleanor Weisberger, *When Your Child Needs You* (Bethesda, Maryland: Adler and Adler, 1987). See also Dr. Burton White, *The First Three Years of Life* (New York: Prentice Hall Press, 1985), p. 151 and Dr. Selma Fraiberg, *Every Child's Birthright: In Defense of Mothering* (New York: Basic Books, 1977).

18. *Wall Street Journal*, March 3, 1987, p. 35.

19. Dale Farran, "Now for the Bad News," *Parents* (September 1982), p. 81. For a sampling of some recent studies suggesting problems with aggression and lack of cooperation among day care children, see Vicky M. Schenk and Joan E. Grusec, "A Comparison of Prosocial Behavior of Children with and without Day Care Experience," *Merrill-Palmer Quarterly*, vol 33, no 2 (April 1987), pp. 231–40; Michael Siegal and Rebecca McDonald Sorrey, "Day Care and Children's Conception of Moral and Social Rules," *Child Development*, vol 56 (1985), pp. 689–703; Carole Peterson and Richard Peterson, "Parent-child

Interaction and Day Care: Does Quality of Day Care Matter?'' *Journal of Applied Developmental Psychology*, vol 7 (January-March 1986), pp. 1–15.

20. Jay Belsky and Laurence Steinberg, ''The Effects of Day Care: A Critical Review,'' *Annual Progress in Child Psychiatry and Child Development*, 1979, pp. 576–61.

21. Jay Belsky and Russell Isabella, ''The 'Effects' of Infant Day Care on Social and Emotional Development,'' in M. Wolraich and D. Routh, eds., *Advances in Developmental and Behavioral Pediatrics*, vol 9 (Greenwich, CT: JAI Press), p. 15ff. Placing baby boys in day care for more than 20 hours a week also appears to interfere with *father*-child attachment. See, Jay Belsky and Michael Rovine, ''Nonmaternal Care in the First Year of Life and the Security of Infant-Parent Attachment,'' *Child Development*, vol 59, no 1 (February 1988), pp. 157–187.

22. Terrence Moore, ''Exclusive Early Mothering and Its Alternatives: The Outcome to Adolescence,'' *Scandinavian Journal of Psychology*, vol 16 (1975), pp. 255–72.

23. Belton M. Fleischer, ''Mother's Home Time and the Production of Child Quality,'' *Demography* (May 1977), pp. 197–212.

24. ''The LHJ Roper Poll,'' *Ladies Home Journal* (May 1988), p. 72.

25. ''1,200 Women Can't Be Wrong,'' *The Washington Post Magazine*, May 24, 1987, p. 20.

26. *The New York Times*, June 5, 1988, p. 22. According to the Census Bureau the breakdown is as follows: children under 5, 23.1% organized child care facilities. Kindergarten, grade school, 0.7%; cared for by working parent 8.1%; cared for by father in home 15.7%; cared for by grandparents in child's home 5.7%; cared for by other relative in child's home 3.7%; cared for by non-relative in child's home 5.9%; cared for in grandparents home 10.2%; cared for in other relatives home 4.5%; cared for in non-relatives home 22.3% (family day care).

27. Harriet Beecher Stowe, *Pink and White Tyranny: A Society Novel* (New York: New American Library, 1988), pp. 178–80.

28. *The New York Times*, June 5, 1988, p. 22.

29. *Ibid*. Note: the article claims 37% of children are in ''family day care,'' but the breakdown provided shows 10.2% of children cared for outside the home are cared for by a grandparent, and another 4.5% by another relative, which is not the kind of arrangement people usually have in mind when they speak of ''day care.''

7

The New
Man Shortage

For years he was a distant figure on the horizon, both feared and longed for, the cavalry that was to ride to the assistance of women beleaguered by babies and briefcases. He was the greatest achievement, the crowning glory of the current social revolution: The New Man.

And now at last he is here among us. Sensitive, warm, helpful, able to leap tall stacks of dishes, while changing roles and diapers with the same hand. The polls scream: 80 percent of new fathers change diapers! 79 percent manned the delivery room! 67 percent feed the baby! 43 percent actually wash the baby![1]

All right, so maybe he's not perfect; maybe, for example, there aren't enough like him to go around; maybe even he's not quite so handy around the house as advertised.

But compared to the Old Man, who avoided children like the plague, retreating behind his newspaper in the slippers while his ever-devoted spouse quietly shooed the children into the playroom like so many gnats at an alfresco dinner party, he's a child care titan, right? Right?

The general impression we have is that men are making incremental progress, agonizingly slow perhaps, but plodding steadily onward just the same. "Men in their twenties and thirties often appear more comfortably participative and involved [with their children] from an early time . . . an increasing number of men are now taking the primary responsibility for child rearing or are sharing equally. There are now more men who fully accept the role of single parent. There are a remarkable number of special men who do not need to have the stereotypical proofs of masculinity to reinforce their own male image, and who find less discomfort with balancing home life with career achievement."[2] This is the New Daddy, a sensitive man who drops out of the rat race, tunes into his kids, and even, like Michael Dukakis, does the dishes.

The only problem with the gender revolution is that men haven't gone far enough. As more men start doing their fair share of child care, women's lives will become more manageable. Maybe even enjoyable, we say, clinging to this vision of progress like shipwrecked sailors, half-drunk with possibility and half-drowned by present reality.

It is our last, best hope, and it is based on an outright lie.

The plain fact is that, as a group, men today are *much less* involved with their children than their fathers. There is a New Man, but he doesn't act like Dustin Hoffman. He lives with women and off women's salary. He refuses to marry and settle down. If he does marry and have children, he won't see any more of them than this father did. If he is single or divorced, he will probably abandon his children.

While society gives lip service to the coparenting ideal, we are actually moving in the opposite direction: toward making women more solely responsible for the care and upbringing of children than at any other point in American history. We'll get a little help, perhaps, from the federal government and the local day care worker, but not from husbands and fathers.

All the praise heaped on the New Daddy is intended to encourage men as they take on new, traditionally feminine household responsibilities. What the image actually does, though, is to disguise the sheer volume of women's productive efforts, and deflect attention from the huge, sudden drop in male responsibility for children.

The gender revolutionaries predicted that as women took on male roles, men would begin to share female responsibilities. Gender boundaries would blur. As women exercised their earning power, men would exercise their dormant nurturing instincts.

This simply hasn't happened. But it has taken us a while to notice that the New Man is a myth, because men and women both conspire to overestimate man's contributions to parenting and household labor. Making married mothers work does not seem to change male behavior at all, except to give men larger disposable incomes. The truth is that even men in intact families are doing little or no more around the house than their fathers did. They refuse to do housework.[3] They do not spend more time with their kids.[4] As a strategy for bringing married men into the family, androgyny has proved a miserable failure.

In 1984, Maxine Margolis concluded, ''All the recent time budget studies have found that women, employed or not, still contribute between 70 and 75 percent of the total time spent on housework; . . . the upper limit in the number of hours men spend on household tasks is about 20 percent, regardless of whether their wives are employed or the age and number of children at home."[5]

In 1975 about 217,000 men gave keeping house as their reason for being out of the workforce. In 1986, 383,000 men—a mere 2.1 percent of unemployed men—did so.[6] That extra 166,000 new men is the gender revolution's concrete achievement. In the best sections of the biggest cities, a handful of men can be seen pushing strollers, toting baby-in-snugglies, showing up at the day care center after work, and in other little ways publicly declaring: Real Men Nurture.

If this were the only change in male behavior over the last two decades, one could call it progress. Infinitesimal, but still progress.

But looking only at the behavior of trendy fathers in intact families misses the point. If current projections are accurate, *a baby born today stands an almost fifty-fifty chance of being largely abandoned by his father.*

Paternal abandonment is not just fairly common, it is fast becoming the new norm. Father absence and father neglect are being institutionalized on a large scale, by the erosion of mores that discourage illegitimacy and by the collapse of those that discouraged divorce.

Look at the raw figures: in 1960 one in eleven American children lived in a single-parent home; in 1980, one in five. Paul Glick of the U.S. Bureau of the Census estimated that by 1990 one in four children will live in a single-parent home and that *50 percent* of all children under age eighteen will have lived in a single-parent family, overwhelmingly father-absent.[7]

These statistics are rather familiar, but in thinking about them, we tend to miss the obvious. These are not just indicators of "social decay," they also say quite a lot about the success of efforts over the last twenty years to forge a new model of male behavior that encourages deeper involvement between men and their children.

When decision-makers think about the social problems caused by illegitimacy, for example, they generally focus on the conduct of the woman. A great deal of intellectual agitation focuses on what sort of social policies may get her to behave. How can we get her to raise her aspirations and close her legs, or at least her cervix? How can she be persuaded to use birth control, have an abortion, give her child up for adoption, finish high school, get off welfare, and get a job?

Very little of our social resources or intellectual energy has been spent trying to figure out ways to make men behave more responsibly, either before or after conception. The very absence of such an effort underscores for women the extent to which we have assigned children to mothers. Women make the babies, women choose not to have abortions, and therefore, women must bear not only the children, but the entire consequences of actions which, by a peculiar moral phobia are publicly acknowledged to be hers, but not his.

The gaps in our thinking about divorce are even wider. We are accustomed, at least, to connect illegitimacy and male abandonment, even if we aren't much inclined to do anything about it.[8] But divorce? Oh, it may be messy and painful for children, but surely divorce isn't the equivalent of paternal abandonment? Well, yes, it's true children commonly are afraid that when their parents divorce they will lose their father. But we generally treat this as an understandable, but childish fantasy on the kid's part. Parents, under the tutelage of socially aware psychologists, read their children the *Dinosaur's Divorce* and carefully explain that even though mummy and daddy are going to leave each other forever, they will never, ever leave their children. Husbands and wives get divorced, but parents and children do not.

Actually, this is a childish fantasy on the part of adults who, having severed the original family connection, wish to believe that all subsidiary connections are inviolable, stone-solid, a rock of family on which all can depend. If parents and psychologists were honest, they would have to warn children of divorce that more likely than not they can kiss Daddy good-bye. Their father will cease to be a reliable presence in their lives.

I have seen too many divorced women trying to shut a despised ex out of their children's lives to believe the blame for child abandonment in every case lies with men alone. But tossing about the guilt doesn't change a central fact in the life of a child of the eighties—the massive defection of fathers from the home.

Look at the epidemic of men failing to meet their modest child support obligations after divorce. In 1985, fewer than half of the five million women awarded child support received the awarded amount. Close to one million did not receive any payments at all. A middle-class father who is letting his children slip into poverty is probably not enjoying a close and warm relationship with them.

Direct surveys indicate the problem is even worse, if possible, than child support statistics suggest. In his 1983 testimony at a Senate subcommittee hearing, Nicholas Zill of Child Trend, Inc., a Washington, D.C., research organization, testified that only about one-fifth of children of di-

113

vorce maintain a good relationship with both parents; only one-third maintained a good relationship with their fathers.[9] Based on a nationwide survey of children in 1981, University of Pennsylvania researchers concluded, "Most outside parents had seen their children rarely or not at all in the previous year. Fathers, in particular were more likely *not to have had any contact at all* than to have seen their children *even once* in the past twelve months."[10]

The mass exodus of men from the family comes just at the time, stimulated in part by feminist concerns, that a wealth of research has confirmed fathers' emotional and psychological importance to children. A father's traditional role is by no means obsolete. Two statistics capture, in broad strokes, the importance of male breadwinners. Married women overall provide only 18 percent of family income.[11] And, 54 percent of all single mothers fall below the poverty line.[12]

But a father is more than a walking paycheck. Dr. George Rekers, professor of neuropsychiatry and behavioral science at the University of South Carolina School of Medicine, recently reviewed the literature on father absence and concluded, "Both developmental and clinical studies have clearly established the general rule that *the father's positive presence in the home is, in the vast majority of cases, normally essential for the existence of family strength and child adjustment."*[13]

Research shows that children without fathers have lower academic performance, more cognitive and intellectual deficits, increased adjustment problems, and higher risks for psychosexual development problems.[14] And children from homes in which one or both parents are missing or frequently absent have higher rates of delinquent behavior, suicide, and homicide, along with poor academic performance.[15] Among boys, father absence has been linked to greater effeminacy, and exaggerated aggressiveness.[16] Girls, on the other hand, who lose their father to divorce tended to be overly responsive to men and become sexually active earlier. They married younger, got pregnant out of wedlock more frequently and divorced or separated from their eventual husbands more frequently, perpetuating the cycle.[17]

The idea that children need active fathers is no feminist fantasy. They do. But how does American society achieve that goal?

How to handle men has been a feminine preoccupation since time immemorial, and lately, it has become a feminist one as well. Especially since the late seventies, it has become apparent that a revolution in sexual roles is not possible, or at least not very comfortable, unless men participate too. As one magazine guru put it (in *de rigeur* sex neutral language), "Of course, the primary source of support for a working parent is a contributing spouse. All the women I talked to stressed how important it is to have a husband who carries his share of the burden. This, they say, is the key to 'making it all work.' "[18]

Well, where can we all get such husbands? That is a question which while intensely personal, is deeply political—or at least social and cultural—as well. What is true for the economy of the United States is true in the economy of eros as well: production precedes redistribution. Not only aren't we churning out the reconstructed man, we've apparently halted production on the older model family man as well.

It is not that no one has been trying to get men to behave. The women's movement, diffused in the general culture, has had several strategies for making men behave.

Problem is, all of them are highly implausible, and none of them have proved successful.

The first idea was simply to force mothers into the work force. If women stopped caring for children, then men would have to start doing so.

Nice try, that one.

A second strategy was to convince men they have a stake in women's liberation. Men as well as women are oppressed by gender stereotypes. Look, now you don't have to support a family all by yourself. (Men appear to have gotten that message.) Now you don't have to miss the joys of parenting. (That one hasn't sunk in.) Unfortunately while receiving occasional tutorials on the joys of family, men have also been absorbing the much louder message addressed to women: that career success is the measure of self-respect, that personally caring for children is oppressive and unfulfilling, and (perhaps most importantly) that having children is not an important part of being an adult, much less of being a man.

But the most common approach has been simply to yell at men. You are abusing women by making them care for children, men are told. You better roll up your sleeves, pick up the diapers and do your fair share, or else . . . or else what?

Modern ideology makes it easy for men to rationalize their defection from family life. They no longer need to have a family to be viewed as real men. Indeed, they never ever really choose to have children—since the actual choice between having a baby or an abortion is always, in the end, the woman's. It is hard to see, under the current consensus which makes choice the foundation of moral obligation, in what sense men are responsible for the issue of their loins. It is only the fading residue of the old moral sense combined with the fatalism of the new welfare mentality ("well, *someone's* got to pay for them") that creates an impression that really, desertion is not quite the thing, and produces fitful, episodic attempts to enforce men's financial obligations to their families.

But justice is a poor paltry weapon in intimate relationships. A judge can divvy up a portion of a man's salary, but he cannot force a man to work overtime to pay for his daughter's braces, or take a second job so his family can move to a nicer neighborhood. No court order can make a man be a father to his children, or to give his wife the support she deserves. Being economically dependent on the state, rather than on a man, offers women with children only a poor semblance of economic independence and none of the satisfactions of marriage and family.

We will never find a solution to the New Man shortage, unless we jettison gender neutrality. The first step towards drawing men into the family is to admit that men are necessary. Men need a role in the family. What men need, loath though we are to utter the word, is a *sex* role.

A central problem in any culture, as Margaret Mead once remarked, is: "What to do with the men?" The male flight from family stems from our failure as a society to come to grips with the need and the dilemma expressed in that question. Women have babies. That is an awesome and indisputably feminine capacity.

My six-year-old son puts a large grey plastic knife underneath his sweater. He then pulls it out and looks up at me, anxiously, testing, and announces, "Women have babies. Men have swords." At a very young age the male senses a certain sterility at the root of his condition and searches for some positive way to assert his sexual identity. "I was joking when I told my wife that if the kid has blond hair and blue eyes, I'm gone," reports another new father. But more than half the men in one survey confessed similar nagging doubts that they were really the baby's father, a fear that they had been left out of something— something as monumental as the creation of life.[19]

How is a man, in the face of his intrinsic barrenness, to feel satisfyingly male? The varying answers which a society comes up with to that question shapes its basic institutions.

The dominant culture in America has only two visions for men in the family: First, to render them unnecessary. Second, to make them useful, but only in a unisex way. An alternate way of expressing the first idea is that we have been trying for some time to render women and children into a self-sufficient unit. "Some analysts speak of female-headed families as a social problem akin to drug addiction and unemployment," remarked *Washington Post* columnist Judy Mann. "Can we stop defining this population as a scourge and view it for what it is, a demographic group that has particular needs, much the same as the elderly or two-parent families with children?"[20]

This, as any single parent knows, is bunk. A single-parent family is not just an "alternate family form" it is an inherently weaker family form, with only one source of income and affection, and very often no emergency support system at all. Two parents are definitely better than one.

But let us take Judy Mann at her word. Let us imagine for a moment that she convinces us all that single-parent families are not a social problem. Male abandonment is nothing to worry about. Women don't need men's help in raising children. If she succeeds, you can forget about drawing men into family life. Men who believe they are superfluous are not likely to become dependable husbands and fathers.

The second tactic of the gender revolution is to admit that two heads are better than one, but to insist that each partner participate equally and interchangeably in the work of making a living and raising a family. Two people may be necessary to support a family, we are told, but there is no particular reason one of them has to be a man.

Modern scholars observed that the male role shifts somewhat from culture to culture and concluded, wrongly, that because the male role is fluid, it is dispensable. The paternal role is not ''natural'' in the sense of being inevitable. We know we can destroy men's fragile attachment to the family. We've done it. America has tried for twenty years to make women less economically dependent and to make men more unisexually involved in family life. The results are not encouraging. When society tries to abolish a male role in the family, men flee in record numbers, women drift into poverty, and children grow up fatherless.

The irony is that as a route to a civilized and satisfying life, the paternal role is much more important for men than the maternal role is for women.

It is not hard to see why women are portrayed as the dependent sex. As feminist therapists Luise Eichenbaum and Susie Orbach observe, women frequently ''carry the dependency'' in romantic relationships. By verbalizing our attachment, women allow men to appear more independent. This is the kind of polite social fiction that enables men to enter marriage without compromising their masculinity. It obscures, as George Gilder has noted, one of the central facts in male-female relationships: By any objective measure, *men need women much more than women need men.*

They may not recognize this need in themselves. Indeed, recent behavior suggests that many men do not. But they ignore it at their own peril.

On average, compared to general population, the single man is likely to be poor and neurotic, disposed to criminality, drugs, violence. He is irresponsible about his debts, alcoholic, accident-prone, and susceptible to disease. Men without women are poor performers, economically and socially. Married men earn some 70 percent more than singles of either sex. A married male high school graduate is four times as likely to eventually make $30,000 a year than a comparable single man. Single men between ages twenty-five and sixty-five are 30 percent more likely than married men or single women to be depressed, 30 percent more likely to show phobic tendencies and "passivity", and almost twice as likely to show "severe neurotic symptoms." They are almost three times as prone to nervous breakdowns, and suffer three times as often from insomnia (when they do sleep they are also three times more likely to have nightmares). The most striking data comes from a study by Leo Stole. In this study, single women were slightly better off than either married men or married women, but single men fared worst of all. Between ages of fifty and fifty-nine, 46.1 percent of the single men in Manhattan suffered "mental health impairment." (Which goes a long way toward explaining some of my recent dates.)

Similarly, single men make up the bulk of felons, rapists, muggers, and murderers. All told, single men have double the mortality rate of married men and three times the mortality rate of single women from all causes. Divorced and widowed men (but not women) show similar signs of distress. They are three and a half times more likely than divorced women to commit suicide and four times more likely to die in an "accidental" fire or explosion. Murder knocks off three divorced men for every divorced woman, as does cirrhosis of the liver.[21]

George Gilder has become a feminist hate figure for pointing out that radical feminists are right. Compared to women, men *are* nasty, brutish, undependable, and prone to crime, alcoholism, and skipping town. They beat each other and (as a sideline) women when their masculinity is unsatisfied. They are given to exploiting "both jobs and women" as a route to short-term satisfaction.

Well, the question is: what are we going to do about it? Channelling male sexual anxiety into the breadwinner role controls male aggression and creates family ties on which women and children can depend. What happens when there is no male role in the family? *What are we to do with the men?*

For men without women are, as a group, dangerous to themselves and others. Denied a male role by mainstream culture, men will increasingly resort to ancient and barbaric strategies for asserting their masculinity. They have sex indiscriminately, with little sense of responsibility toward the women they sleep with. They create violent subcultures in which women, even if we cared to, could not compete. And when all the roles connected with the family feel either feminine or unisex, men's attachment to their children becomes increasingly weak and vulnerable.

An astonishing number of men are articulately aware of their need for a sex role, of the gap between their own and their wives' importance in the family, of their need to earn their children. Husbands of working wives, it seems, do not object to their wives' careers. Nor do they feel they are overly burdened with housework or child care (as indeed, statistics suggest they are not). Instead, husbands of em-

121

ployed wives are tormented by what researchers call "breadwinner anxiety," a profound distress at their own inability to adequately provide for their families.[22]

For the same reason, married men find work more satisfying than single, cohabiting men do. Pepper Schwartz and Phillip Blumstein discovered that contrary to their expectations, "...husbands actually enjoy their work more than cohabiting men do. We feel that providing for other people infuses their work with greater meaning, so that even a tedious job can reward them...The responsibilities of caring for a family may help him to focus his efforts and cause him to be more serious about making himself a success."[23]

Certainly many new fathers report just such a transformation. In a rare study of expectant fathers, Jerrold Lee Shapiro, an associate professor of counseling psychology at the University of Santa Clara, uncovered ample evidence of what one might call The Gilder Effect. "One day I was going along happy-go-lucky. The next day I was the sole support of three people," said one twenty-two-year-old who had been a father for three days. More than 80 percent of the fathers from all economic strata expressed a similar feeling. "I became aware, when Mary was pregnant, that I no longer had any right to die," said another. "...I stopped taking such huge risks. I found myself driving slower, avoiding rougher areas of town, actually listening to a life insurance salesman...All for the reason that I was now important to this little thing, and I couldn't die because he needed me."[24]

Women also feel the need for a male role in the family. As the wife's income rises, the probability of divorce increases dramatically as her husband's inability to make an equal contribution to the family becomes intolerable to them both. Women who make more than their husbands adopt all kinds of stratagems to cushion what is obviously felt by both as a blow to his masculinity. Wives who earn more than their husbands on a regular basis are very rare. One-quarter of working wives earn more than their husbands, but half of these are working-class or middle-class women temporarily out-earning men who have been laid off, or are disabled, or are retired. Many of the rest are supporting husbands while they pursue higher education.

Only about 4 percent of working wives hold professional or managerial positions and make more money than their husbands. These women are the avant garde of the gender revolution.

Millie Stephens is one of this tiny avant garde, a twenty-eight-year-old manager for Bell of Pennsylvania who earns $46,000 a year. Carl, her husband, earns $31,000 as a Pennsylvania state trooper (a job which offers more masculine satisfactions than most). To disguise her salary, they put all of her earnings in the bank and live off his income. Mrs. Stephens also makes a point of washing dishes and ironing her husband's shirts. "I want to make him realize that even though I make more money, I can do all those womanly things," she says, "I don't mind treating him like a man."[25]

Masculinity isn't something men impose on women. It is something women insist on from men, refusing to marry or to stay married to men who cannot live up to its demands. I look around at the single professional women I know. Women in their late twenties or early thirties who self-consciously long for a husband and family. In almost every case, some nice man is in the background who would be willing to marry us. In many ways they are very eligible bachelors, exactly the kind of egalitarian helpmates women are supposed to be looking for. Men who could provide 50 percent of the income and show no sign of wanting to oppress us with their desire for dominance. Yet none of these women are tempted. Instead women with self-confessed longings for marriage and children, whose biological clocks are ticking away, flatly refuse to consider, as women with high incomes choose to divorce, men who have been unable to achieve a status equal or superior to that which they have achieved on their own.

The gender revolutionaries are right about a lot of things. It is important for men to spend time with their children. And it *is* culture that makes men commit to their children, but not by merely yelling at them for failing to meet unisex standards of justice and certainly not by promising to bring out their hidden femininity if they do. Culture binds men to families by offering them an essential role to perform, a role which is masculine in character and which society recognizes as such. In pursuit of gender, men will accomplish much.

For achieving a sexual identity is both a more difficult and yet more urgent task for men than for women. As Gilder writes, "Almost nowhere in the anthropological records is found evidence of Freudian penis envy (except among other men), but womb envy is ubiquitous. It confirms female sexual superiority as a basic reality of human life, universally apparent but feverishly denied—and aggressively countervailed in action—by posturing men in all societies."[26]

A male role in the family is threatening only to those who reflexively believe that whatever the men are doing is more significant and satisfying that whatever the women are doing, like the feminist who refused to join an elite women's club in Manhattan, saying she was going to hold out for a seat in the all-male Century Club.

Certainly, a male breadwinning role doesn't imply a life of obedience and subordination for women. Indeed, one of the most striking and least remarked findings in *American Couples*, is that the vast majority of homemaking wives enjoy egalitarian marriages. Sixty-three percent of all homemaking wives are in "marriages where power is shared equally."[27]

I am not arguing that biology is destiny. We may very well be able to alter our social institutions so that the single man is less oppressed by his sexual condition. Indeed, the gender revolution has been remarkably successful in achieving that goal. Over the last decade, the relative happiness of men and women has changed dramatically and in an odd direction. Married women remain the happiest group, but the percentage of wives who report being very happy declined somewhat from 43 percent in the 1972 to 1976 period to 39.7 percent in 1982 to 1986.

Among members of my generation, the change is even more striking. The percentage of married women age eighteen to thirty-one who say they are "very happy" plummetted from 43.7 percent in 1972 to 34.7 percent in 1986. On the other hand, the happiness quotient of single men in this age group tripled, leaping from 11.1 percent in 1972 to 31.3 percent in 1986.[28]

This is an *extraordinary* change. It appears we are busily restructuring our society to suit the least productive and most dangerous element of the population: single men. Their happiness is being gained at the direct expense of women and children.

That, surely, is a revolution of sorts, but not exactly what we were promised. An ideological commitment to gender neutrality blinds us to the obvious: pushing women out of the home is not a promising strategy for drawing men into it. When we get it out of our heads that forcing women to support children is liberation, and when children are recognized as an essential public good, rather than a private hobby, then and only then will intense pressure be brought on absent fathers to make them meet their financial obligations to women and children. And when men are made to feel that in their behavior to women and children their masculinity is on the line, those pressures may no longer be needed.

The New Man is a myth, but the need to involve men in families is not. Children need men actively committed to families. So do women. A culture which refuses to satisfy men's lust for gender deprives children of fathers, women of male support in raising families, and men of the incentive they need to live rich, productive, responsible lives. Both married and absent fathers must be made to meet their responsibilities to their children. But that will never happen as long as the creators of taboo remain more appalled at the idea of gender, than they are by the increasing poverty of women and the anguished bewilderment of children abandoned by their fathers.

Endnotes—Chapter 7

1. Gallup/Levi Strauss poll, *The Washington Post Magazine*, October 16, 1983, p. 13.

2. Dr. Morton H. Schaevitz, "How Men Really Feel," in *The Superwoman Syndrome* by Marjories Hansen Shaevitz (New York: Warner Books, 1984), pp. 55–56.

3. There is an extensive body of scholarly literature on household division of labor pointing to this conclusion. For example: "Husbands of employed women spend little or no more time in housework than husbands of non-

employed women (Ferber, 1982: Fox and Nickols, 1983; Walker and Walker, 1976).'' (Glenna Spitze, "Women's Employment and Family Relations: A Review," *Journal of Marriage and the Family,* vol 50, no 3, August 1988 p. 600.) A 1986 Rutgers University study of husbands of employed women also found these men spent little or no more time doing housework than husbands of full-time housewives. (Staines, Pottick and Fudge, "Wives' Employment and Husbands' Attitudes Toward Work and Life," *Journal of Applied Psychology* 1986 vol 71, no 1, pp. 118–128.) A fall 1988 survey, reported in the October 5, 1988, *New York Post,* well after Kramer v. Kramer first plunged the housedaddy into the spotlight, found that 8 out of 10 women, whether they work or not, do all the food shopping. 84% of women say they accept that cooking is their responsibility. And a 1989 survey reported in the February 9, 1989 *New York Times* found that 98% of working mothers, including those who work full-time and make more money than their husbands, say they are responsible for making child-care arrangements.

4. Working wives tend to make their husbands more ambitious, suggesting that far from freeing men to spend more time with children, wives' employment plunges men more intensely into the work force, in order to insure that her work achievements don't eclipse his. (See for example, Blumstein and Schwartz, *American Couples,* pp. 162–4). Other researchers have found that working mothers strive to make up for lost time away from the infant during the day.'' (Jay Belsky and Russle Isabella, "The Effects of Infant Day Care on Social and Emotional Development," MS. accepted for publication in M. Wolraich and Dr. Routh, eds. *Advances in Developmental and Behavior Pediatrics,* vol 9 (Greenwich, CT: JAI Press), pp. 15.24.26; 41: cited by Bryce J. Christensen, "Day Care: Thalidomide of the 1980s?" *The Family In America,* (November 1987). A study by Belsky and Rovine found that 50% of baby boys in full time day care were insecurely attached to their fathers compared to 29% of baby boys in day care for less than 35 hours a week. See Jay Belsky and Michael Rovine, "Non-maternal Care in the First Year of Life and the Security of Infant Parent Attachment," *Child Development,* vol 59 (1988), pp. 157–67. Another study of 922 families conducted in 1981 by the Institute for Social Research (ISR) at the University of Michigan found that fathers spend an average of 8 minutes a day on weekdays and 14 minutes on the weekends in "quality time" activities with their children, such as reading, conversing, or playing with them. Husbands with working wives, the researchers concluded, did not spend any more time with their children than husbands of full-time housewives. See Joshua Fischman, "The Children's Hour," *Psychology Today* (October 1986, p. 16.) After reviewing cross-cultural research literature on parental accessibility, Harvard psychiatrist A.M. Nicholi concluded "Parents in the United States spend less time with their children than in any other nation in the world, perhaps with the exception of England...Research shows that in Russia, fathers

spend as much as two or three hours a day with their children. But, in this country, according to a study out of Boston, fathers spend on the average of about 37 seconds a day with their young children." (Nicholi, 1984a, cited in Dr. George Rekers, "Fathers at Home," *Persuasion at Work*, April 1986, p. 2.)

5. Margolis, *Mothers and Such, op. cit.*, p. 177.

6. Sara E. Rix, ed., *The American Woman 1988-1989: A Status Report* (New York: W.W. Norton & Company, 1988), p. 2.

7. George Rekers, "Fathers at Home," *Persuasion at Work*, a publication of the Rockford Institute (April 1986), p. 2.

8. Indeed, current strategy on unwed teen mothers is actually to encourage male abandonment, on the theory that teen marriages are inherently unstable, and that women who marry in their teens tend to become (ugh) housewives. Given the current instability of adult marriages, this reasoning seems questionable, to say the least.

9. Dr. Nicholas Zill, Hearings before the Subcommittee on Family and Human Services of the Senate Committee on Labor and Human Resources, March 22 and 24, 1983, p. 86.

10. *Insight*, October 13, 1986, pp. 14-15. For a similar estimate see Judith A. Seltzer and Suzanne M. Bianchi, "Children's Contact with Absent Parents," *Journal of Marriage and the Family* 50 (August 1988), pp. 663-77. According to Seltzer and Bianchi, 24.4% of children see their fathers less than once a month while 35.2% never see their fathers. Interestingly, absent mothers are somewhat more reliable: 30% see their children less than once a month and 19% never see them.

11. George Gilder, "Women in the Work Force," *Atlantic* (September 1986), pp. 20-24.

12. Bumpass and Sweet, *American Families and Households, op. cit.*, p. 105.

13. Rekers, *op. cit.*, p. 2, emphasis in original.

14. Rekers cites Bach, 1946; Biller, 1976; Biller & Baum, 1971; Carlsmith, 1964; Drake and McDugall, 1977; Hetherington & Deur, 1971; Lynn, 1974, 1976; Matthews, 1976; McCord, McCord & Thurber, 1962; Mead & Rekers, 1979; Nash, 1965; Nicholi, 1985b; Reis & Gold, 1977; Rekers, 1981, 1986; Stolz, 1954.

15. Rekers cites Hoffman, 1961; Nicholi, 1985a, 1985b.

16. Rekers cites Apperson & McAdoo, 1968; Bene 1965; Berg & Kelly, 1979; Beiber, 1962; Earls, 1976; Evans, 1969; Greenstein, 1966; Mussen & Distler, 1960; Santrock, 1977; Stoller, 1969; West, 1959; Winch, 1949.

17. Rekers cites Hetherington, 1972; Hetherington, Cox & Cox, 1976, 1978, 1979.

18. Karen Levine, "Survival Tips," *Parents Magazine* (November 1988), p. 69ff.

19. Jerrold Lee Shapiro, "The Expectant Father," *Psychology Today* (January 1987), p. 39.

20. Judy Mann, "Helping the Strong," *Washington Post*, March 13, 1987, p. C3.

21. Gilder, *Men and Marriage, op. cit.,* pp. 61–68.

22. Graham L. Staines, "Wives' Employment and Husbands' Attitudes Toward Work and Life," *Journal of Applied Psychology,* vol 71 no 1, (February 1986), p. 118ff.

23. Blumstein and Schwartz, *American Couples, op. cit.,* p. 157.

24. Shapiro, *op. cit.,* pp. 36–42.

25. Laurie Hays, "Pay Problems: How Couples React When Wives Out-Earn Husbands," *The Wall Street Journal*, September 19, 1987.

26. Gilder, *Men and Marriage, op. cit.,* pp. 31–32.

27. Blumstein and Schwartz, *op. cit.,* p. 139. The authors instead focused on the fact that wives with full-time jobs were very slightly more likely than wives with part-time jobs or no jobs to enjoy egalitarian marriages. They judged 63% of homemaking wives enjoyed "marriages where power is shared equally," compared to 68% of marriages where wives are employed full time.

28. Norval D. Glenn and Charles N. Weaver, "The Changing Relationship of Marital Status to Reported Happiness," *Journal of Marriage and the Family* 50 (May 1988), pp. 319–320.

8

The Search for the Secret Self

"I have an abiding love for you—the deepest thing in me," wrote the author Neith Boyce to her husband Hutchins Hapgood more than three generations ago, "but in a way I hate your interest in sex, because I have suffered from it. I assure you that I can never think of your physical passions for other women without pain."

Neith Boyce and her husband were one of a group of avant garde intellectuals living in Greenich Village who in the early years of the 20th century self-consciously adopted a new moral code. They listened to Havelock Ellis, the first great sexologist, when he asked, "Why...should people be afraid of rousing passions which, after all, are the great driving forces of human life?" and agreed that sexual indulgence must be "ever wonderful, ever lovely."[1] Marriage was a bourgeois superstition, or worse, a chain yanking vibrant womanhood down to the status of property. They renounced sex roles and monogamy and announced that hereafter men and women shall live with perfect sexual equality in perfect sexual freedom.

Those pre-War radicals discovered, as we are discovering, that sex is more powerful than ideology. As Neith told her husband, "my reason doesn't find fault with you. But it's instinct and it hurts. The whole thing is sad and terrible, yet we all joke about it every day." For his part Hapgood, like many other male radicals, found free sex with sexually-free women less satisfying than expected. In his autobiography *A Victorian in the Modern World,* he admitted he longed for a wife who faithfully loved and cared for him.[2]

Eighty years ago these radical intellectuals had already formulated the two key strands of what would become the avant garde politics of the seventies: liberation consists of abandoning both sexual inhibitions and gender stereotypes. Today the sexual revolution has fallen into a certain amount of disrepute. But the once radical theory of androgyny has become *de rigueur.* Yet the two theories share certain peculiar views about sex and human nature.

Sexual liberationists declare, in effect, that sexual repression is contrary to human nature. Civilized mores are a mere crust holding back the volcanic polymorphic passions which are our true lusty selves. A man is what his sex is and his sex is what it would be, undampened by social convention. Ditto for women. It's a Freudian updating of Rousseau's noble savage, in which the id is the I and the ego merely the stubborn residue of social training. We'll never be truly free until we find our way out of sexual bondage.

And so the search begins for new and varied routes to

orgasmic fulfillment: sex with your clothes off, sex with the lights on, sex in the bathroom, sex standing up or sitting down, sex with the wife on top, sex with the husband behind, sex with honey and whip cream, premarital sex, extramarital sex, sex with men, sex with women, sex with inanimate objects, interspecies sex, love triangles and orgies with extra butter, please. Arise oh shackled bourgeoise, you have nothing to lose but your inhibitions.

Gender liberationists are motivated by a similar vision of human nature: underneath the layers of social conditioning lies a more genuine being, undistorted by gender, delightfully flexible, uninhibited, neither masculine nor feminine but in full possession of a divine, free personhood. So begins the search for the Secret Self.

For women, the Secret Self is our better self: what we would be like if we had not all been stuffed into little pink pajama sleepers at birth. To gender revolutionaries, a female role is in itself the offensive thing. Their dream is a world in which each individual in perfect freedom, that is without any outside influences, chooses his or her own lifestyle, goals, personality traits, even costumes. In this view, the very idea of a communally recognized feminine and masculine, whatever the content of the concepts, is offensive to personal liberty.

"Precisely because the concept of femininity is artificially shaped by custom and fashion, it is imposed upon each woman from without," writes Simone de Beauvoir, the first and most influential of modern feminists. "She can be transformed gradually so that her canons of propriety approach those adopted by the males: at the seashore— and often elsewhere—trousers have become feminine. That changes nothing fundamental in the matter: the individual is still not free to do as she pleases in shaping the concept of femininity."[3]

It began with de Beauvoir, but it is so much fun intellectuals won't stop doing it. One after another they tumble to record in exquisite detail all the awful things we do to turn little girls into women. We make them wear dresses and wash their hands and put their hair in pony tails, and their nonexistent breasts in training bras and who knows what other degradation.

Apparently, all one must do to show that women are oppressed is to show that we have been shaped by culture. Of course, all human beings we have ever encountered have been enculturated in one way or another, but that doesn't stop gender liberationists from assuming there is some fundamental opposition between being a free human being and having parents, teachers, friends, neighbors, lawmakers, and matinee idols who influence you.

The other side of the gender debate has been playing its own game: Fun with Darwin. Ever since Edmund O. Wilson proposed that all human behavior has a biological base which can be explained in evolutionary terms, pop-sociobiologists have had a field day, creating biological fairy tales to explain the reproductive value of every observable sex difference.

"[T]he origins of the basic contours of the human mating game are no longer a mystery," proclaims Robert Wright. "No one playing strictly by the rules of science can reasonably subscribe to any explanation other than the Darwinian one."[4] Men philander because men who philander leave more children than those who play by the rules. The sins of the father are genetically visited upon the sons. Women want marriage because our children stand the best chance of surviving if we can count upon the resources of the father. Women who did not care about such things did not reproduce as successfully, and are therefore statistically under-represented among current women. It is all impressively imaginative, and quite possibly true. It is also totally irrelevant to the current political debate.

The trouble with sociobiological ''explanations'' is that they do not explain. If true, it is but a tautology: only that which has been reproduced, exists. And if true, sociobiology is also self-enforcing: only that which reproduces will survive. Evolution will go on blindly selecting whatever we say or do. So why should we worry about it?

Pop-sociobiology gets its political power from the same source as Marxism: a natural human tendency to root for the winning side. If the proletariat will inevitably overthrow the bourgeois capitalist society, then let's root for them. If sex roles are ineluctable, then we have to embrace them. But confronted with this proposition, any red-blooded American, feminist or not, is likely to reply to a sociobiologist: ''Why should I care what's good for my genes?'' In the long run, there is no refuge from morality in hormones. People have been known to die for their convictions and they may be willing to risk genetic suicide as well.

The argument from biology also fails when it encounters a fundamental human reality: freedom of the will. Free will may be (as certain sociobiologists claim) a mere illusion. But it is an inescapable one. All of the minute acts which together make up sex-typed behavior are within our control. A teacher says ''men'' but she could have said ''people.'' A man bites his lip, but he could break down and cry in public. A woman screams, but she could pull out a gun and make our day.

The wholesome American response to the claim that biology is destiny is: well, okay, maybe we can't eliminate

134

sexual stereotypes, erase femininity, create a perfectly free unisex society, but you can't stop us from trying. Maybe, as Stephen Goldberg argues in *The Inevitability of Patriarchy,* men will always fill the majority of powerful positions because on average they have a lower dominance threshold and will fight harder to do whatever is necessary to obtain high status. Still, we can be Japan, or we can be Sweden. We know that we can create a nation in which 18 percent of the lawyers are women, rather than 7 percent as in 1975.[5] We know because we've done it. How about a society with 28 percent female lawyers? What about 48 percent? Let's try it and see. Maybe there are biological limits, but why not keep pushing until we find them. Anyway, if sex roles are really so unchangeable, what are you antifeminists so worried about?

The sociobiologists' mistake, argues Ann Fausto Sterling in *Myths of Gender,* "lies with the very notion of human essence—not with the idea that there is a human nature, but with the thought that there is a *particular* human nature, visible when all culture and learning is stripped away."[6] But gender liberationists like Sterling pursue the same false idol, trying to strip off layers of artificial culture in order to liberate our real androgynous selves.

Feminists and antifeminists have agreed to fight it out on the same confused terms: that gender behavior is *either* biologically based and therefore determined *or* culturally created and therefore infinitely malleable. The gender debate sheds so much heat and so little light because it currently revolves around the wrong set of questions. Do genes cause gender or does society? Sociobiologists insist it is the former. Is femininity an inherited or an acquired defect? Mainstream feminists have the dubious distinction of insisting it is the latter.

135

Few recognize how odd this nature-nurture debate is. It asks, "If I grew up without the distorting influence of culture, what would I be like?" We know the answer to that question from research on children raised in the wilderness: most likely, deaf, dumb, blind, or dead. We've grown so used to the question that it is hard to see how strange it is. Is language unnatural because it is learned?

Personally, I am not very interested in whether my desire to care for my son is biologically ingrained or culturally imposed. I do not view my desire as false because it may be (in greater or lesser degree) learned any more than I so regard my culturally-imposed inhibitions against traipsing into Godiva's on Fifth Avenue and surreptitiously making off with a box of chocolates. In neither case do I view my actions as a suppression of my "real" self. The distinction between culture and biology, though no doubt scientifically fascinating, breaks down for the individual, and therefore from the political perspective as well.

Whatever influence biology has on human behavior, it always exercises it through culture. One might say that culture is man's biologically ordained condition. For a man raised outside of culture is, as Aristotle said, a beast or a god. Experience suggests he is almost certainly the former.

Unlike animals, in which instinct frequently rules behavior, for human beings there is no clear distinction between "learned" and "biologically-based" behavior. Take aggression, for example. Men exhibit more aggressive behavior than women, and boys exhibit more aggressive behavior than girls. Yet we know that aggression is, to a large extent, a learned response. One 1967 study of preschool children found that "when a child was positively reinforced for an act of aggression, he was likely, subsequently, to repeat the same action toward the same victim. If he was negatively reinforced, the likelihood of a repetition decreased. Thus we see a process of conditioning of aggressive behavior at work."[7] Yet though aggressive behavior is frequently learned, boys appear to learn it more easily than girls. As Maccoby and Jacklin observed in their comprehensive review of the scholarly literature on the subject, "[I]t would appear that girls do not add aggressive actions to their repertoires of potential behaviors as readily as boys do through observing aggressive events."[8]

If it were possible to raise boys and girls from the same culture in totally separate environments—to raise the boys in a nonviolent, pacifist environment and inculcate the girls in an aggressive one, then the adult women may turn out to be more aggressive than the adult men. This is the Amazon fantasy. But egalitarian child rearing won't do it. When boys and girls are raised in a relatively egalitarian fashion, the boys pick up and respond to aggression cues more often than the girls. Though men in some cultures are more violent than men in other cultures, there are no societies in which women are more violent than men.

Gender revolutionaries assume that we are born gods—and would remain so but for the oppressive influence of culture. Suppose, for a moment, that they are right: gender is entirely a social construct; our bodies place no limits on our sexual nature. There is no reason to suppose, on that account, that gender will be any easier to eradicate.

Culture is a powerful force. When visionaries attempt a complete and radical transformation of society, the first step is usually spilling blood. There have been many attempts in many societies in this century to establish a New Man. Even with the gulag, the gas chamber, and mass

137

starvation at their disposal, revolutionaries have never completely succeeded in extirpating an existing culture. After several generations, as we are seeing now in Russia, the older culture generally reasserts itself. Let us suppose that women's connection to children is in many ways a cultural artifact. It will not necessarily, on that account, be any easier to force us to detach from children or to begin behaving like men. But the attempt to make us do so will create many painful casualties.

The preoccupation with hormones and DNA misses the point. In the end, the argument for femininity is not that it is unavoidable, but that it is *good*. Society urgently requires the femininity it now punishes in women. And women require men and society to recognize our values and contributions if we are to continue our work safely. That recognition will never emerge as long as elite women, afraid to acknowledge the value of women's work, maintain taboos against femininity. As long as we repress gender, our culture deprives both men and women of the many benefits of sex.

The idea that gender has a purpose is almost shocking to the modern ear. Many concede that sex roles *used* to be functional. In the early 19th century, women produced an enormous amount of goods for household consumption, everything from soap to candles. Most men worked twelve hours a day at jobs demanding physical labor. It would have been hard for women in such circumstances to work outside the home as well and still find ''quality time'' for the six kids.

But sex roles are still functional. This is true on many levels. In the first place, sex still leads to children, though I hesitate to mention this in public. We have so successfully separated sex and reproduction in our minds that it seems almost indecent to point out that we are not really in control of our bodies, though control is what we pride ourselves on. Today, to get pregnant without planning (even if one is married) is to have an "accident," like a toddler in training pants. (Abortion is the way to wipe up the mess, privately.) But still, eggs go on meeting sperm all the time without asking our permission first.

As long as this remains true, a crucial purpose of sex roles is to prompt men to take responsibility for their progeny. Creating a male role in the family insures women the support we require in raising children, and children the fathers they need. Gender-neutral social institutions render men unreliable even while making women more dependent on men.

When it becomes the social norm for both spouses to work (even when there are small children in the household), both spouses soon have to work. Few families with one income can compete with those with two incomes (especially the child-free ones) for resources, such as housing. This is particularly true when government, through the tax code and day care subsidies, subsidizes women in the workforce and penalizes women who care for their own children. When it takes two incomes to raise children in middle-class comfort, women become more, rather than less, economically dependent on men who become less rather than more family-centered. In a society founded on androgynous assumptions, women become doubly vulnerable: both outside marriage and within it.

But sex roles serve more than an economic function. Gender is a universal human need. Sex roles are a cultural contrivance invented to satisfy that need while at the same time insuring that the two great tasks of civilization—

taming the disruptive aggression of men and insuring the care and nurturing of the next generation—are performed.

However great or small biologically-based sex differences are, culture always exaggerates them. This frustrates and shocks the modern intellectual. "But clearly biological femaleness is not enough," complains Susan Brownmiller. "Femininity always demands more." She is right. Culture exaggerates sex differences to make them more gratifyingly real—to satisfy our lust for gender.

Women are naturally less hairy then men: with depilations and razors we make ourselves hairless. The fashions change, but always emphasize difference. Men and women may both wear tight jeans, but they aren't unisex: they practically outline the fundamentals of sex. Fashion cycles alternate. Women strive to be full-bosomed fertility goddesses or tomboyish Annie Halls, but either fashion exaggerates our femaleness. There's nothing more feminine than Cher in a black leather motorcycle jacket.

When talking about how people acquire gender, social scientists revert to mechanical concepts such as "social conditioning." They imagine a process in which parents, teachers, and media moguls cram childish souls into little gender packages from which we escape only with extraordinary difficulty. If this were the case, creating a gender-neutral society, while very arduous, might be possible. But the truth is children do not passively permit themselves to be gendered. Instead they hunger for it, actively reaching out for ways to establish a sexual identity. They too, lust for gender.

In her book, *Girls and Boys, the Limits of Non-Sexist Childrearing,* Sara Bonnett Stein notes that even parents devoutly committed to raising children free of gender stereotypes often end up with daughters who want pink dresses and sons who go "bang-bang" with guns. Children learn about gender by observing the world around them, quite independent of the androgynous sermons parents and teachers explicitly preach. According to the survey results in *The Motherhood Report,* about half of American mothers are trying to raise their children without sexual stereotypes. It's not easy.

One woman, for example, taught her son to help out with housework, as her husband often did. One day while her son was vacuuming, her brother-in-law remarked, "You mean you get pushed into doing woman's work?" That stray remark undid years of nonsex role training. "For weeks, he put up a fuss about housekeeping," the mother moaned. "The fact that my husband vacuumed, too, made little difference. My son's response was, 'So what? So he's been pushed into doing woman's work, too!' "⁹

Her son had two choices: either he could follow his father's example, vacuum and thereby affirm that vacuuming was a unisex activity, or he could label vacuuming women's work, and affirm his own masculinity. Pursuing gender offered psychic rewards that accepting androgyny did not.

Another woman took special care to make sure both her daughters and sons took turns doing all household chores. The girls mowed the lawn and took out the garbage; the boys learned to cook, wash dishes, and clean. "Then, during the summer, the kids spent a couple of weeks on my brother's farm. Upon returning home," she reports, "they would then identify jobs as boy's jobs or girl's jobs. It took weeks before I could get them to stop."¹⁰

Again, what is astonishing is that children shucked off years' worth of nonsexist instruction at the least provocation. Offered a gender stereotype, they grabbed it and ran, much to their parents' dismay. Sex roles are stubborn in part because they satisfy a basic human need. The sexual liberal's great dream, a society in which gender is irrelevant, is everyone else's nightmare.

Six year olds are some of the most determined chauvinists in the world. Gender, being newly-acquired, is all the more passionately valued. The boys are convinced that boys are bigger, brighter, smarter, faster, better, more wonderful than anything else in the world. And guess what? The girls think the same about girls. In this culture, high sexual self-esteem for females lasts through college and then subsequently declines somewhat. It doesn't have to be that way.

In many highly-gendered societies, adult women have had a quite adequate self-image. Women naturally tend to persevere in their little girl certainty that women are best. It is of course possible for any woman, or a whole society of women to lose this belief. One sure way to deprive women of it is to tell them that their most cherished contributions to society are inferior, that their deepest feelings and values are but self-delusions, that indeed, their very selves are lost as long as gender lives.

The myth of the Secret Self arises in our times from many sources. Anthropologists, for example, quite sensibly maintain that it is impossible to understand a primitive culture unless one suspends judgment long enough to see social institutions as the natives do. Unfortunately, anthropologists and many other intellectuals influenced by them mistook this analytic tool for a moral insight. If you were raised among the Kafe in Papua New Guinea, they tell us, you would believe that when a girl first menstruates she ought to be locked up in the house for a week and allowed to eat only sweet potatoes roasted in the fire. It is only because you were raised in New Rochelle that you think the proper way to acknowledge budding womanhood is with a Sweet Sixteen party. If so much of what we do or believe is a result of mere accidents of geography, they implicitly ask, can any of those beliefs or actions be part of our real selves? They ask us to imagine that the accumulated experience, knowledge, education, relationships, and social roles of many years are not really part of us—that the question, "what would you think if you were born into a different family, in a different age, in a different culture?" is conceptually coherent when it is not.[11]

Academic philosophy has done its part as well. John Rawls is something of a phenomenon. In a century in which philosophy has been largely kept safely locked in the ivory tower, Rawls has won for himself the academic equivalent of a household name, a fame which exceeds the narrow confines of his academic specialty. His book *Social Justice,* gave liberal democrats what they had been lacking for at least a century: the pretense of an objective moral basis for their passionately held political preferences. How did he do all this? With the help of the Secret Self.

Rawls gave us a mental exercise. Put on, he tells us, "the veil of ignorance." Strip yourself of all the specific content of your personality: your beliefs, social position, family relationships, talents, inclinations. Now, understanding that you might be born any kind of person in any social situation, what kind of social institutions would you prefer?

Rawls wants us to conclude, that stripped of the biases of our social situation we would do anything to avoid being born poor. That choice precisely reflects the risk-averse psychology of the average academic. But a more daring individual might easily decide that a society in which most people lead interesting lives but there is a one in fifteen chance of being condemned to a life of abject poverty is preferable to a society in which no one is poor, but opportunities for great achievement are restricted. People do take chances all the time.

The only proper answer to the question of what you would want if you didn't know who you were is: "how the heck would I know?" There has never been a human being without content to his personality. How could such a being prefer one social state to another?

The most powerful progenitor of the myth of the Secret Self is 20th century existentialism, the philosophy out of which feminism was born. Simone de Beauvoir is very frank about her intellectual debt to Jean Paul Sartre. "Of course, in philosophical terms, he was creative and I am not...I always recognized his superiority in that area. So where Sartre's philosophy is concerned, it is fair to say that I took my cue from him, because I also embraced existentialism for myself..."[12]

For Sartre, there is an inextinguishable contradiction between social roles and personal liberty, a contradiction rooted in his rather odd conception of what it means to be a self. As Alasdair MacIntyre writes, "Sartre...has depicted the self as entirely distinct from any particular social role which it may happen to assume...For Sartre the central error is to identify the self with its roles, a mistake which carries the burden of moral bad faith as well as of intellectual confusion.[13] De Beauvoir applied Sartre's analysis to sex roles.

But there is an essential contradiction in de Beauvoir's work. To understand it, we have to step back for a moment and consider the intellectual ancestor of de Beauvoir's existentialism: Friedrich Nietzsche. In a democratic age, Nietzsche joyfully asserted a ruggedly aristocratic morality.

Virtue was not open to every man, or to the average man. Only the man great enough, bold enough, courageous enough to carve a morality for himself out of pitiless uncaring nature could possess the good—a good that he himself created.

Like the later existentialists, Nietzsche proclaimed that values are not discovered, they are made. There is no value without a Valuer. But Nietzsche argued that this task of creating morality out of chaos was difficult and immense and magnificent and that only the greatest of men could accomplish it. The rest of us live upon the faith of one or another of the great men "who saw that it was good." Nietzsche, in a Godless world, elevated a few to the status of gods and relegated the many to the status of herd animals, effectively eliminating the category: human.

Existentialists like Sartre, on the other hand, breezily claimed that creating a morality to live by was a task open to all men. Freedom is ours and only bad faith explains why we don't seize and act on it. Twentieth century existentialism, it turns out, is Nietzsche diluted for the masses. It is also therefore a lie.

In the first place, very few men have been able to live without believing that the good is larger and more secure than their love of it. In the second place, existentialists were incredibly impressed with themselves for being one of the few who could do so. Sartre's existentialism is existentialism for the masses largely in the sense that it is existentialism in fear of the masses, an elitism behind a democratic facade. Existentialism is an aristocratic morality in disguise, in retreat, in *bad faith*.

This bad faith is evident in the work of de Beauvoir, who combines a pervasive contempt for women in particular with a profound and urgent passion for the well being of

great women, those unrecognized in the past, and yet unborn to the future. "With all the respect thrown around it
by society, the function of gestation still inspires a sponta-
neous feeling of revulsion," she writes.[14] Through maternity, women are chained to the claims of the species and so
remain on an animal plain compared to men. It never oc-
curs to de Beauvoir to wonder how is it possible that bearing and raising human children could be a less than fully
human endeavor. So, she concludes, the woman who devotes herself to raising children is a "parasite," one who
"buries her will and her desires," and (my personal favorite) "a bamboozled conscious being and a practitioner of
bamboozlement."[15]

Worst of all she is a Temptress: "What is extremely
demoralizing for the woman who aims at self-sufficiency is
the existence of other women of like social status, having at
the start the same situation and the same opportunities,
who live as parasites," de Beauvoir chastises. "A comfortably married or supported friend is a temptation in the way
of one who is intending to make her own success; she feels
she is arbitrarily condemning herself to take the most difficult roads; at each obstacle she wonders whether it might
not be better to take a different route...."[16]

It is only on the highest level, as de Beauvoir insistently repeats, that women's accomplishment in art, literature, and philosophy do not rival men's. But getting women
to that highest sphere of power and accomplishment is de
Beauvoir's—and orthodox feminism's—obsession:

> [T]he majority of men have the same limitations; it is when
> we compare the woman of achievement with the few rare
> male artists who deserve to be called "great men" that
> she seems mediocre...

Art, literature, philosophy are attempts to found the world anew on a human liberty: that of the individual creator...
The men that we call great are those who—in one way or another—have taken the weight of the world upon their shoulders; they have done better or worse, they have succeeded in re-creating it or they have gone down; but first they have assumed that enormous burden. This is what no woman has ever done, what none has ever been *able* to do.[17]

The elitism of which the current wave of feminism has been accused is not a mere accident of history. It is not the consequence of the white, upper-middle-class status of its founders, women like Friedan and Steinem. Feminism's elitism is lodged in the philosophical assumptions on which it is based, which lead sexual revolutionaries like de Beauvoir to care little about what happens to ordinary women so long as they succeed in giving birth to the *Uberwench.*

That is why liberal feminists have such contempt for any proposal to improve women's lives which rejects androgyny. If reformers wish to give women an opportunity for diverse, productive, meaningful lives, they will search for ways to give us the opportunity to make many kinds of public contributions without downgrading or undermining our work in nurturing families.

But if the goal is, as it seems to be, to make sure the best and the brightest women don't get distracted by the temptation of love and motherhood—the feminine role— then a different set of solutions is in order. Then there must be "no turning back the clock" on divorce. Then women must be permanently at risk of abandonment and poverty, so that we will be forced to work continuously. And if society must make special accommodations for motherhood, these benefits must be structured so as to keep women on the job, lest the most ambitious women feel odd or awkward because they aren't fulfilling traditional female roles. In keeping with this goal, the achievement of women as mothers and wives must be downgraded and suppressed because there is no way that cultivating the feminine virtues in ourselves will help us write original philosophy or become great statesmen.

But of course only a handful of men in history have produced, in their working lives, achievements of that magnitude. To build social institutions chiefly to accommodate such men and the women who wish to join them assumes the rest of us, as Nietzsche shouted out loud and existentialists like de Beauvoir whispered furtively, are really only fodder for their achievement.

Liberal feminism triumphed by telling a lie about nearly all women—and men. The work women do in families may not perhaps, seem great compared to oh, inventing a new morality, or discovering the cure to cancer. But it compares quite favorably, in value, meaning, and social productiveness with being a vice-president for public affairs of General Motors, say, or a partner in an advertising firm. And it is necessary that we start saying so.

The search for the Secret Self starts as a quest for freedom: from tradition, from inherited obligation, from family, religion, geography, and gender. It ends in elitism and even tyranny. Before the truth we are all equal. If all values are social constructs imposed on individuals by culture, then all political argument becomes propaganda, a mere expression of the will to power. A person can choose silence and indifference. But to the extent one steps into the social arena at all, to the extent one tries to please, persuade, convince, reward, admire, applaud, disapprove, or support any single other human being, one is necessarily being manipulative: trying to make another person conform to one's own arbitrary vision. This belief will disarm and disenfranchise most people who will discover they no longer know how to defend what are artlessly called traditional values. But it makes those who are running the game and are quite confident that they know the real desires of others' Secret Selves, vastly more powerful.

If existentialists are right, only two choices are left a citizen seeking to influence the state: she can either impose her own vision of the good on everyone else; or she can accept that others will impose their vision on her. Orthodox feminists try to escape this dilemma by positioning themselves as champions of the right to choose. They can have their cake and eat it too by defending, not an actual individual's right to choose, but the right of the individual's secret self—unconstrained by social influence—to choose. So long as any social influence remains, the choices women make are not free and need not be respected or protected.

Secret selves are wonderful devices, for outside parties can pour judgments and aspirations into them. In this way, essentially authoritarian political philosophies can be disguised, even to those who hold them, as democratic and individualistic.

No, no, you don't really want what you think you want: it's only a spasm of false consciousness. And anyhow even if you do really want it, if you had only been raised differently you wouldn't, so what makes you think we have to pay any attention to what you want anyway? It is peculiar, an irony of history, but in this way orthodox feminism institutionalized the practice of ignoring female desire.

When a political movement defines choice not in terms of what people do and want, but what they would do and want if society didn't oppress our secret selves, there is no way to check ideology against reality. As one very nice radical feminist cheerfully proposed to me in a debate, "We don't even have the language yet to describe what society will be like when men and women truly participate equally in both public and private realms." If a woman becomes a nurse, it's a sign of social oppression, not personal choice. If women choose to drop out and have families, it's because we've been excluded from higher pursuits. Any amount of violence or poverty or personal trauma is acceptable as a means of prodding women out of our stodgy ways, of liberating our secret selves.

The answer to androgyny is not biological destiny but uncommon sense: we've seen the future and it doesn't work. Actually, of course, it works fairly well for those older women who've already raised their families and who have not been callously impoverished by legally-sanctioned male abandonment. Orthodox feminism has done pretty well by the Betty Friedans and the Jeanne Kirkpatricks of the world. But there is no reason, when creating new avenues for female achievement, to tear down the social institutions that make it possible for women to devote themselves to the nurture of children. No reason, that is unless your ultimate goal is eliminating sex differences, no matter how much it hurts.

The costs of sexual repression have been high: In less effective parenting and the repression of female desire; in the poverty of single mothers and the pain of children abandoned by their fathers; in a generation of women overworked in the name of a future utopia its proponents lack the language to describe; in a generation of children left at the mercy of institutionalized care which (given the state of public schools) is not likely to be helped by a massive infusion of federal aid.

If sex roles are too stifling, the obvious answer is to widen the range of opportunity contained in the role, not to extirpate gender altogether. What is the result of attempting to abolish sex roles by proclamation? Men, abandoning a civilized male role, increasingly turn to promiscuous sex and violence as their primary route to male identity. Women remain in our traditional role as caretakers of children—poorer, overworked, more vulnerable to male abandonment and abuse. And children, both male and female, become the most vulnerable of all.

The result is not a gender-free society. If we do not offer our children—by deed and word—a constructive sense of gender, destructive sex roles will emerge to fill the vacuum. While we try to repress gender by banning sex roles in public images, in our television shows, and sex manuals, and public school textbooks, our children will eventually emerge with a new sense of gender based on what they observe in the world around them: women are poor and have children. Men make love, money, and trouble. Something very like this conception of gender appears to have emerged in America's ghettos.

An ideology is an idea that is afraid. Like all frightened things, it seeks first and foremost to defend itself no matter what the cost. In this sense an ideology is always reactionary in temperament, though it dresses itself in the rhetoric of progress as easily as that of orthodoxy, authority, and decline. Today androgyny is an ideology promoted, maintained, and fiercely defended primarily by women. The costs of trying to impose androgyny are also being born primarily by women. But not necessarily the same women.

I believe mainstream feminists are compassionate individuals, motivated by a genuine concern for women. Their error is not of the heart, but of the head. Because they have appropriated to themselves the right to define women's rights, women's desires, and women's needs—addressing what they perceive as the needs of our Secret Self, and scorning the "reactionary" desires of our actual selves—the new female elite must accept considerable responsibility for the dramatic decline in women's status and well being.

Considerable, but not sole responsibility. The search for the Secret Self has prospered only because it resonated, as we shall see, with other deeply rooted strands of American thought, which together made it possible for intelligent people to entertain the idea that culture is the enemy of human liberty.

No, gender is not the only area in which we remain charmingly, alarmingly ignorant of the facts of life.

Endnotes—Chapter 8

1. John D'Emilio and Estelle B. Freedman, *Intimate Matters: A History of Sexuality in America* (New York: Harper & Row, 1988), p. 230.

2. *Ibid.*, p. 224.

3. de Beauvoir, *The Second Sex, op. cit.*, p. 759.

4. Robert Wright, "Why Men Are Still Beasts," *The New Republic*, July 11, 1988, p. 30.

5. Rix, ed., *The American Woman 1988–89; A Status Report, op. cit.*, p. 344.

6. Ann Fausto-Sterling, *Myths of Gender: Biological Theories About Women and Men* (New York: Basic Books, 1985), p. 197.

7. Eleanor Emmons Maccoby and Carol Nagy Jacklin, *The Psychology of Sex Differences* (Stanford, California: Stanford University Press, 1974), p. 240.

8. *Ibid.*, p. 236. "Girls do not notice and retain the details of modeled aggression to the same extent that boys do. In the Bandura experiment, even under the incentive conditions, girls recalled less. Maccoby and Wilson (1957) found that girls recalled less of the aggressive content. In the work by M. Moore (1966), children in the age range 8–16 were shown pairs of pictures in a stereoscope, one picture showing a violent scene, the other a nonviolent one. Boys more often reported seeing the violent scene. Kagan and Moss (1962) found that in tachistoscopic presentation of aggressive scenes, girls required longer exposure times than boys to recognize the picture."

9. Genevie and Margolies, *The Motherhood Report, op. cit.*, p. 302.

10. *Ibid.*, p. 302.

11. This concept of the null self undoubtedly prepared the ground for the importation and sudden popularity of New Age doctrines like reincarnation which hold just that: the essential self can jump from being a king, a peasant, or a cockroach with equal facility.

12. Alice Schwarzer, *After the Second Sex: Conversations with Simone de Beauvoir*, translated by Marianne Howarth (New York: Pantheon Books, 1984), p. 109.

13. Alasdair MacIntyre, *After Virtue: A Study in Moral Theory*, 2d ed. (Notre Dame, Indiana: University of Notre Dame Press, 1984), p. 32.

14. de Beauvoir, *The Second Sex, op. cit.*, p. 165.

15. For example, from *The Second Sex*. "It is through gainful employment that woman has traversed most of the distance that separated her from the male; and nothing else can guarantee her liberty in practice. Once she ceases to be a parasite, the system based on her dependence crumbles. . ." p. 755; "If the difficulties are more evident in the case of the independent woman, it is because she has chosen battle rather than resignation. All the problems of life find a silent solution in death; a woman who is busy with living is therefore more at variance with herself than is she who buries her will and her desires; but the former will not take the latter as a standard. She considers herself at a disadvantage only in comparison with the man." p. 763; "The fact is that the traditional woman is a bamboozled conscious being and a practitioner of bamboozlement; she attempts to disguise her dependence from herself, which is a way of consenting to it." p. 789.

16. *Ibid*, p. 777.

17. *Ibid.*, pp. 791–793.

Section 2

SEX AND JUSTICE

The Curse of Contract

One evening, not long ago, I was standing in the kitchen arranging pink carnations in a vase. My date, a very intelligent and well-educated man in his late twenties, walked up to me, put his arms around my waist and said, "Well, here we go lapsing into sex roles again." I slapped his face. Well, not really, but I ought to have. Oh, it wasn't his fault. He was only being what every thinking person longs to avoid being: a product of his times.

What is distinctive about our times? While we were busy making choice the sole standard of social justice, we also made social justice one of the chief goals of personal

relations. As a slogan, ''The personal is the political''
meant not only the eminently reasonable point that women
(like all voters) ought to make our own needs the basis for
political demands. It came to signify as well that women
ought to introject a commitment to political justice into our
personal relationships. That is how we have reached a point
where women are not permitted our own natures. Because
gender justice demands we exclude or eradicate or sup-
press that within us which is contrary to the first law, the
law of sexual equality.

Seeking social justice may be a noble thing. Demanding justice in personal relationships, though, is an unnatural
act. For justice is the least men may claim from us. Justice
is giving to each man exactly what he deserves and no
more. Justice is what we offer those we cannot love. Justice
is for strangers. And to have a passion for justice, in the
personal sphere, is to long inexpressibly for what is forever
second rate.

Many subtle theoreticians preoccupied with social justice have traced the ways personal relationships affect
power structures. Women, they tell us, fail to achieve
power, wealth, and fame in the same proportions men do
because we remain enmeshed in family concerns. For
these intellectuals there is only one answer: reshape the
family so that it no longer interferes with women's path to
glory. To achieve this narrow vision of social justice, they
create and promote a new conception of the family. The
family, they tell us, will no longer be the realm of unchosen
relationship, of bonds of kinship. A family is (or ought to be)
a collection of freely-choosing individuals seeking self-
realization.

Eradicating gender is part of this ambitious attempt to
reshape the family. The theory goes something like this:

Once gender stereotypes which tie women to children break down, men will give in to their heretofore repressed feminine desire to nurture. Men's increased attentiveness to children will, in turn, liberate women to compete in the marketplace, which is the only place where freedom, power, and self-actualization can be won. As we saw in chapter 5, it hasn't really worked out that way. In practice, the effect of the choice ideology in gender has been that society—and men—get to exploit women's capacity for love without ever having to pay for it.

In the realm of family law, the results of the choice ideology have been similar. In today's America, getting married or having children has been redefined as a private pleasure that choice-enhancing individuals select from an array of possible pleasures. Individual men and women are supposed to work out the terms of marriage and parenting without being oppressed by gender stereotypes or social norms. The consequence of the gender-neutral conception of family is that women, who remain stubbornly devoted to children, are left to shoulder both the traditionally male and traditionally female work involved in the critical task of raising the next generation, with a little help from government subsidies perhaps, but not from men.

America's elite has sought to sacrifice the benefits of gender on behalf of a non-existent ideal of existential freedom. But the sacrifices do not stop there. Other key social institutions have become casualties of our determined pursuit of perpetual and perfectly "free" choice.

The rapid deterioration of women's lives is not an accident. Nor is it the fruit of a cabal of wicked feminists or, as one Rutgers law student suggested to me recently, the result of the machinations of "the male establishment." The painful choices women face are a direct consequence of a profound and widespread intellectual misconception, a fundamental error in philosophy which occurred when we began articulating the moral basis for human institutions, such as the family, which in the past had never been seriously questioned and therefore required no explanation. What is taking place in America today is a massive attempt on the part of that corporate mind we term culture to introduce justice in intimate relationships by understanding family obligations as contractual in nature.

The great thrust of the classical liberal tradition (to which both contemporary liberal and conservative movements are, in their separate ways, heir) has been to eliminate hereditary rights and obligations. As Sir Henry Maine wrote in 1864, "The movement of the progressive societies has hitherto been a movement from *Status* to *Contract*"[1] Liberal social programs, from affirmative action to wealth redistribution are attempts to redress accidents of birth, to neutralize hereditary advantages.

Modern liberals understand only too well the role government sometimes plays in creating freedom of choice. "To leave people entirely to their own devices offers no respect for individuals in a world where the distribution of resources often results from luck, historical accident, family inheritance, or injustice," write David Kirp, Mark Yudof, and Marlene Franks, authors of *Gender Justice* and self-avowed liberals.[2] Make sure all players, no matter who their parents are or how much money they have, enjoy exactly the same opportunities, then Play Ball. But what the modern liberal refuses to recognize is that very often gaining one choice eliminates others, and that government programs as frequently narrow as facilitate choice.

Conservatives, on the other hand, emphasize that a man has no status obligations, at least few or none that are enforceable by the state. This impulse to personal liberty reaches its perfection in the libertarian vision that only the individual has concrete reality, and that no abstraction—no nation, community, church, has any moral claim upon an individual except upon his consent.

But the Elysian vision of the sovereign individual, self-created and self-governing, runs smack into the most ancient of human institutions: the family. Because the core of family, what gives it its distinguishing character and transformative power, is that family obligations are not contractual in nature. One is born into a web of relationships, full of confusing and often demanding obligations (including legal ones) towards people you never chose and may, in fact, dislike.

Here in the grand American experiment, a country which exalts the power of the individual to shape his own destiny, the family is a stubborn remnant of status obligation and a distasteful reminder that we are never really solely responsible for all that we achieve.

A naive conception of individual choice is not the exclusive property of any part of the political spectrum. It grows out of the very core of American political traditions. What is more American than the self-made man? But the image of the self-sufficient individual, that part of the American heritage endlessly promoted by the right is, of course, a myth. It is the sort of useful social myth that points to certain psychological truths and obscures others, including this: Every individual choice, from property to marriage, requires a social structure to maintain and uphold it, to forge out of the chaos of nature a space in which human choices can be made.

In pursuit of the widest field for individual liberty, extended family obligations have been shucked off one-by-

161

one, leaving the reproductive core: father, mother and 1.8 children. In the last two decades, we have gone post-nuclear and deeply weakened men's sense of obligation to their offspring, encouraging the formation of a yet more liberated family: the single parent household. And with new institutions like surrogate motherhood, we are prepared to go one step further: The mother-child dyad itself will be broken down. Women will be liberated from the burden of knowing that the child in our womb is our responsibility. All these various developments are, at the deepest level, one and the same phenomenon.

The backdoor way to destroy the family is through contract. Re-imagining bonds of kinship as bonds of contract leaves women and children dangerously vulnerable. But making contract the basis of kinship is more than dangerous, it is false. The contract model does not explain how families are formed or sustained; in fact it makes families inexplicable.

When we begin to view choice and contract as the foundation of family ties, ordinary family behavior comes to seem extremely peculiar. Raising children is arduous, time-consuming, and brings no obvious rewards. Why are parents obligated to care for their children? Why is society, for example, morally justified in punishing child neglect and enforcing child support? Doesn't that infringe on individual liberty? No, no, no goes the modern falsetto chorus, you have a duty because you *chose* to have children.

Parents today are supposed to have chosen their children for the gratification they bring. One consequence of this doctrine has been a decreased tolerance for the inconveniences children impose on adult society, and the increasing isolation of mothers who care for their own children. As the feminine mystique collapsed, more men

162

and some women became unashamed to admit they dislike children. Get a babysitter, parents are told, although just where we are supposed to find the ever-handy neighborhood teen in a world of one-child families is never made quite clear.

The contract model predicts that the more choice you inject into personal relationships, the better people will behave and the more harmony there will be in families. "Every Child a Wanted Child," the slogan goes, conjuring up visions of identically happy, pink-skinned babes cradled in identically loving maternal and paternal arms.

There's only one problem with this theory: it's just not true.

The experience of the last twenty years does not indicate that turning children into objects of choice will rescue them from poverty, battering, or sexual abuse. On the contrary, it appears that an intact family, planned or unplanned, offers children the safest haven in an increasingly dangerous world.

Some research suggests that planned children may actually be more likely than accidental babies to be physically abused (see chapter 13). Though that finding may shock those who see in choice the wellspring of all virtue, to those with an older conception of family it comes as no surprise. Parenthood can seem an act of insanity if you tote up all the discomfort, anxiety, pain, work, and drudgery gained, not to mention the money lost. Under the choice ideology, parenthood is not a duty made easy by affection, but a decision weighed on the scale of human fulfillment. The question to prospective parents is: are the pains of staying up all night, rocking crying infants, and changing dirty diapers, worth the pleasure of a baby's smile? The victims of this new ideology are children, for the answer to exhausted parents very often seems: no.

And if the conditions of modern society make parenting very difficult, if mothering is isolated to a degree unheard of in the awful Fifties and essentially unrewarded, if the tax code punishes families in general and pampers double-income-no-kids cohabitators, if parents are made to feel like social pariahs rather than praised for contributing to the community, if women with children teeter on the brink of poverty or exhaustion, if it ever seems as if children really aren't worth the bother, well, it is your own damn fault: after all, you chose to have children.

The problem with importing the contract model into the family is not that it is morally wrong, but that it is empirically false: Concepts of contract, choice, and objective justice do not describe how families come into being or are sustained. Insistent attempts to define choice and contract as the foundation of the family distort our ability to see what actually takes place in these relationships. And public policy that is based on this unreal vision will be, and indeed has been, a disaster.

When a culture begins to pursue the ideal of the contractual family, the effects can be seen immediately in the quality of everyday life. But to really understand the curse of contract, we must travel far from average ranch house in the suburbs to the realm of an exotic new form of family life.

Endnotes—Chapter 9

1. Henry Maine, *Ancient Law* (Boston: Beacon Press, 1963), p. 165.
2. David Kirp, Mark Yudof, and Marlene Franks, *Gender Justice* (Chicago: University of Chicago Press, 1986), p. 21.

10

Baby M: The Art of the Deal

It was the kind of story that makes Geraldo Rivera's mouth water: A tale of sex and money, love and greed, eager hope and cruel betrayal. It was the stuff of soap operas, cheap tabloids, and pulp fiction: On Mar. 27, 1986, Baby M was born.

Everyone knows the basic story by now. For ten thousand dollars, Mary Beth Whitehead agreed to bear Bill Stern's child and give her to Stern and his wife. After she gave birth, Mary Beth changed her mind. She refused the ten grand and kept Baby M for four months, fleeing to Florida after a New Jersey court granted the Sterns temporary custody.

A snapshot from Baby M's family album: on a sunny day in Florida, four-month-old Baby M sleeps peacefully in a crib in her grandma's home. Her mother is out but her half-sister Tuesday, ten years old, is brushing her hair in the bathroom. Hearing a strange man's voice, Tuesday rushes into the hall to see what is happening. Three men stand in front of her sister's room. They see the crib. One man snatches up the baby and runs toward the front door. To Tuesday, it looks like a kidnapping, but it's all perfectly proper: these men are officers of the law. Tuesday takes her hairbrush and starts beating on the nearest sheriff, screaming: "No! No! No!"

Bill Stern got his daughter back. Mary Beth Whitehead was permitted to visit Baby M for two hours twice a week (at a local home for troubled youths.) At first, Baby M, smelling her mother's milk, nuzzled at Mary Beth's neck, but the court-appointed chaperone wouldn't let Baby M nurse. That might create a mother-child bond, and the state of New Jersey had not yet decided whether Mary Beth was permitted to be Baby M's mother.

Though reams have been written about surrogate motherhood, the underlying issues are seldom named. A great soap opera took place right before the public's eyes and much of the discussion sounded like a page ripped from a *National Enquirer* primer: See Mary Beth cry. See Bill Stern cry. See Bill Stern's childless wife cry. Who's sorriest now?

The case is now over. Judge Sorkow's ruthlessly consistent order completely stripping Mary Beth of her parental rights was overturned by the New Jersey Supreme Court. Today, she retains the vestiges of her maternity, shrunk to two hour visitations. But the legal, moral, and intellectual struggle continues. At stake in the debate over surrogate motherhood is our fundamental concept of the family—are family relationships created by and therefore at the mercy of the state? Are men, who may not legally purchase sex, entitled to purchase the fruits of sex: to legally create, as it were, the world's first truly disposable woman?

Surrogate motherhood allows men to enjoy the benefits of a woman's sexuality while undertaking only extremely limited and carefully delineated responsibilities towards her. For Bill Stern, Mary Beth Whitehead ceased to exist after services rendered. Now she is nothing but a large and potentially unruly obstacle.

To the Catholic church, surrogate motherhood, like artificial insemination by donor, is adultery. That shocks us, because as a matter of mental hygiene we have abstracted reproduction from sexual relations, a remarkable intellectual feat. "What does having babies have to do with sex?" we ask with touching naivete, like those savage peoples unacquainted with basic biology.

Advocates of surrogate matings do not want us to think about the issue in those terms. They have successfully sold the public on the idea that surrogate matings are the fruit of a revolutionary new technology. "There was not one state in fifty that was ready for this scientific revolution," Gary Skoloff, the Sterns' attorney, proclaimed during a court recess. "The technology of surrogate motherhood did not exist until recent years. History, when faced with the unprecedented, cannot pretend to teach lessons," wrote a Harvard professor of history (who, also being a physician, ought to have known better) in a letter to the *New York Times*.[1]

Those who oppose the practice are supposed to be intellectual Neanderthals: antimedicine, antiprogress, antiscience. Not only do Americans love technology, we are loyal to it. It is as difficult to persuade an American that he can successfully resist the advance of technology as it is to persuade a Marxist that he could resist the march of history. Even those who oppose surrogate motherhood usually describe it as a kind of Frankenstein's monster, a moral horror brought on by science out-of-control.

But the only thing new about surrogate motherhood is our willingness to tolerate it. Its sudden emergence in the latter half of the twentieth century is not evidence of a technological revolution, but of a social, sexual, and intellectual one. The term surrogate motherhood was originally coined to describe a somewhat complicated medical procedure in which a woman's egg is extracted, mingled with her husband's sperm, and implanted in a biologically-unrelated host mother who carries the baby to term. But almost all surrogate mothers today are really surrogate wives— women who agree to conceive a child with a man through artificial insemination, and then hand it over to him.

The first recorded case of artificial insemination took place in 1790. The procedure is so simple women can easily perform it themselves. All you need is a mechanical device to suck up and then expel liquid. One woman I spoke with used a syringe without the needle. A turkey baster will also do.

Carol Pavek is a lively and articulate woman, difficult not to like. She has a husband, a son, a college diploma, and a distinct Texas accent. A Christian, Mrs. Pavek says she volunteers for a number of Amarillo charities, mostly working with sick or handicapped children. Why do women like Mrs. Pavek agree to have a child for a strange man? The money, of course plays a part. The $10,000 Mary Beth Whitehead was offered appears to be the going rate, though I was told of one surrogate (a college graduate) who held out for $40,000. But there are other motives at work as well.

Mrs. Pavek was in search of the perfect "birthing experience." Her first son's birth, she says, "didn't go as we had planned. My husband and I teased each other we'd have to give birth until we got it right, but then what would we do with all the kids?" Jan Sutton, one of the founders of the National Association of Surrogate Mothers, has had two babies under surrogate arrangements. "I always loved being pregnant," she explains. "That's a thing we surrogates all share. I got the notion when I was thirty I wanted to be pregnant again before I was 35."

So do I. When you explain it that way, it makes a lot of sense. (tic-toc tic-toc tic-toc) But surrogates don't have much sympathy for women like Mary Beth who want to keep their babies. "I think the court should definitely give the baby to the Sterns," Jan Sutton says. "There needs to be legislation. People who would create problems should be weeded out."

Mrs. Pavek is less cerebral: "Oooh, I'd like to get my hands on her," she exclaims, "Once you make a commitment, you stick with it. An egg doesn't make a baby, nor a mother either."

Well, then what does? This is the crux of the debate, which more than any other current political issue illuminates our deformed sense of the relationship between sex and family, the moral confusion that cripples public discourse on a hundred other, ostensibly unrelated topics. It is as if the consummate intellectual defect of the age had been sliced, affixed to a slide, put under the microscope, backlit, and enlarged a hundred times its natural size.

And yet this bizarre tumor has grown so slowly, so naturally over the last hundred years, millimetering up on us, one layer crusting on another, that even now, when it's as plain as elephantiasis on your face, many people cannot recognize the oddity, the ugliness, the *irrationality* of their beliefs about sex and family.

If an egg does not make a mother, then sperm does not make a father either. For surrogate advocates, Stern is Baby M's real father, not because half her DNA comes from Stern (for that argument only underscores that half came from Mary Beth), but because he thought her up. Like Athena, she burst from his brain full born, instead of descending from intestinal regions like ordinary mortals. The long tumultuous months of pregnancy are just a technicality, mere flesh and blood technology which will eventually be replaced by the more obedient metal and plastic kind. Bill Stern is Baby M's father because he chose to have children. And choice is the only form of relationship we know how to acknowledge.

How nice. We've been verbally transported beyond the bonds of "mere" biology. Eggs and sperms may come together to make babies but they cannot make anything out of *us,* the adults, wrapped in our proud, self-deluding autonomy.[1]

The most important sign of this rebellion against the flesh is the mysterious emphasis on contract in the Baby M case. After all, marriage is a contract too. But Judge Sorkow in his long career on the bench hasn't shown the least interest in holding men and women to specific performance of that promise. Contract, sadly, hasn't reigned supreme in business transactions for many years. Yet suddenly contract, the law's poor neglected stepchild, became a general favorite.

Something about this case, the circumstance of this transaction alone, caused contract to rise from the grave, made its inviolability so appealing, so necessary, so self-evidently sacred. It is not merely that we think people ought to keep their promises, for the law lets people break their promises all the time. If Mary Beth Whitehead had been buying a car rather than selling her baby, she would have been granted forty-eight hours in which to renege on the deal.

Behind the logic of valorizing contract in this case is an attempt to escape the messy, fleshy reality that we are not only gendered we are embodied; that "its" actions are our actions. "Nobody, including [Mary Beth Whitehead] ever intended her to be the mother," said Gary Skoloff, the Sterns' lawyer. "So you're not terminating a mother."[2] If intention is the key, then, parenting is no longer a thing of the flesh, subject to involuntary processes, outside of our control. Reason has tamed its most stubborn opponent, not of course, actually by controlling the body, but by the simple expedient of refusing to recognize anything that falls outside reason's domain. Our bodies cannot make us parents, we make ourselves mothers and fathers in the most respectable of all fashions, by making deals.

Family law scholars, many of whom call themselves feminists, are busily at work now charting and quantifying the permutations of legally enforcing intent-based parenthood. For example one nouveau theorist argues in the *Yale Law Journal:* "When the child's existence begins in the minds of the desiring parents, biological conception of the child declines in importance relative to psychological conception with respect to the full life of the child. The mental concept of the child is a controlling factor of its creation, and the originators of that concept merit full credit as conceivers."[3]

Yale is apparently a hotbed of reproductive revolutionaries. Carmel Shalev in her November 1985 Yale JSD dissertation abstract, argues "...the control of reproduction afforded by bio-medical science is seen to portend a movement from status to contract in the establishment of a parent-child relation, which is to say that reproductive activity becomes a rational matter of contriving means to meet pre-conceived ends."

I wonder if these scholars are aware of the effects their theorizing will have when it migrates (as ideas inevitably do) out of the narrow confines of exotic birth practices into ordinary family law. Intent would be a practically fool-proof defense in paternity suits, for example. After all, the average guy rationally intends only to put peg A in hole B. Or maybe, if he's a really nice guy, he intends to express his deep affection and to give his woman rapturous pleasure. In other words, put peg A into hole B. If a baby comes out nine months later, that's not his fault, is it? It's more of an Act of God—like hurricanes, earthquakes, and other natural disasters. Let the Red Cross pay for it.

It is to such absurdity that the rationalizing champions of surrogate motherhood are rationally committed. This example is not particularly far fetched. Something very like this attitude is rather common among single, and even some married men. Many women have abortions because their lovers and husbands threaten to abandon them entirely if they go through with the pregnancy. Among the felt grievances of men's rights groups is a legal case in which a woman quit using birth control without informing her sexual partner and then sued the father for child support. Since it was her choice, they argue vehemently, let her pay. The manipulativeness of the mother, in their view, deprives the child of the right to a father and the father's support.

If surrogate advocates are correct about the source of parental obligation, then it is not only difficult, but also morally wrong to impose financial burdens on the growing ranks of absent fathers. If it is choice that makes parents of us all, then it is wrong, unjust, and unnatural, that a man should suffer for a baby he did not will and to whom therefore he is unrelated.

Am I wrong in sensing that this conception of parenting is adolescent? One thing that makes young adulthood so tumultuous is the intolerable burden of being connected to people one did not choose. Though the burden of family may be far greater later in life, never before or after does its imposition seem so unjust. After I published an article opposing surrogate motherhood in the conservative magazine, *National Review,* I was not surprised to find that many of my younger college-aged friends disagreed with me. People who are busy trying to break free of childhood are not in a very good position to think about how families are formed and sustained. What did surprise me was the number of adults, citing logic and waving the flag of reason, who disagreed even more violently.

The ideological fissures revealed by Baby M tantalize. It's not an issue easily categorized as right or left, or even pro or antifeminist. The Vatican opposed surrogate motherhood, which automatically makes that a "conservative" position. But then so did many radical feminists. And a number of prominent liberals joined with conservatives to endorse surrogate motherhood as an institution as American as apple pie. Thomas Sowell, a distinguished right-wing intellectual, even managed to work up a bit of righteous indignation about opponents of the practice: "The real issue is whether we are going to watch human freedom destroyed, bit by bit, just because the anointed

173

have ringing rhetoric and airs of moral superiority...all of us stand to lose if political snipers are allowed to pick off different groups, one at a time."[4]

Surrogate motherhood cuts through old ideological lines, dividing feminists from each other, setting conservatives head-to-head. It reveals a political secret hidden under mounds of caustic rhetoric—American conservatives and liberals share many of the same premises. Americans are all descendants of classical liberalism, the great intellectual and moral movement which sought to free men from the bonds of hereditary status and obligations and replace them with freely-negotiated contracts not only between business partners but between buyer and seller, servant and master, man and the state.

In this intellectual nexus, the moral and legal status of biological relationships becomes extremely problematic. A family, to paraphrase Robert Frost, is the place where, when you have to go there, they have to take you in. It is the realm of unchosen relationship, of the accident of birth. Consequently, liberals see the family as a socially-constructed and at least potentially oppressive superstition. Conservatives, on the other hand, think it violates market principles.

But the family, by its nature, cannot ultimately progress from status to contract without dissolving in the process. Contract doesn't describe how families come to be, or are maintained. To legally impose the notion of contract on families is not to liberate people, but to try to coerce them into behaving in ways more like the models of human behavior constructed by choice-enhancing intellectuals. The contract model doesn't free individuals, it frees the state to rip babies from mothers arms and award them according to a judge's perceptions about "the best interests of the child."

For enforcing contracts, and adjudicating disputes about them, is the realm of the state par excellence. Reimagining the family in contract terms constitutes an enormous invitation to the state (which experience suggests it will hardly refuse), to rearrange our most basic human relationships, tailoring them to suit the moral fashions of that extremely odd and unrepresentative class of human beings: judges and lawyers. The state will not succeed thereby in creating a fundamentally new type of family. It may succeed in destroying the old one.

"Ms. Gallagher makes what can only be described as a naked emotional appeal to her readers in her depiction of the seizure of the child from Mrs. Whitehead's residence in Florida," wrote a disgruntled reader, responding to an article I wrote attacking surrogate motherhood, echoing complaints of many others. All right, all right, I confess. I did it. I exhibited unclothed emotion. *And on purpose.*

I am even more shameless than he thinks. I don't know if the man who wrote that complaint, or any other man, can fully experience the emotions I intended to stir in pleading for Mary Beth Whitehead's right to nurture her child. Does he understand what it would be like to hold your baby rooting for the breast and be unable—forbidden—to feed her? The most vivid impression I have from my own son's infancy is the panicked feeling that somehow somewhere for a few minutes or (God forbid) a few hours my baby might be hungry and I would be unable to satisfy his needs: that the formula will have run out in the middle of the night, or the nipple would be lost, or, or I don't know what. Nowadays, of course I tell him he has to wait for dinner. The intensity of the old fear and the attachment that generated it, seem almost as amusing and incomprehensible to me as it undoubtedly would to the State of New Jersey.

But what is this thing called emotion? Is it as inconsequential, as dispensable, as *misleading,* as the advocates of surrogate motherhood imply? For this same "instinct" (to use an inadequate word to describe the unification of persons which is love), this sense of inalienable connection, this fusion of egos, that appears from the outsiders, even the father's perspective, so touchingly ridiculous is the same "irrational" emotion which society depends upon to create and nurture the next generation.

Whether this bonding is "instinctive" or not, any culture requires for its continued existence that women will fall in love with their babies. For the state to refuse to consider Mary Beth's inconvenient emotion, is to use women, all women. It thereby announces its intention to exploit our capacity for love, where it is useful to society, and to demean it where it is deemed inconvenient. It tells mothers we will count on you to have these emotions; we need you to have these emotions; we may even (though this grows rare) praise you for having these emotions; but what we will not do is officially recognize these emotions when they conflict with some more important social goal, like getting a man the baby he wants.

At present, surrogate contracts operate in the grey market, neither sanctioned nor explicitly banned. They appear to violate laws banning payments (other than medical expenses) to mothers who give their children up for adoption. Enforcing surrogate contracts also appears to violate state laws that refuse to allow women to surrender a baby for adoption before the baby is actually born. Most states, even after birth, offer natural mothers who give up their infants for adoption a grace period in which to change their mind.

Men who want the services of a surrogate sign a letter of intent, usually promising to pay the mother a fee, plus medical expenses, and to accept the child regardless of physical or mental defects. The cost, counting legal fees, medical expenses, and the surrogate payment, runs as high as $40,000. The women they hire sign a letter of intent promising, among other things, that they will not "form or attempt to form a parent-child relationship." But these are not legal contracts. Surrogate lawyers routinely warn their clients that most of the documents they sign are not legally binding.

This may soon change. In the early eighties, Kentucky, like a number of other states, passed a law barring payments (in excess of medical expenses) to a mother who gives her baby up for adoption. In 1981, the attorney general of Kentucky tried to use this law to put Surrogate Parenting Associates of Louisville, Kentucky, out of business. On Feb. 6, 1986, the Kentucky Supreme Court reached a decision in *Surrogate Parenting Associates, Inc. v. Commonwealth of Kentucky*: surrogate contracts are not illegal *per se*, because the Kentucky law was designed "to keep baby brokers from overwhelming an expectant mother or the parents of a child with financial inducements to part with the child. The central fact in the surrogate parenting procedure is that the agreement to bear the child is entered into *before* conception. . . [Surrogate motherhood] is not biologically different from the reverse situation where the husband is infertile and the wife conceives by artificial insemination." Invoking the kindly spirit of advanced technology, the majority wrote that "The courts should not shrink from the benefits to be derived from science in solving these [fertility] problems simply because they may lead to legal complications.''

The judge here throws his lot with the rational-intent scheme of parenthood. Why is it wrong to shower women with financial inducements to give up their children after getting pregnant, but not before? The answer must be that being pregnant makes women slightly touched in the head, and therefore unable to make a rational decision. But, the court reasons, as long as the decision to sell a baby is made coolly, before the pregnancy, there's nothing wrong with it.

That court's reasoning has been echoed by many others. *Washington Post* columnist Charles Krauthammer, for example, asks, ''Why the sudden concern with the few dozen surrogate-mother cases a year . . . when sperm donations (the reverse kind of artificial insemination where the husband is infertile and the wife conceives an outsider's child) is routine?''

I am amazed at how many people can overlook the obvious. Chalk it up to an indigenous form of couvade, a sudden outbreak of womb envy. I hate to have to be the one to point this out, but masturbating into a little cup is not at all like having a baby. Men are connected to children through DNA and marriage. Women have other ways.

''It is the woman who conceives, bears, and suckles the child. Those activities that are most deeply sexual are mostly female; they comprise the mother's role, a role that is defined biologically,'' George Gilder writes in *Men and Marriage*. ''The nominally equivalent role of father is in fact a product of marriage and other cultural contrivances. There is no biological need for the father to be anywhere around when the baby is born and nurtured.''[5] This is more than an anthropologist's abstraction. The transaction that takes place when a man donates sperm is no different really, than the one he undertakes in sleeping with a woman he hardly knows. Unless entirely chaste, a man can never be sure that somewhere out there, some young woman he met in a bar isn't raising his eldest son, or hasn't aborted him. He can never be sure.

Until the very recent development of foolproof genetic tests, it was in fact impossible to determine any child's paternity. Visitors to Oneida, the 19th century commune which practiced complex marriage, often wondered aloud how children knew who their fathers were. "They have no more proof than other children," came the stock reply, "only the testimony of their mothers."[6] Fatherhood depends on "marriage and other cultural contrivances"—and ultimately on the virtue of women.

The practice of artificial insemination may not be as benign as we currently think. We do not yet know, for instance, what effect (if any) having a sperm bank for a father has on the psychological health of the child. In any case artificial insemination is, at least, anonymous and uncertain. The man who offers up his sperm to posterity may have children running about somewhere or maybe his sample never "took." (The success rate in artificial insemination by donor is quite low.) He'll never know. A surrogate mother, on the other hand, does not just sell "the idea of children in general" she gives up an actual child in particular, and for money. A man is selling his seed; a woman sells a baby.

Some commentators have made a great deal of the distinction between "selling a baby" which is verboten and "selling one's parental rights," which is considered more benign. This is a semantic game. If you put your '72 Buick up for sale, you can say you are "selling a car" or "selling your rights to the car." It's all the same to the buyer, unless you don't have any rights to the car, in which case it's fraud. It's true that the rights obtained in buying a baby are not exactly the same as those in buying the car. But that only makes the surrogate child a special class of property, like an IRA account or a discount airline ticket, for which certain legal restrictions apply.

The trouble with commercial transactions is that they are impersonal ones. I do not mean that money taints, or that participants in commercial activities cannot be filled with love and goodwill to all men. It is not the motives of the buyer and seller that are suspect, but the nature of the transaction itself. A sale implies fungibility; a certain amount of this good—money—equals a certain amount of that good—a baby. A human being can remain priceless, it turns out, only if he or she may not be sold. What is it like to live in a society where we know exactly what each person is worth? What is it like when children suspect that every mother has a price?

Adoption emerged as a social and legal institution because emotional bonding is not enough; ordinarily, a child needs the support of a two-parent family. The justification for adoption, for giving away one's own child is the hard defense of necessity. Legalized surrogacy, on the contrary, makes it acceptable for one to weigh the gratification of having children against some other good, like a new car, and if the you would prefer the latter to the former, well, then go ahead.

In this sense, the institution of adoption is the fulfillment, not the negation, of parental responsibility. But the surrogate mother, unlike the mother putting her child up for adoption, does not admit she has any special obligations to the child she bears; she does not even admit that it is hers. The child cannot obligate her, she obligates it: it is a product conceived for sale and use.

The personhood of the infant is also destroyed, for she has been reduced to her exchange value. After all, as Ronald Reagan pointed out, the surrogate mother is not giving up much; she can always make another. "The agreement was violated by one party. The individual who had made the arrangement could not have a child otherwise. And the surrogate mother in this case can have a child at will and has had them, and it just seemed to me that it was wrong for her to then turn around and make the decision she did," President Reagan remarked.[7] A surrogate baby isn't priceless and irreplaceable. Her mother can always make another. Her father can always buy another.

Almost all commentators blame state legislatures for failing to regulate surrogate motherhood. What they find scandalous is not that there is a market in babies, but that it's a free market; unscreened women making up their own minds, people without medical degrees opening clinics, men and women entering into surrogate relationship without benefit of a psychologist's guidance—unlicensed people making *babies*.

Horrid as it may be to contemplate, people make babies all the time without so much as a by-your-leave to the government. The problem is not lack of regulation but lack of intellectual courage: a surrogate contract is a polite term for baby-selling. If it is not, then a surrogate mother ought not to have to surrender her parental rights to obtain her fee.

In acknowledging the connection between mothers and their children I do not mean to imply that fathers aren't important. On the contrary, a great body of evidence confirms fathers play an essential role—economically and emotionally—in the complicated job of rearing healthy and productive children. One of the central problems of our society is convincing men to undertake that difficult task. Part of the horror of surrogacy is that it inverts natural relationships, and sets the father against the mother of his child, totally, ruthlessly. There are a number of other raw, unpleasant, "emotional" scenes from Baby M's family album. Filing a petition to declare Bill Stern the baby's father, Stern's lawyer alleged that Mary Beth and her husband were unfit parents. On the basis of this allegation, without evidence from a social service investigation and without offering Mary Beth an opportunity to be heard, Judge Sorkow issued an order transferring custody of Baby M to Bill Stern, effective immediately. When the police showed up on her doorstep, demanding "Melissa Stern," Rick Whitehead escaped with the baby out the back window. "Man seen running with infant," blared a voice over the police radio. Terrified her baby would be shot, Mary Beth rushed outside to the Stern's car.

"Don't look at her, Bill," commanded Betsy Stern.

"Look at me," Mary Beth pleaded, as she stood barefoot while blood from the yet unhealed wounds of birth streamed over her legs.

Look at me, she begged, pleading with him to raise her into something more than a "surrogate uterus," as one of Stern's experts called her in court, desperately trying to become recognizable in his eyes as a whole person, as the mother of his child.[8]

Surrogacy is in many ways like prostitution, another sexual contract the state refuses to enforce. Prostitution turns women into nonpersons, figures to the exact penny how much men who use them owe for the rental of their sexual organs. Once paid, a whore has no claim upon the man who uses her. She doesn't exist for him, in relation to him. In *Intercourse,* Andrea Dworkin explores a Tolstoy story in which the hero worried obsessively because he had not been able to pay a woman with whom he had had sex. He could find no peace until he hunted her down and paid her: "The money repudiated the possibility of any human sameness between him and her; and this put him at ease." He had sex; she had money. "Real debauchery," as Tolstoy wrote, "lies precisely in freeing oneself from moral relations with a woman with whom you have physical intimacy."[9] What prostitution does to women for men in the realm of orgasmic sexuality, surrogate motherhood accomplishes in the realm of procreative sexuality. Women are reduced in their relations with men to their sexual organs.

As Katha Pollit said in the her May 23, 1987, article in *The Nation:* "What William Stern wanted, however, was not just a perfect baby; the Sterns did not, in fact, seriously investigate adoption. He wanted a perfect baby with his genes and a medically vetted mother who would get out of his life forever immediately after giving birth. That's a tall order, and one no other class of father—natural, step-, adoptive—even claims to be entitled to. Why should the law bend itself into a pretzel to gratify it?"

Permitting artificial insemination is only recognizing the inevitable. If a small number of women want to have babies with strange men, you cannot stop them. Surrogate motherhood, on the other hand, cannot thrive unless it is institutionalized. Surrogate advocates maintain that if outlawed, the practice will only go underground, but it is difficult to imagine a practice the state could more easily ban. Recruiting surrogates is a very public endeavor. Having a baby for money is not a quick and private transaction, like scoring some coke.

But making surrogate motherhood illegal is not nearly as important as making it deviant—making sure the law recognizes that the parental bond is based on something larger, more secure, more outside its control, than mere contract.

If the state merely enforces all the normal procedures regarding termination of parental rights (forbidding payments, giving birth mothers the right to decide after birth whether they will surrender a child for adoption), the practice will not have much of a future. There may be a few men who are willing to pay $40,000 to help create a baby they have no legal right to collect, but not many. If the common law regarding illegitimate children prevails (as it should), surrogate fathers could very well end up paying child support and receive only visitation rights in return. And if (as frequently happens in custody disputes), a surrogate father does get custody, how many wives are going to want to face being relegated to stepmothers, and to seeing their husbands indissolubly connected to another woman through a child?

Surrogate motherhood can prosper only if society sets up special institutions to nurture its growth. And what those special arrangements come down to is this: a guarantee by the courts that they will strip a woman of her parental rights, not because she abandons or neglects her child, but because she is *unwilling* to do so.

Though the mother-child bond is the core of all societies, legal institutions that affirm and protect the primacy of that bond are not inevitable. They are, for the most part, a modern invention. Today a woman's right to mother is undergoing slow erosion in ordinary divorce and custody cases. The push to legalize surrogate contracts represents a frontal assault on that right.

The avant garde of this force are the surrogate mothers themselves. They cheerfully produce infants and hand them over, without admitting pain or grief or guilt. "I feel a little guilty because I didn't feel more of a maternal bond," says Jan Sutton, "The feeling I have for her is just like the feeling I have for the kids of other good friends." Surrogate moms are the female counterpart to those men, molded by the welfare culture, who cheerfully recount the number of children they have sired whom they neither see nor support. (This is not an entirely fair comparison, to be sure, since surrogate mothers have more reason to think their babies will be well cared for.)

A detached delight in one's fertility is not evil, it is primeval. But for a woman to experience a child growing inside her body and all the while pretend that it is not *her* child—what is that but a form of temporary insanity? For the state to enforce surrogate contracts is to applaud such an aberrant mental state. Indeed, the system attempts to induce this irrationality in women. Law-abiding surrogate mothers will "neither form, nor attempt to form a parent-child relationship," as they are directed by the contract and the court.

Some surrogate mothers may naturally feel this estrangement from her child, but the men who profit from surrogate arrangements also take great care to promote it. Some clinics, like the Surrogate Parenting Associates, keep surrogate mothers and fathers separated in an attempt to make it psychologically easier for the woman to give up her child. Other clinics adopt the opposite strategy, and women are encouraged to have at least a brief meeting with the prospective father and his wife, so that the surrogate mother can emotionally bond with the (usually) infertile wife.

If empathy doesn't do the job, clinic personnel may use threats to get the surrogate to obey. According to one recent book favoring surrogate contracts, prominent surrogate lawyer William Handel tells each surrogate, "I don't know if we're going to be able to enforce the contract if you decide to keep the child...If you decide to keep the child, we'll sue you for intentional infliction of emotional distress. You'll have ruined this couple's life. And we'll make it awfully expensive for you to hold on to the child."[10]

Forcing a woman to believe the child of her womb isn't her child is the kind of irrationality that results from the current effort to rationalize parenting, to bring it out of the realm of the too-too embarrassing flesh. It fulfills the dream of those early church theologians who imagined that, before the Fall, the male member rose on the command of reason, and performed the sacred duty of procreation without desire. We at last have found a way to make ourselves children of reason, not of lust.

The article I wrote for *National Review* opposing surrogate motherhood generated more mail than any other article I have written, and also more negative mail, especially from men. "Perhaps the surest end to debate is her focus on biology," sniffed one reader, "If any theme binds all definitions of civilization it might be the transcending of mere biology—*against* human instinct—for the sake of political, philosophical, or spiritual abstractions." The biological relationship which is family now inspires a pervasive fear of the natural; not of what *is* natural, but of the very idea of the natural, that it may in some way confine us, deny us our freedom. We are terrified that biological functions of human beings are somehow animal and not human. We suffer existential anxiety at the first hint our bodies may be ourselves.

This terror is part of a scheme in which human "instinct" is seen as dehumanizing, and freedom as the triumph of the mind over the body. To achieve this rational utopia, society must refuse to recognize the existence of inconvenient emotions which restrict perfectly "free" and rational choice. It means aggressively rooting out gender, reducing sex to pleasure alone, and eschewing "bonding"—an emotional state in some sense thrust upon us—in favor of the dignity of freely-willed intention.

Our prevailing conception of the relationship between our bodies and our selfhood is a relic of the materialist superstition. When God died in the 19th century, there arose a fear: Human beings are just walking protoplasm, like everything else; random atoms that arrange themselves for a fleeting moment into consciousness before scattering again, like dust in the wind. Faced with a conclusion intolerable to our pride, Western culture retreated into reason. Our reason, having been glorified by a long religious tradition, then sanctified by the vast, proud progress of science in the 18th and 19th centuries, began to appear the only human thing about us. We shrank our self-identification to that one part. That which is not under rational control is not us, it is the "it," the other. And so in our minds we sit perched precariously on top of our bodies, trapped inside this solid flesh, perennially struggling to break free.

The lure of the contract model of the family is that it breaks the bonds of flesh. Contract is clean, contract is disembodied, contract gives us the illusion of control. That is all it gives us. We may choose not to have children, but we never choose the children we have. They come to us a gift, or a burden, a joy or a disappointment, with their own personalities, needs, desires, temperament with a cavalier disregard for all our carefully-drawn-up contracts. Contract as a blueprint for families fails because the key party, the child, isn't a cosigner. And because there is no meaningful way for children to consent, family imagined as a contract is tyrannically insouciant about the interests of children in order to grant adults the illusion of control. It is a psychological reversion to the old paterfamilias—the Roman man of the house had truly planned parenthood, because he was free to sever his relationship with his children, along with their heads, at will.

Shulameth Firestone states the choice model in its purest form when she argues that the only solution to women's "oppression" as mothers is to abolish childbearing and the family and replace them with artificial reproduction and contractual households filled with adults and children who agree to share their lives for a finite period of time.[11] Reading Firestone one can feel the tortuous burden, the lethargic weight, the inescapable heaviness of inalienable connection. To be related is to be trapped by an accident of birth, to writhe helplessly under the weight of a connection founded not on rational tastes and preferences, but ugly, contingent flesh and oleaginous blood. It is the despairing cry of the adolescent whose parents walk into the teen party, smiling, loving, gauche: What have I to do with these people? When will I be free?

Adolescence fades. New families form. Adulthood, in an individual or a society, is the act of shouldering the responsibility for the future. And it is also the act, and this is in some sense the same act, of coming to terms with death and the messy reality of imperfect control. To a child, a mother or a father is an almost omnipotent being. An adolescent, instead of merely worshiping that power, reaches for it, and claims it as his own. Adulthood begins at the moment an adolescent glimpses that the promise of unlimited control will never be fulfilled; our parents never had it, and neither will we. At that moment of profound disappointment, the child who would be an adult summons the courage to embrace the future, joyfully if he can, dutifully if he must. Adulthood is the refusal of a woman or of a man to be paralyzed by the fragile tragedy of flesh, the human bond and bondage of being alive, self-conscious, and death-bound.

We can deny the family, but we cannot escape it through the conjuror's trick of contract. A relationship based on contract is not a family relationship. Family is more secure than partnership or friendship precisely because it does not depend on self-interest or mutual affection, though it often generates both. The security of the child rests in knowing that he belongs to his mother and father and that his mother and father belong to him.

Contract promises control. But because families cannot be created by choice, what the contract model delivers is chaos. What begins in a promise of perfect ordered liberty, ends in blunt coercion as judges and legislators try to reshape family obligations according to their own peculiar conceptions of social progress. What is heralded as a mark of social progress, ends with the progressive disintegration of civilized communities. What is billed as the triumph of science and reason in family life, results in the ascendancy of brutality, violence, callousness, and unreason in our daily lives. What begins as a paradise of freedom, ends with the abandonment of children, the impoverishment of women, and the increasing barbarization of men. A society that tries to ground family relationships in choice sacrifices happiness, wealth, and the liberty of social order, in pursuit of a divine omnipotence that will remain forever out of reach.

It is not hard to see where the illusion of contract begins. It begins with the effort, the visible social and personal strain, of taking two unrelated individuals and making them into one single family. It begins, that is, with marriage.

Endnotes—Chapter 10

1. Leonard Groopman, "Baby M Writes a Chapter in History of Families," *The New York Times*, April 12, 1987.

2. E.R. Shipp, "Parental Rights Law," *The New York Times*, April 8, 1987.

3. Andrea E. Stumpf, "Redefining Mother: A Legal Matrix for New Reproductive Technologies," *The Yale Law Journal* (November 1986), pp. 195–196.

4. Thomas Sowell, "The Deep Thinkers Sound off on Baby M," *New York Daily News*, April 10, 1987.

5. Gilder, *Men and Marriage, op. cit.*, p. 6.

6. Raymond Lee Muncy, *Sex and Marriage in Utopian Communities: Nineteenth Century America* (Baltimore: Penguin Books, 1974), p. 178.

7. "Ron Back's Baby M's Dad" *New York Daily News*, April 12, 1987, p. 20.

8. Mary Beth Whitehead with Loretta Schwartz-Nobel, "My Fight for Baby M," *Family Circle*, February 21, 1989, p. 100ff.

9. Andrea Dworkin, *Intercourse* (New York: The Free Press, Macmillan, 1987), p. 11.

10. Lori B. Andrews, *New Conceptions: A Consumer's Guide to the Newest Infertility Treatments* (New York: Ballantine Books, 1985), p. 216.

11. See, for example, Shulamith Firestone, *The Dialectic of Sex* (New York: William Morrow, 1970).

11

The Murder of Marriage

In 1970 Mary, a nice Catholic girl in her early twenties, tried to commit an illegal act.

She and her boyfriend Jim had just graduated from a small Catholic college near San Francisco and like many other young couples they decided to wed. They had blood tests and proper licenses; a priest officiated at the ceremony; the bride marched up the aisle in a white dress, they exchanged vows, she took his name, and over the years bore two children. To all outward appearances, Mary and Jim were married. Everyone said so.

But 1970 was the year the state of California imposed no-fault divorce. With that act, quietly, with little public fanfare or political debate, the state of California outlawed marriage.

Mary did not find out till nearly a decade later when Jim decided to fly down to Los Angeles to scout out law offices for a new practice. Two days later, Mary received a long letter in which Jim explained that he had married too young and needed to "find himself." She was left with two toddlers, $12,000 from the sale of the house and $300 a month in child support.

When Mary agreed to live in the same house with Jim and accept his financial support and offer her own paid and unpaid labor to the household, to sleep in the same bed and to bear his children, she did so because she thought she was married. Had Jim asked her to do these things for him without getting married, she would have slapped his face. Mary knew what marriage meant. The example of her parents, and the teachings of her religion gave her a concrete idea of the unwritten law. It meant the two became one flesh, one family. It was a lifetime commitment.

But the state of California later informed her that she was not allowed to make or to accept lifetime commitments. No-fault divorce gave judges, at the request of one half a couple, the right to decide when a marriage had irretrievably broken down. They decided by and large that wanderlust would be a state-protected emotion, while loyalty was on its own. In a cruel display of raw judicial power, the state of California made Mary a single woman again, without protecting her interests and without requiring her consent.[1]

What happened to Mary in California in 1970 happened again and again to other men and women in other parts of the country as state after state feverishly established no-fault divorce laws. By the early eighties, the revolution was all but complete: eighteen states plus the District of Columbia had eliminated fault grounds for divorce all together, almost all the rest added no-fault as an option for a divorcing spouse. Unlike many European countries, which attach waiting periods as long as five years before a man or a woman may divorce an unconsenting spouse for no reason, American state legislatures opted for quick and speedy spouse disposal. Most American jurisdictions require a year's separation or less for a no-fault divorce.[2] Not surprisingly, already rising divorce rates soared.

No-fault divorce was supposed to permit a couple to get a divorce by mutual consent. What no-fault divorce actually did is create unilateral divorce. During the seventies, Americans gained the right to divorce-on-demand and in the process lost the right to marry. And this is the remarkable thing: *no one noticed.*

Men and women continued to walk up the aisle, exchange rings and vows and become Mr. and Mrs. Families sent presents, garters were thrown, cakes cut, households set up, children born, and people continued to use the same old word marriage to describe this new social institution, which more closely resembles taking a concubine than taking a spouse.

Divorce reformers imagined they could let a few disgruntled individuals slip out the back door of a bad marriage and yet retain the institution of marriage intact. Unilateral divorce, they said and we believed, is only a humane way of disposing of already dead marriages; it doesn't affect the vitality of the truly married.

The reformers did not calculate what would happen once the message contained in the new marriage laws sank in. They never wondered what it would be like to get married, and yet know one's spouse could leave at any time. They never contemplated the anxiety of young men and women today who consider betting their futures in a game

193

heavily weighted in favor of the unfaithful, the immature, the betrayer.

For Americans, choice, like technology, is not only a good but a good that cannot be resisted. To the idolators of choice a man or a woman who wants to leave a marriage is an irresistible force encountering an all-too-movable object. Even if Americans could summon up the courage to say that a man's deeply fulfilling, and life-affirming decision to abandon his family to poverty for the consolations of a coed is wrong, what could we do? Tie him to the trash masher?

What the divorce advocates never got into their heads is that some choices preclude others. If everyone can choose divorce then no one can choose marriage. The ancient Greeks had a saying: "Call no man happy until he is dead." Our modern variant is: Call no woman married until she is dead. Men and women no longer have control over the terms of our marriages. We do not know what bargain we have struck getting married and it hardly matters since the culture and the court will not enforce any bargain. The rule is: he who wants out, wins.

A person now stays married only if both partners constantly choose to. Like the attempt to abolish gender, this scheme runs on existentialist fantasies of choice in perfect freedom: Would we choose to be feminine if we were free of all personal qualities that might influence the choice? Would we choose to accept the obligations of marriage in a world where such obligations do not exist? Neither question makes much sense.

The murder of marriage is a particularly appalling legal atrocity because it was entirely the act of an elite. In 1966, before the wave of divorce reform, only 13 percent of the adult population felt divorce laws were too strict.[3] As Harvard law Professor Mary Ann Glendon notes, "Discontent with fault-based divorce seems to have been felt more acutely by mental-health professionals and academics than by the citizenry in general."[4] No cry from the anguished breast of a populace chained by marriage vows demanded divorce as a right. The revolution was made by the determined whine of lawyers, judges, bureaucrats, psychiatrists, marriage counselors, academics, and goo-goo reformers who objected, of all things, to the amount of *hypocrisy* contained in the law.

Fault-based divorce, they believed, created unnecessary acrimony between departing spouses. Couples who wanted to split were often forced to fabricate evidence of adultery or mental cruelty to petition for divorce. And judges were forced to pretend to believe fabricated evidence to grant them their divorces.

Because divorce is so widespread and has caused so much evident pain, we lie about it to ourselves and in public. We try to evade responsibility for the world we have made and the values we have endorsed through institutions we ultimately control. First the government passes laws allowing unilateral divorce and society surrounds those new laws with rhetoric about how courageous it is to end a dead marriage. Then when divorce rates skyrocket, we announce there's nothing anyone can do about it. We put up a big sign that blocks any serious debate. Warning: Historical Forces At Work.

A fifty percent divorce rate is not a historical inevitability; it is a political decision. It's not something that happens, it's something we do to ourselves, to each other, and to our children. In 1792 France made it easy to get a divorce. Six years later divorces outnumbered marriages in Paris. In 1816 divorces were outlawed altogether and the divorce rate, naturally, plummetted.[5] In America in the fifties and sixties when judges expanded the grounds for fault-based divorce, the rate began to climb. Since 1970, when both law and culture actively began to encourage unilateral divorce, the divorce rate has more than doubled.[6] Twenty-five years ago, only 4 percent of divorces happened among people married more than fifteen years. Today, the figure is 25 percent.[7]

Much has been written about the economic consequences of divorce, which are devastating for women. Lenore Weitzman calculated that a woman can expect a 73 percent drop in disposable income one year after divorce, while her ex-husband experiences a 42 percent increase. Fifty-four percent of single-parent families live below the poverty line, many of the rest teeter uneasily just above it. Thirty-four percent of all divorced female heads of household are on welfare.[8]

Unilateral divorce not only increases the number of women in poverty, it makes their poverty worse. In the past, for example, a woman might protect herself and her children by threatening to drag out divorce procedures unless her husband came up with an adequate settlement. Now that the law sanctions haste, a wife has less to bargain with. Between 1978 and 1985, child support awards adjusted for inflation dropped 28.4 percent.[9]

Successful men in their thirties and forties trade in their aging wives, unashamed to express repugnance at wrinkles and grey hairs. Their middle-aged ex-wives grow old alone and close to poverty. In psychologist Judith Wallerstein's study none of the women aged forty years or older at the time of divorce had remarried after ten years; 80 percent were financially insecure and almost half had witnessed a decline in their standards of living in the last five years. A 1985 Census Bureau survey showed that only

11 percent of divorced women remarry in their forties and only 3 percent remarry in their fifties.[10]

It had been almost a decade since people began noticing that divorce is impoverishing women. Yet no one appears the least inclined to do anything but bemoan the fact. There have been efforts, laudable in themselves but woefully inadequate, to enforce child support orders more vigorously. But an extra two hundred dollars or so a month from an ex-husband, while a welcome addition to the family budget, will not rescue women from the economic terrorism of divorce. There is no sign that the women with children can be expected to care for children and maintain a family at a middle-class standard of living by ourselves. Nor any reason that we ought to be asked to do so.

The feminization of poverty has become a popular phrase; in practice it means nothing but that society is licensing men to abandon women and children. But no-fault divorce injures even women who are still married. Divorce on demand makes women less powerful in marriage as we become aware that we and our children are only a divorce away from welfare.

For adults, the psychological results of divorce are mixed. Ten years after the divorce, Wallerstein found in the overwhelming majority of couples, one ex-spouse is much happier than before the divorce, while the other is not. In only 10 percent of couples do both husband and wife say they are better off a decade after divorce. "Looking closely, we find that by and large the person who wanted the divorce is the one doing well, while the one who opposed it is doing less well."[11]

This is not surprising. The spouse who makes the decision has a liberating sense of mastery, of control, which is one of the key components to personal happiness. The act

197

of leaving, breaking free, the exhilarating headlong embrace of change with psychic echoes of the original break from the family at adolescence can boost self-esteem.

But being divorced reinforces just the opposite sense of life. No one can pretend that being divorced is an act of great personal courage, for it is not an act at all. It is something that happens to you and over which, thanks to no-fault, you have no say at all. The spouse who leaves learns that love dies. The spouse who is left learns that love betrays, that society approves of betrayal and sides with the betrayer. He is empowered legally and you have been disenfranchised.

Over the past twenty years we have accumulated an enormous body of evidence about the effects of divorce on children. Though almost all the news is bad, you might not guess this by glancing at newspaper headlines. Writers and intellectuals and psychologists determinedly put on their happy faces when talking about divorce.

One study of the effects of parental loss on children was recently reported in the *New York Times* under the reassuring title ''Nurturing Can Offset the Trauma of Loss in Childhood, Study Says.'' The lead of the article: ''The loss of a parent early in life through death or divorce does not necessarily make a person more susceptible to depression or other major problems as an adult, a new study found.'' Dr. Alan Breier, who directed the study, concludes that ''poor parenting'' rather than parental loss itself leads to emotional problems in adulthood.

This sounds very comforting for parents who are or want to be divorced. Buried deep in the fine print is the astonishing bad news: in this study 77 percent of those who lost a parent to death or divorce suffered at least one serious episode of psychiatric disorder as adults.[12]

The trouble with Dr. Breier's reassuring theory that poor parenting, not divorce itself, inflicts psychological damage on children is that divorce makes it much harder to be good parents. "In the crisis of divorce," writes Dr. Wallerstein, "...mothers and fathers put children on hold, attending to adult problems first. Divorce is associated with a diminished capacity to parent in almost all dimensions— discipline, playtime, physical care, and emotional support."[13] To say that poor parenting, not divorce, inflicts psychological trauma is like saying that lack of food, not poverty, causes malnutrition.

A woman's husband comes home one night and announces he's found bliss with his secretary. He moves out, leaving her to handle the anger and the hysterical longing of her children. She watches the man who pledged to love, honor, and cherish try to weasel away with as few financial obligations as possible, and no one blames him, much. Her lifestyle is upset, she may have to leave her home, few couples call on her any more. Men start hitting on her at work, or men never call her and she worries no one will ever touch her again. She must start working, or work longer hours, her children act up in school, and still her standard of living plummets. She lives in poverty or at its edge with anger and anxiety as constant companions. What do you suggest Dr. Spock?

Judith Wallerstein's study is the only one to track the same families over a fifteen-year-period to determine how divorce affects the quality of adults and of children's lives. But her findings are perfectly consistent with other studies on the affect of father absence (see chapter 5). After reviewing the scholarly literature, Dr. George Rekers concluded, "It seems that millions of parents have purchased their own relief from marital conflict with a divorce that forces their children to pay the price in unhappiness, stress, and adjustment problems that could persist for a lifetime. Victimless divorce is either rare or nonexistent when children are present.''[14]

A wealth of recent research suggests that children of divorced parents suffer disproportionate rates of emotional and mental problems, and are more likely to run into problems at school as well.[15] Children of divorce are more promiscuous than children from intact families, or from families in which a mother or father had died.[16] Among the white, mostly middle-class children Judith Wallerstein studied, one-quarter of the girls became sexually active in junior high school.[17]

The wealth of evidence leaves the reformers untroubled. It's not divorce which causes trauma, they say, it's the social stigma attached to divorce. Or else it is family conflict that traumatizes children and as badly as they do, these children would do even worse if their parents had continued the marriage. We need to compare children of divorce not with children in happy intact families, but with children in unhappy conflict-ridden families, say these experts.

Dr. Rex Forehand, a psychologist at the University of Georgia, headed a study which did just that. He compared children in four categories: low-conflict intact families; low-conflict divorced families; high-conflict intact families; and high-conflict divorced families. Children in low-conflict intact families did significantly better than any other group; children in low-conflict divorced families did somewhat better than children in high-conflict intact families; and children in high-conflict divorced families did the worst, considerably worse than children who remained in homes where their mother and father fought constantly.

"Divorce may be a plausible option if it leads to less parental fighting, but it is a horrendous option if it does not," says Dr. Forehand. "High conflict in conjunction with divorce was significantly more detrimental to the functioning of adolescents."[18]

Unfortunately, low-conflict divorces are rare. In encouraging divorce, Americans are betting the welfare of our children on the unlikely proposition that people who fight in marriages will stop fighting once they leave. We have a great deal of experience with divorce now, and we've discovered the obvious: that isn't the way human beings work. Wallerstein found that ten years later 50 percent of the women and one-third of the men are still intensely angry with their ex. "Nearly one-third of the children were party to intense bitterness between the parents. True, some couples were no longer standing in the same kitchen screaming at one another; they were screaming on the telephone instead. Or they fought face to face while dropping off or picking up the children."[19]

Divorced parents can argue about the usual range of child rearing issues and a whole bundle of new issues as well: visitation, child support, unexpected medical bills, vacations away from home, college educations, where to spend the holidays. Among divorced parents, every new child rearing aggravation arouses and feeds on the all the anger, the hurt, the shame, and the betrayal of the original divorce, creating a blacker hatred than two people who live together generally allow themselves to feel. Indeed, divorce, rather than defusing anger, often takes marital bickering to new heights.

The divorce process itself exposes children to scenes

different in character from the ordinary conflicts of married life. In Wallerstein's study, over half the children in the study witnessed physical violence between their parents, whereas before one partner initiated divorce proceedings 75 percent had never seen physical violence in the home. One study of violent marital rape found that incidents frequently occur as the couple go through the early stages of divorce.[20] Children of divorce "share vivid, gut-wrenching memories of their parents' separations. 'I saw my dad beat up 'my mom,' says twenty-two-year-old Tom. 'That is a scar I think of every day.' *Every day.*" Despite the fact they may have witnessed only a single violent incident, many of these children found themselves in physically abusive relationships in their teens and early twenties.

Opinion-makers often talk about divorce as an escape route from physically abusive marriages (as it should be) but we rarely recognize that high rates of divorce itself expose more children to physical violence. "Mom and Dad were fighting in the bathroom and Mom ran out into the bedroom and Dad went after her. I tried to stop Dad and he belted me across the room. And I could hear him punching her. And I could hear her gasping in the bedroom," one child told Wallerstein, "I don't know how anyone can *do* that."[21] Even a single act of family violence can leave a lifetime of trauma in its wake, as children watch love twisted into hate.

Even for adult children, divorce is a major emotional disruption. Gunhild Hagestad, a sociologist of the College of Human Development at Pennsylvania State University conducted one of the few studies of the effects of divorce on grown children, in this case college students. "Our first surprise was how difficult it was for most of them. These

interviews were extremely emotional, very often teary...
there's an enormous sense of loss. Many of them did say
their world was falling apart."[22]

Judith Wallerstein, like most modern psychologists, is
not opposed to divorce; her book is a plea for divorcing
men and women to behave in a civilized fashion. "Although
our overall findings are troubling and serious, we should not
point the finger of blame at divorce per se...A divorce un-
dertaken thoughtfully and realistically can teach children
how to confront serious life problems with compassion,
wisdom, and appropriate action."

Certainly, men and women on the brink of divorce
ought to behave with as much emotional maturity as adults
facing intense emotional pain, financial ruin, and personal
betrayal can be expected to behave. If Wallerstein is right,
those that succeed may avoid inflicting long-term economic
or psychological damage on children and the abandoned
spouse. But that possibility, itself a slim hope for all but the
very emotionally and economically secure, hardly settles
the question.

Divorce causes great, intense, lasting pain. After five
years the majority of children still hope their parents will
reconcile, often mistaking polite gestures as augurs of possible remarriage. After five years, they are still furious at
their parents for getting a divorce. The question Wallerstein, and others who have been much less honest, help us
avoid is: how can it be right to cause so much pain to those
we love?

If I had an aching pain in my abdomen, and a shaman
promised me I could relieve it by giving my baby a series of
painful electric shocks, would I do it? I don't think so. And
it would not much matter to me that "no lasting damage"

to my baby would result from the pain. Yet this is the bargain of divorce: adults purchase emotional relief at the expense of their anxious, bewildered, grief-stricken children.

Marriage exists not to punish people, but to help them achieve their objective: to create a successful family. The evidence suggests that many of us who can do this within the framework of marriage are unable to do so without it. "Psychologically, the very structure of marriage helps maintain adulthood," writes Wallerstein. "When the marriage collapses, many impulses are no longer contained."[23]

Many people who are good parents within marriage, become abysmal ones outside of it. During his ten years of marriage, Dale Burrelle was an active father. He enjoyed coming home to his three little children, reading them bedtime stories and tucking them in for the night. But then his wife Betty became very depressed and erratic for a period of some months. It probably had something to do with the fact that her mother had died recently in a car accident, but Dale didn't seem to think of that when he told her he enjoyed living alone.

The divorce settlement left Betty with $360 a month to maintain three children. Dale moved to New York and had a good job as a hospital administrator. After five years, he was $5,000 behind in payments. Contact between father and children dwindled to a few letters a year.

Today, ten years later, Dale is convinced he was a good father. "If they need anything, they can get it." He keeps their pictures by his desk, but he is so detached from their actual lives, he simply isn't aware of the pain he has caused them. "The tragedy of the Burrelle family is that Dale wants to be a father, tries to be a father, but cannot do it outside the marriage," says Wallerstein.[24]

Dale is not an unusual case. Divorced men commonly

become emotionally detached from their children. Middle-class fathers let their children live on the edge of poverty. Wealthy fathers refuse to pay for college educations. The average divorced father sees his children erratically or not at all.

Bad spouses are not necessarily bad parents. "Children," Wallerstein points out, "can be quite content even when their parents' marriage is profoundly unhappy for one or both partners." Only one in ten children in her study say they felt relieved when their parent divorced.[25] Happy adults do not necessarily make good parents and unhappy parents do not necessarily take their grievances out on their children. Marriage provides a structure for good parenting, and the structure often turns out to be more important than the individual temperaments, moral convictions, and abilities of the adults within it.

Even as unilateral divorce was making it easier for a woman to be abandoned by her spouse, a wave of gender-neutral child custody laws was making it easier for her to lose her children in the bargain. This time the goal was more choice for judges. Lawmakers abandoned the "tender years" doctrine, which guaranteed women custody of young children because "it did not permit much discretion for judges to deviate from maternal custody. The newer emphasis on the 'best interests of the child' greatly expanded judges' discretion in custody cases..."[26]

The new law promises much and delivers less than nothing. The "best interests of the child" rule asks judges to make decisions they are not qualified to make. A judge may be expected to recognize a manifestly unfit parent, but hardly to make nice distinctions between the good and the better parent. The best interests rule has not made custody decisions better. It has made them much less predictable, and more unhappy for almost everyone, including children, who become living scorecards for their parents' bare-knuckle bouts, while they wait for months or years to find out with which parent they will live.

Abolishing maternal custody was part of a larger drive in America to make gender publicly invisible, to deny the reality that sex roles are the basis of marriage, and to encourage androgynous experimentation. The harm to women, as Phyllis Chesler documented (perhaps unwittingly) in *Mothers on Trial*, has been considerable. Even mothers who get custody live in fear that their ex-husbands may come along and take away their children. Because a judge may reassign custody whenever he thinks it's in "the best interest of the child," many women must significantly alter their life plans and practices to avoid appearing unconventional.

Avoiding eccentricity may not be enough. Simply being poor and remaining unmarried may cause a woman to lose her child. An affluent ex-husband with a new spouse may claim to offer more resources and a more stable homelife than the woman he impoverished can provide. Money talks louder than ever when, in pursuit of androgyny, culture cancels out the value of mothers.

It's Baby M all over again, and all over the country. When the law disregards the intense emotional connection of a mother to her children, women lose their bargaining power. If what children need is "caretaking" and that can be done equally well by fathers, babysitters, au pair girls, or day care workers, then a new stepmom is certainly as good as any old biological mom. Androgyny, by refusing to recognize women's work, renders women defenseless.

Richard Neely is a justice of the West Virginia Supreme Court of Appeals and author of *The Divorce Decision*. As the maternal custody rule gave way to a gender-neutral "better parent" rule, Neely noticed a cruel new trend. "Mothers who wish to get custody of their children without a fight are routinely forced to sacrifice necessary financial support. This distasteful form of barter is one of the reasons that single women with dependent children are becoming a new class of the poverty stricken."

Neely knows this is true, because as a lawyer, he's done it. One of his clients was a railroad brakeman, married with two kids, with a taste for motorcycles and motorcycle mammas. Neely asked his client if he wanted custody. He said, emphatically, no. "Nonetheless it occurred to me that if he told his wife that he would fight for custody all the way to the U.S. Supreme Court, we might settle the whole divorce fairly cheaply. That night he went home and began a guerrilla campaign centering on the children." His wife agreed to accept modest alimony and support in exchange for custody.[27]

Today only six states have a strong maternal presumption for custody, while twenty-one states explicitly forbid favoring mothers. Women still retain custody of children in about 90 percent of cases, but at a higher cost. When men decide to contest custody they win two-thirds of the time. "The pendulum has swung," comments Nancy D. Polikoff, director of the Child Custody and Child Support Project of the Women's Legal Defense Fund. "...Today even outstanding mothers are losing custody to fathers who did little caregiving during the marriage because society has devalued the maternal role by assuming there is a 'new man' who actively participates in child rearing."[28]

The divorce plague relentlessly undermines marriage, all marriage, including intact marriages and marriages yet and perhaps never to be. I have talked to men who are afraid to marry because they fear divorce, and to married women who are afraid to have the children they long for, because any tension in their marriages reminds them they cannot guarantee their children a father. Children everywhere are nervous about divorce, none more so than children who have experienced it.

The children of divorce are careful, cautious, and ever so sensible. They speak of commitments to traditional values. They despise divorce, infidelity, selfishness, and lack of commitment. They want love, home, family, and faithfulness more fiercely even than children from intact families. Yet they are less likely to achieve them.

They believe in screening lovers and potential mates carefully, and they talk about putting off children until they know the marriage will work. Yet even as the marriages of people who cautiously live together first are more likely to fail than those who take a blind leap of faith, this very anxiety about divorce causes marriages to break down. It makes women unwilling to have children, or more than one child. It makes men guard their assets jealously with prenuptial agreements. When conflict arises (as it inevitably does), the constant tension of wondering whether divorce is the answer, and the horror of watching their friends' divorces turn lovers into hated enemies, takes its toll. I have watched couples spend years wondering whether or not they should get divorced. They do it, one finally suspects, simply to end the intolerable suspense.

Today all of us are children of divorce however happy our parents' marriage. We see what happens to an uncle, a neighbor, a brother or a sister, or a friend. When it happens often enough and in the best of families, the psychological destruction of marriage is as complete as its legal prohibition. People dare not invest in a relationship when they know the one who leaves first clearly wins.

We have chosen to treat divorce as a private decision; indeed as the unilateral choice of one partner. The divorce plague is not a private problem because marriage is not solely a private good. Those who remain securely married provide enormous benefits to society, for which society need never directly pay, while those who abandon their spouses and children create an enormous public burden. The divorced are far more likely to be mentally and physically ill, economically underproductive, or dependent on public assistance than either married or never-married people. Their children are far less likely to contribute to making ours a healthy, productive, reasonably happy, and sane society. Dr. Armand Nicholi of Harvard Medical School predicts an unprecedented incidence of mental illness if the divorce plague continues. Crimes of violence will increase as well as child abuse and suicides.[29]

But there is another more powerful sense in which marriage is not a private good. For, though marriage confers vast benefits on those who enter into it, and those who issue from it, people cannot create it for themselves.

We did not, in the first place, create the erotic drama that marriage embodies. We do not make Eros, it makes us, and the world. The service of Eros takes up, if only we could admit it, the greater part of our whole lives, and gives or withholds almost all that we know of happiness and grief. Eros's imperious power is seen in the desperate attachment to every faithless lover or disappointing husband; the devotion to every ungainly, too numerous, or expensive child; the irrational and unexpected grief at the passing of parents for whom love had been long lost to pain and anger.

Worshipers of contract, right or left, love to talk about

the virtues of private bargains, privately agreed to. But in the most libertarian society, the law shapes private bargains, indeed makes them possible. It would make no sense to talk about contracts or agreements in a world without private property, or the legal determination to protect it. And yet greed is but a shadow of Eros and no mythmaker has ever made him a god. It makes far less sense to talk about merely private marriages, unsupported by laws binding the parties to their promised performance. It makes still less sense to do so when children appear, whose consent to the deal was never asked.

It is children who show finally that marriage is not too little a thing to be contained in contract, but too great. Children are the great sign of Eros, who make nonsense of contract because they make nonsense of everything, because they make no sense at all. If greed or reason ruled the world instead of Eros, there would be no children. Greed and reason are for individuals, alone. By themselves they could not even justify children by the need to perpetuate the race (what need, after I am dead?) never mind the mad desire to create a family.

In *Man and Superman,* George Bernard Shaw predicted that while England and America would never tolerate the idea of abolishing marriage, "nothing is more certain than that in both countries the progressive modification of the marriage contract will be continued until it is no more onerous nor irrevocable than any ordinary commercial deed of partnership."

He was wrong. We have diluted the marriage contract until it is *much less* binding than the average business contract. Since the seventies, marriage has been one of the few contracts in which the law explicitly protects the defaulting party, at the direct expense of his or her partner. If business contracts were treated as cavalierly as marriage contracts, America would face economic collapse. Once businessmen and women recognized that deals were no longer binding, business would grind to a halt unless some ruthless private enforcement mechanism, say, Don Corleone, stepped in to fill the vacuum created by the withdrawal of law. In India, when dowries were banned (that is no longer enforced by the law), bride-burning emerged as the local solution to default on the dowry contract.

The semblance of marriage continues because, as Mary Ann Glendon put it, the kind of marriage imagined by our current laws is not the only kind of marriage imagined by the populace. Other stories of family, devotion, loyalty, commitment, of courage—the wild daring to make an irrevocable commitment to another person—remain, subtly camouflaging the stark, brutal invitation to abandonment contained in our marriage laws. Our erotic ties to each other remain much stronger that the weak words of contract we use to describe them to ourselves. But slowly, inexorably, the story contained in the law is becoming the only story our culture has to tell about marriage. This is inevitable, for the story told by the law has, for an increasing number of people, become the story of their lives. We see it in crumbling lives all around us; we fear it for ourselves.

The very least a free society must do is offer us the option to marry. For in creating the marriage relation, society creates an opportunity we cannot create for ourselves. Love cannot create marriage. A family generates affection, but affection cannot alone generate a family. What makes family ties unique is precisely that they are not voluntary in the way that friendships are. Your brother is your brother, whether or not you like him. A father must provide for his son, even if he considers him a snot-nosed punk. The reason divorce is so traumatic for children is that it breaks up a child's reassuring sense that family connections are indissoluble. If Daddy behaves badly, then Mommy leaves. If I behave badly, then Mommy will leave me too. Love becomes, not the benefit a family provides, but it's eliciting condition. I am under protection of family only as long as I am loveable.

Marriage is not, as confused people now say, "a public affirmation of love." Many fine and important relationships are created by feelings of intimacy, affection, and mutual pleasure. Drawn by their feelings, people become friends, and comrades, and lovers. And it is a great thing to have a friend, a comrade, a lover. But none of these relationships is marriage. Many cultures, for example, have allowed men both wives and legal concubines. How can one tell the difference between the two? Largely this: a wife is part of her husband's family, a concubine is not. The distinctive feature of marriage, as opposed to other long-term personal relationships, is that two unrelated individuals come together to create a new family which (usually) extends itself via children into the next generation. The purpose in taking a concubine on the other hand is personal pleasure—not merely pleasures of the flesh, but of intimacy, feminine refreshment, including artistic or intellectual refreshment, as courtesans were frequently better educated than wives.

The thing now called marriage, which has been created by unilateral divorce and the social and cultural attitudes that support it, is also a relationship based on pleasure. Two adults contract to live together for a period of time in the hopes that they might like it better than living apart. If one of them finds it less fulfilling than planned, the relationship based on mutual pleasure can be dissolved at the displeasure of either.

The basic outline of the family in America, a man and woman and their children bound together with strong affectionate ties was drawn by the late 18th century. Our recent innovation is to imagine that these feelings of intimacy, rather than being one goal of marriage, are the marriage itself. Marriage has become socially-sanctioned sexual intercourse in an age where pretty much any kind of sexual intercourse is socially-sanctioned anyway.

This is not, as trendy sociologists like to call it, serial monogamy, a new form of polygamous marriage. This is the destruction of marriage and the erection of a new social institution, mutual concubinage, in it's place. It consists of using people until they are no longer useful and then discarding them in search of better growth opportunities. It is entrepreneurship in the realm of love. Along with junk bonds we have junk marriages, empty promises backed by no assets.

Blinded by continuity of language, we find it hard to see how radical the change has been. The difference between a spouse and a concubine is the same as that between an adopted child and a foster child. You cannot tell the difference from outside appearances. A foster parent and an adopting parent may go through the same motions for a child: feeding, clothing, and playing with him, but they are not doing the same thing. In adopting a child, an adult makes a biologically unrelated individual a part of his family; the foster parent knows he may terminate his relationship with the child at any time and for any reason. In the same way, men and women may continue to have weddings, move in together, and have children, but that doesn't make them married. Only a legal and social institution strong enough to allow men and women to bind up a new family where there was none before can do that.

Marriage attempts to bind not only other people, but to bind one's self in pursuit of a great goal. For marriage, lovers need the law. They cannot do it alone. They have never been able to. In traditional or tribal societies the law may have looked more like what we call custom. In the Age of Faith it may have looked more like what we call moral sanction. But those who bumped up against either knew it was the law.

But it is the law that has killed marriage and wounded family and it is the law that must be changed. In defense of some choices, it is time Americans began taking away others: the choice to use a woman and then abandon her to poverty, the choice to beget children and then forget them.

The old marriage contract, we are told, was horribly oppressive. But imagine if today's marriage licenses set down the new marriage contract in black and white, explaining that a husband has the legal right to leave his wife for a younger woman, and to take her kids along too, if he wants, or leave her with the burden of supporting them, if he does not. If we were handed this new marriage contract judges and legislatures and reformers have written for us, how many of us would sign? Is this what we want in wanting marriage? Is this what we mean when we say "I do"?

Giving people the right to marry does not mean abolishing divorce. American law has permitted divorce, generally in the case of adultery, impotence, or desertion, since the colonial days. Cruelty was added to the list of grounds for divorce in most states in the 19th century. Fault-based divorce does not prevent marriage. Even allowing divorce by mutual consent erodes, but does not erase the possibility of marriage.

Only unilateral divorce has succeeded in deforming marriage out of recognition, in depriving Eros of a durable dwelling place in the relations between men and women. In an insane triumph of mood over monogamy, no-fault divorce gives all the odds to the itch and ignores the seven years. In worshipping choice we destroy it. We build a world in which commitment is illegal and find that choice is just another word for faithlessness.

People enter marriage with a variety of expectations. For many individuals, children, family, and the future may not be at the top of the list. But while a man and a woman are entitled to marry without making children the focus of their relationship, they are not entitled to demand that society restructure the institution of marriage to suit their ends. For those ends are purely private, and government really has no business aiding or hindering the enterprise in any way. Couples who define marriage as long-term intimacy don't need a piece of paper; their own hearts must show them the way. Two unrelated individuals who wish to create a new family do need the law, for a family is not something two individuals can create by themselves. We need to draw on all the resources that history, tradition, law, and religion can provide. We need to be given, by law and society, the right to bind ourselves in the indissoluble connection which is family.

Endnotes—Chapter 11

1. Mason, *The Equality Trap, op. cit.*, pp. 54–60.
2. Mary Ann Glendon, *Abortion and Divorce In Western Law: American Failures, European Challenges* (Cambridge: Harvard University Press, 1987), p. 68.
3. Herbert Jacob, *Silent Revolution: The Transformation of Divorce Law in the United States* (Chicago: The University of Chicago Press, 1988), p. 28.
4. Glendon, *op. cit.*, p. 66.

5. Paul Horton and Lawrence Alexander, "Freedom of Contract and the Family: A Skeptical Appraisal," in *The American Family and the State*, edited by Joseph R. Peden and Fred R. Glahe (San Francisco: Pacific Research Institute for Public Policy, 1986), p. 251.

6. Rekers, "Fathers at Home," *op. cit.*, p. 1.

7. *Wall Street Journal*, January 21, 1985, p. 12.

8. Richard Neely, "Barter in the Court," *The New Republic*, February 10, 1986, p. 13.

9. Mason, *op. cit.*, p. 50.

10. Wallerstein and Blakeslee, *Second Chances, op. cit.*, pp. 49–51.

11. *Ibid.*, p. 40.

12. Daniel Goleman, "Nurturing Can Offset the Trauma of Loss in Childhood, Study Says," *The New York Times*, December 1, 1988, p. B22.

13. Wallerstein and Blakeslee, *op. cit.*, p. 7.

14. Rekers in "Fathers at Home," *Persuasion at Work*.

15. For example: "...most of the research has generally ignored longer-term consequences of parental divorce, such as the effects on adult behavior or achievement....More recent studies, however, suggest that parental divorce does have a negative impact on children (Ambert and Saucier, 1984) and on adult status and behavior. McLanahan (1985) found that educational attainment was lower for young adults who had experienced parental divorce earlier in life. Glenn and Kramer (1985) also found diminished psychological well-being among adults whose parents divorced." [Verna M. Keith and Barbara Finlay, "The Impact of Parental Divorce on Children's Educational Attainment, Marital Timing, and Likelihood of Divorce," *Journal of Marriage and the Family* (August 1988), pp. 797–809.] Keith and Finlay's own study found children of divorced parents have lower educational attainment and that daughters (but not sons) of divorced parents have a higher probability of being divorced, perpetuating the cycle. For other summaries of recent research on the effect of divorce on children see Rekers, "Fathers At Home," *op. cit.*, and Vance Packard, *Our Endangered Children: Growing Up in Our Changing World* (Boston: Little, Brown, 1983), pp. 185–202.

16. Alan Booth, David B. Brinkerhoff, Lynn K. White, "The Impact of Parental Divorce on Courtship," *Journal of Marriage and the Family* (February 1984), pp. 85–94.

17. Wallerstein and Blakeslee, *op. cit.*, p. 163.

18. Dr. Forehand found that children in low-conflict intact families rated highest in cognitive abilities, social competence, communications skills and had lower rates of disruptive conduct in school. In teacher ratings of cognitive competence, low-conflict intact families scored the highest with 3.75. Next were those from low-conflict divorced parents, with 3.58. Children from high-conflict intact families rated somewhat lower at 3.16. But the group which consistently

fared worst of all, much worse than children whose parents remained in angry, unsatisfying marriages, were children in high-conflict divorced families, with an average rating of 2.46. "Parental Fighting Hurts Even After Divorce," *The Washington Post*, November 12, 1986.

19. Wallerstein and Blakeslee, *op. cit.*, p. xviii.

20. "A wife's leaving or threatening to leave her marriage frequently provokes a marital rape...In our study over two-thirds of the women in our sample were raped in the waning days of a relationship, either after previous separations or when they were making plans to get out. Among the eighty-seven marital-rape victims in Diana Russell's study, ten were raped after they were separated. For six of the women it was the first time their husbands raped them." David Finkelhor and Kersti Yllo, *License to Rape: Sexual Abuse of Wives* (New York: The Free Press, Macmillan, 1985), p. 25.

21. Wallerstein and Blakeslee, *op. cit.*, pp. 23–24.

22. "Divorce Exacts Its Price from Parent and Child Alike," *Insight*, October 13, 1986, p. 16.

23. Wallerstein and Blakeslee, *op. cit.*, p. 305.

24. *Ibid.*, p. 144.

25. *Ibid.*, p. 11.

26. Jacob, *op. cit.*, pp. 130–31.

27. Neely, *op. cit.*, pp. 13–16.

28. Sharon Johnson, "The Odds On Custody Change," *The New York Times*, March 17, 1986.

29. Susan B. Garland, "American Children Growing Up Too Fast, Too Soon," *The Oregonian*, June 12, 1984.

12

Abortion and the Children of Choice

When I was in high school and much of college, I believed in all the cliches of my generation. I believed in reproductive freedom. I believed that abortion "cured" the problem of unwanted children, and that every child has a right to be loved and wanted. I believed that no one had a right to tell me what to do with my body. I believed that sex was an expression of affection between two people who respected each other. I believed that abortion was a positive good: in time it would make all children one of the Chosen People.

Over time, as I began looking at the choices open to me, I learned that for adults, choice is an overrated virtue; applied to children, it is a disaster. What propagandists for choice ignore is the power of Eros. It is those erotic ties, not our flimsy choices, that tie families together. Ties that are powerful enough to last never feel like a choice at all. We fall in love with our children soon or not at all, in which case our careful planning will be very cold comfort indeed in the long years to come.

If parents choose children expecting pleasure, and they get a great deal of frustration and anxiety (as all parents do), they are likely to feel cheated. This isn't what they signed on for. They chose to have children because they thought it would improve their quality of life. To a generation drunk on choice, parenting can come as a surprise and a trap. For once our children are born, we are stuck with them whether we like it or not.

Children of choice are a new phenomenon, but not, as many people say, because of recent advances in contraceptive technology. Long before the Pill, married couples had exercised control over their fertility. Urban middle-class families in America have been limiting births for more than a hundred years. But only in this generation have we created the dangerous fantasy that planned parents are better parents and that "accidental" children are less valuable, less happy, less *wanted* than children who have been made to order.

Choice is the opiate of the liberal. It blinds his eyes and hardens his heart. It makes him dull and stupid and complacent. Where choice is, the sexual liberal believes, justice flourishes and happiness will reign. Children of choice will of course be the happiest children of all. You can see the beginning of this hallucination in adoption literature of the fifties which downgrades mere "biological" ties in order to reassure adoptive parents. It picks up steam in the political controversies over contraceptives in the sixties. But it did not become the ruling ideology until 1973, when the Supreme Court of the United States made abortion on demand the law of the land.

Roe v. Wade did the unthinkable. It reestablished as a Constitutional principle an idea we thought died on the blood-drenched battlefields of the Civil War: that there can be human beings who are not persons.

The humanity of the unborn is not and cannot be an issue. Peering into the womb, scientific technology has settled a question our ancestors could only ponder: human life begins at the moment of conception. The fetus is alive and (being a human fetus) is human; it is a human being.

But what we have come to believe in the long years since seven Supreme Court justices took it upon themselves to inflict an abortion crisis on this country, is something else; something dark, dangerous, arrogant, and ominous: we have come to doubt that being a human being is enough.

The debate over abortion has come to turn over the *personhood* of the fetus, just as feminism, as Betty Friedan wrote in 1981, is about "the personhood of women." A person is someone who cannot be sold into slavery. To kill a person is murder. What *Roe v. Wade* did is destroy the idea that all human beings are people. Since *Roe*, being a human being no longer gives you any human rights. Since *Roe*, you must meet some other vague and undefined criteria—the ability to reason, the ability to make choices, the ability to live on your own, the ability to make adults go ooooooh and aaaah while they tickle your toes. Some ability, it's not clear what, earns for you the right to life.

There is no rational distinction between a fetus and a baby. At some barely-suppressed level of consciousness many women know this. "Most women when they have an abortion don't really know what they are doing—they're either so young, so ignorant, or so frightened," one social worker at Abortion Hotline, a crisis counseling and referral center in Portland, Oregon, told me. "Down the line, five, six, or seven years when they have children, some kind of trauma almost always comes up . . . and down the line, most women do think of the aborted fetus as a living being, as a baby."

To sexual liberals even babies are beginning to seem less than fully people. "Children," as one academic writes, "it seems, are not on a par with adults after all; they are not to be accorded exactly the rights adults enjoy because they lack 'experience,' 'rationality,' 'the capacity for choice,' or some other 'adult' faculty or attribute. It would appear then, that we think children are persons—but not quite persons."[1] Our current confusion stems from the fact we think morality flows from choice, so that it seems absurd to say that children are people—moral agents—and yet incapable of making decisions for themselves. A lot of people, in their guts, feel one achieves personhood at about the same age at which one can intelligently discuss Ayn Rand's epistemology (an age which continues to elude many of us).

This is a misplaced faith in a misidentified quality. The trouble with making the ability to choose, or the ability to reason, the criterion for personhood is that every one of us is sporadically subject to temporary incapacity in this regard. A man who is asleep, for example, or dead drunk, or in a temporary coma, is still a person, though he may not be able to walk, or talk, or make it to the bathroom unassisted. A dog makes many choices and an incapacitated human being cannot. Does that make Lassie more of a person than John Tower on a binge?

The key to the humanity of babies (besides how much

fun they are) is continuity of identity. The baby my mother held in her arms, was me. It was me that grew in her womb. Infancy, like a drug-induced stupor, is a temporary condition from which people normally recover.

I am the human being I was and I am the human being I will be, though in ordinary speech we might say the *person* that I am can easily change. This is why the new idea of "personhood" is so dangerous. Our "personhood," defined as the sum total of the choices we make, shifts and dies and is reborn constantly. Our self-consciousness alters beyond recognition, we abandon the companions, the ideals, the tastes of our youth, remodel our selves and our futures, and constantly rewrite our own histories. But nonetheless through all this shifting and changing and transformation, we each remain the same human being that we were, from conception through birth, teething, childhood, puberty, adolescence, adulthood, and senescence until death do we part from our humanity.[2]

If it is reason that makes us human, then most of us, judging from our behavior, could be considered fair game. The sacredness of human beings, it if does not come from God, must come from our human possibilities not from our actual accomplishments. Most of the great achievements of reason, or of reason combined with great moral courage, remain out of the average person's reach. This is what we and the fetus have in common: For most of us, most of the time, being a potential person is about the best we can do.

Many people today have a very difficult time accepting the idea that a developing child is just as valuable as a fully grown adult. Generally, these people do not care to reason or dispute about the matter. They just point to an unborn child and say, "You don't mean to suggest that eentsy weentsy little amphibian is as important as *I*, an actual ten-

ured professor of biopsychology at a very well-regarded institution of higher learning with a very large endowment,
am? Surely, madam, you jest.''

Clifford Grobstein, professor emeritus of Biology and
Public Policy, expresses a very common sentiment in his
book *Science and the Unborn*. ''Can a single cell be a human being, a person, an entity endowed with unalienable
right to life, liberty, and the pursuit of happiness?...it
seems ludicrous to suggest that concepts appropriate to
that realm should be extended to an individual cell at the
bare limit of visibility.''[3] So, to many people, it does.

But that emotion should make us suspicious. If we find
it so hard to take a tiny little unborn embryo who has never
done anything gauche in its life seriously as a human being,
how can we expect to handle the idea that there is something self-evidently sacred about PeeWee Herman, or Al
Sharpton, or that great slob of a next door neighbor of
yours whose dirty T-shirts don't quite cover his enormous
beer belly?

Self-consciousness does not always seem so awe in-
spiring if you look at the uses people put it to. Put aside
even the cases of great and awful evil, the Adolf Hitlers and
Joseph Stalins, and look at your ordinary run of the mill
made-for-TV-Movie news story. Oh, we can be a pathetic
enough species when we put our minds to it. If Jimmy
Swaggart is a person, what's so exalted about being one?

Once we trust ourselves to start deciding who is sufficiently personable to live and who is sufficiently alien to be
killed, it is rather hard to find any principled stopping place.
Through the barbarism of abortion, we've begun separat-
ing the humans from the persons. And once you accept the
idea that simply being a human being isn't enough, you

have (by definition) made it no longer self-evident that all men are created equal and endowed with inalienable rights.

This is the problem with "sensible" liberals like Charles Krauthammer, who argues in the pages of the *New Republic* that only those persuaded by faith could believe that personhood begins at conception ("life obviously does, but then again even a sperm is living").[4] Krauthammer is appalled by the brave new world unfolding before us, in which women will be paid to turn their wombs into fetus farms, out of which doctors will harvest the heart, the liver, the pancreas, the brain cells of the unborn. But Krauthammer, denounces those "hard-liners" at the Vatican who insist that all human life deserves protection.

Like the sensible liberal that he is, he suggests we draw a bright line at fourteen days, after which experimentation on the unborn will be considered disrespectful of human life. Before that time, embryos may be created, implanted, discarded, and experimented on as much as prospective parents and doctors little hearts' desire.

A fourteen day limit, says Krauthammer, preserves the human dignity of the fetus. But what kind of dignity can a human being have if it may be disposed of at will? Conversely if the unborn is not a person, but only an undignified mass of cells, why shouldn't we use its death to save real, actual humans? And why shouldn't we grow more blobs of cells to save more real people? The fourteen day line allows us to do what we want—explore artificial birth technologies—and prevents us from doing what Krauthammer says we do not want—turning unborn children into spare parts. The only trouble is that Krauthammer cannot explain why we do not want it.

Krauthammer's fears in this regard are hardly exaggerated. Fetal transplants offer promising cures for a number of diseases from diabetes to Parkinson's disease. Several companies already do a brisk business in fetal parts. And already at least one woman has offered to become pregnant and then abort the unborn baby and use the tissues to help cure her father's illness.

Scientists pant to experiment on children in the earliest stages of development, both in and outside of the womb. One scientific philosopher goes so far as to say it is "disrespectful" to human life not to make use of the bodies of very young unborn humans for such scientific purposes: "If the preembryo cannot realize its highest potential as a person—the preferred option—preembryos have other very substantial values. They may provide essential cells and tissues to others. Or they may be the subject of research studies yielding important benefits to all of humanity. In contrast to such possibilities, casual or even ceremonial discard of preembryos amounts to disrespect, in that it fails to appreciate them. . ."[5]

The value of unborn human beings in this sense is use-value. We "appreciate" them for what we can get out of them, in the same way an African cannibal might "appreciate" the human tissue he consumes. In the brave new world unfolding, we shall eat our young and gain thereby eternal youth for ourselves and our loved ones.

Krauthammer finds fetus farms instinctively repulsive, but he does not (and apparently cannot) explain why. I admire his instincts more than the pseudosophistication which leads him to call the Vatican's principled position "biological Luddism" and yet replace it with little else but a quick "Yeecch!" and a lengthy consultation of public opinion. ("If drawing lines against fetal abuse is the object, drawing them at a place where they will not be accepted is not prudent.")

225

On July 3, 1989, the Supreme Court took the first step in the long process of overturning *Roe v. Wade*. The debate unleashed by *Missouri v. Webster* already has engulfed the country. As the battle shifts to state legislatures, the debate over abortion threatens to preoccupy and divide the country like no other issue since the great civil rights struggles of the 1950s and 1960s. It is a debate over what it means to be a person.

Abortion devalues some human beings in defense of a frail and limited concept of personhood: the right to choose, and right to be one of the Chosen People. Abortion is both the necessary tool and the cultural embodiment of those who believe that families are formed by choice, that choice nurtures and sustains them.

Academics and activists who make choice the source of family obligation are struggling with the problem: how can woman be morally and legally held responsible for the great burden of caring for a child? This is the current answer: because she *chose* to have children.

A woman sufficiently alienated from her body might be made to believe it. As her belly swells with life and her breasts swell with milk, she might just be deluded into believing that it is her disembodied mind which connects her to her child. Then, like me, she will be in for a surprise. I was twenty-two and unmarried when my son was born, just a few months after I had graduated from Yale University. I remember sitting in the hospital bed, holding my tiny naked son. It came as such a shock to me, more powerful than and yet akin to the shock of falling in love, this sense of absolute and unbreakable connection. At that moment, he was the most important thing in my life, and though I have endured, as other mothers do, the usual quota of baby messes, emotional aggravation, missed deadlines, and deferred gratifications, I have never doubted it since.

Why hadn't anyone told me it was like this? They were too busy telling me (and I believed them) about my right to self-determination, bodily and otherwise. I have always been intensely ambitious. Before Patrick was born, I believed I did not want to have children. Once he came into my life, I found to my profound surprise that I wasn't going to let any ambitions of mine get in the way of caring for his needs.

I have since talked to many women of my generation to whom motherhood came in the same way: as an intense gratification, and an unutterable shock. I made the choice, as every woman must today in a society in which abortion is easily available and widely promoted, to give birth. But I never succumbed to the delusion that my measly little act of choice had anything at all to do with what I felt for my son.

The horror of abortion is not just that a woman destroys a child, but that a woman destroys *her own* child. We have a duty not to kill any human being, but we owe our own children much more: care, protection, the effort of daily love. Abortion is the refusal to acknowledge the unconditional claim children have on our lives. In an aborted society, parental love is hedged in with conditions. I will care for you only if: it seems like it would be gratifying; if it doesn't interrupt my education; if it doesn't interrupt my marriage; if I have the time, and it doesn't interfere with my career; if you love me enough to make it worth my while.

Every woman who has a child she loves knows the lie of abortion. Through the long months of pregnancy, the being that grows in the womb is not a blob of cells. The grief a woman who miscarries feels is not for a potential human being, it is for her baby. The careful euphemisms used in abortion clinics are evidence of the bad faith of the abortion culture. Women are never told (and orthodox feminists fiercely oppose laws requiring doctors to inform us) that the blob of cells may have tiny fingers, toes, a beating heart, and brain waves. Clinic personnel do not even refer to this developing human being as a "fetus"; nor is the word "abortion" used. It might be too painful for women to face what we are doing. So we are reassured. The nurse tells us "the procedure" will eliminate "the blob of cells" from the uterus. Then the "product of conception" (my personal favorite euphemism) will be disposed of. A day off, a few aspirin, and, presto, good as new.[6]

The abortion culture devalues born children as well as unborn children by turning them into objects of choice. But it is not just children that are affected. I was a teenager in the mid-seventies when I first heard the argument that abortion could lead to infanticide and the killing off of the elderly. I dismissed it as absurd. Daniel Callahan did the same at more scholarly length in his influential 1970 book, *Abortion: Law, Choice and Morality.* But we were both wrong. It took less than fifteen years, but now retarded babies with birth defects may be legally starved to death. Old people, if they are unconscious or have other cognitive defects, may already be ordered killed by their relatives with the approval of a judge.[7]

Dr. Grobstein acknowledges the link between the disposing of unborn children and killing off elderly, retarded, or comatose people. "[Embryos] are not yet persons but they clearly are on the way to becoming such; they are semi- or quasi-persons...This transition of the embryo roughly and reciprocally parallels the course of elderly people who are suffering from senile dementia... The two situations are not, of course, identical. But each represents a transitional state to, or from, typical personhood. Elderly people with severe cognitive defects might not be admitted to personhood if their status were to be reconsidered on strictly definitional grounds. But by general consensus and for complicated reasons, their status is continued as an entitlement."[8] Lucky for them. Once that consensus is disrupted, say by close relatives overburdened with medical bills or distant ones hungry for an inheritance, so is their entitlement.

The link between abortion, infanticide, and the legal murder of the elderly and the handicapped is the new concept of personhood which is rapidly superseding our old faith in human rights. The thin line that now separates murder from medical practice is that we do not actively kill off these unwanted patients. Instead, a judge orders that it is in the patient's "best interest" that food and water be withheld. The victims die a terrible, slow death from dehydration and we claim that we merely eliminated "heroic" means to sustain life. But giving food and water to those unable to feed themselves is not a heroic measure. The thin line, which is a lie, will not hold. Soon "quality of death" will replace "quality of life" as a slogan, and rather than watch our chosen victims suffer, we will kill them off directly. It is doctors who will do this and it will be called a medical procedure, though, like abortion, it has nothing to do with healing.

"Abortion is a service of sorts, and it is now performed by doctors, but it is no more a *medical* service than is a haircut," as John Wauk put it in the *Human Life Review*. In the Middle Ages, barbers gave haircuts and performed surgery because the same scarce tools were needed for each. In the new dark ages, doctors will heal the sick and kill the unwanted and because scalpels and shots are used for each procedure, we will be fooled, for a while, into believing that killing and healing are just different branches of the same thing: medicine.

The continuity of human life in the face of radical transformations of "consciousness" is what makes many women who are feminists and pro-choicers uneasy and ambivalent about abortion. Two pro-choice feminists, Linda Bird Francke *(The Ambivalence of Abortion)* and Kathleen McDonnell *(Not an Easy Choice)* wrote books about this uneasiness. In the Apr. 11, 1989, issue of the *Village Voice,* Lynn Chancer argues for Abortion Without Apology. No, counters a friend of hers, "Destroying a fetus simply cannot be equated with going to the dentist and having a tooth removed; it has to be 'weird,'...for one is always conscious of the potentiality the fetus represents."

Potentiality is a potent word. It hints at, without fully capturing, the continuity of identity that exists from womb to grave. The "person" who will be comes from the human being that now is in its mother's womb. A wordless baby, a babbling child, a vigorous mother, a dying old woman, and a tiny thirty-two-cell embryo are all stages of the life of the same thing: a single human being.

Tormented by widespread ambivalence about abortion, the inner compromise Americans have settled on is that women may have abortions so long as we feel *bad* about them afterwards. The psychic pain of women is the anesthetic which dulls our social conscience. Women are told we may extract the frightening pound of flesh as long as it hurts us. If having an abortion is a painful and troubling decision for a woman, then she is good, not callous. The gods are satisfied; values have not been abandoned. Women admit they are vulnerable and the social order remains intact. It is sadism as a substitute for morality.

The abortion ethic is the denial of tragedy. The interests of mothers and children never diverge, it tells us. Unwanted children are better off dead anyway, so we might as well kill them off before they can claim due process rights. This denial of tragedy, a staple of the cheerful, death-denying American character, also pops up among many pro-lifers. I have sat across the dinner table and heard two anti-abortion men (both now active in Republican politics) describe the act of giving birth to a child and giving it up for adoption as a mere "inconvenience" to a woman.

Tragedy is real because other human beings are real, and therefore it is possible for human interests really to clash. The tragedy of that clash is real and unavoidable and also at the same time testimony to the value of what is at stake. Denying the tragedy of abortion is averting one's eyes to the suffering and the limitations of being alive and human, out of fear that if we saw the pain, *really* saw it, we would no longer believe that life was worth living. At the heart of abortion is a lack of courage.

Abortion is the death of tragedy and the birth of nihilism. The abortion ethic places avoiding pain at the center of existence—the pain of childbirth, the pain of illegitimacy, the pain of being connected to a child you may not be able to support, the pain of being an unwanted child and an unwanted mother and worse, the pain of being unloving. The abortion ethic makes us believe it is an act of healing for doctors to kill and an act of love for a mother to refuse her children life. It says explicitly of children and implicitly of mothers: some human lives are not worth living. Abortion is nihilism with the abyss.

Or is it a cheerful nihilism proclaiming an absolute right

to pleasure? Getting pregnant interferes with a woman's sex life and so abortion must be legal. The right to orgasm, in this view, supersedes our children's right to live. Pleasure is good. Sex is magnificent. But can we remain persons ourselves while maintaining that sex is more important than the life of a human being?

The force which drives our bodies together in lust and the force which binds us to our children are one and the same. Maternal love is an intensely sexual experience, more sexually-satisfying than any feeling produced by the manipulation of body parts. Far from freeing women's sexuality, abortion is an antisexual act. "To say that in order to be equal with men it must be possible for a pregnant woman to become unpregnant at will is to say that being a woman precludes her from being a fully functioning person . . . Of all the things which are done to women to fit them into a society dominated by men, abortion is the most violent invasion of their physical and psychic integrity," writes New Zealand feminist Daphne DeJong, "It is a deeper and more destructive assault than rape, the culminating act of womb-envy and woman-hatred. . ."[9]

Many women who have had abortions know this only too well. Sexual relationships almost never survive an abortion, and a woman in love with her child's father who receives any encouragement from him seldom has an abortion. In turn, many women who have abortions report suddenly feeling sexually cold. Their bodies are not sources of pleasure or abundance, but of sexual rejection. Their lovers reject the fruits of their bodies, or they themselves do. It makes little difference, the result is the same. The femaleness of their body, their sexuality, has proven a tremendous liability. In their womb is death and the vagina is a pathway to it. How much better to be a man and permanently barren and therefore impregnable.

The myth of abortion is that choice sets parents and children free. Today, women alone choose to have children and increasingly, women alone bear the responsibility for raising them. Choice is an escape hatch for men and a lie for women: a lie because giving life is a leap into the future for which nothing in the past can prepare one; no one ever knows in advance what raising children will be like.

But the obsession with carefully-planned parenthood does serve one important social function; it keeps us from noticing some perfectly obvious causes of the current epidemic of battered children and broken lives.

Endnotes—Chapter 12

1. Lyla H. O'Driscoll, "Toward a New Theory of the Family," *The American Family and the State*, edited by Joseph R. Peden and Fred R. Glahe, (San Francisco: Pacific Research Institute for Public Policy, 1986), p. 81.

2. Continuity of human identity is also the reason why using brain waves as the criteria for personhood falls short. We accept the cessation of brain waves as evidence of death in adult human beings only because we conclude (after repeated observation) that once the brain stops waving it never starts up again. If brains generally shut down and started up again, then the stopping of the brain would no longer signal death. Today, brain waves in the fetus are being discovered at earlier and earlier stages in the womb, from at least 8 weeks, as our technology for sensing them becomes more sophisticated. But that is beside the point; even with brain waves neither a fetus, nor a baby, nor your average 3-year old, is capable of much rational thought. You can probably communicate more effectively with your German shepherd than you can with a 2-month old baby, and the dog will certainly be more responsive than your average 2-year old. The absence of brain waves in an unborn child (unlike a grown person) is not irreversible.

3. Clifford Grobstein, *Science and the Unborn: Choosing Human Futures* (New York: Basic Books, 1988), pp. 5–6.

4. Charles Krauthammer, "The Ethics of Human Manufacture," *The New Republic*, May 4, 1987, p. 17ff.

5. Grobstein, *op. cit.*, p. 138.

6. The euphemisms of abortionists are matched only by those of scientists experimenting on the unborn. "Fetus ex utero" (rather than premature infant) is the term of choice when an abortion produces a live baby rather than a dead one. Another creative research team labelled the not-yet-dead children surgically removed from their mother's womb "intact feto-placental units." Perhaps they are also from Regulac and consume mass quantities.

7. For a roundup of some recent cases, see David N. O'Steen, "Climbing Up the Slippery Slope," *Window on the Future: The Pro-Life Year in Review*, edited by Dave Andrusko (Washington, DC: National Right to Life Committee, 1987), pp. 73–87.

8. Grobstein, *op. cit.*, p. 141.

9. Daphne de Jong, "Legal Abortion Exploits Women," *Abortion: Opposing Viewpoints*, edited by Bonnie Szumski (St. Paul, Minnesota: Greenhaven Press, 1986), p.164.

13

Child Abuse and the Liberated Family

On Nov. 2, 1987, Daddy Steinberg took his darling six-year-old Lisa, with the shy eyes and dirty, broken fingernails, into the bathroom and beat her senseless. Six hours later, she died and a major news story was born. In all the hoopla that followed, here is a question nobody thought much about: just why *was* Lisa a member of Joel Steinberg's family?

In a society in which choice is the highest virtue and the source of all moral obligation, children are hard to explain. The change in the divorce laws that took place over the last two decades has fueled the illusion that family relationships and families are the products of choice.

The current watered-down version of marriage is based on the modern watered-down version of contract.

Our relationship to our children, though, takes contract one step further: Not agreement, but free and sovereign choice—on the part of the parents—binds us to our children. We are proud of ourselves for having outgrown the social fictions of duty and biology. We will be better than our own parents, and our children will be better off.

America has embraced the myth, assiduously promoted by organizations like Planned Parenthood, that carefully-chosen children are happier than carelessly-conceived products of biology. "All of us who believe that every child should be born wanted and loved must stand up and be counted now," a recent Planned Parenthood of New York City fundraising letter on behalf of abortion rights proclaims.

This is the new ideal of family: a group of people who are not bound together by biological ties or moral obligations they cannot escape. This is the new freely-chosen family. Once every child in America is freely-chosen, then the problems of unwanted children will disappear. To sexual liberals it makes perfect sense: if you choose to have children you must want them and if you want children you will treat them better, right?

People who talk like that don't seem to have noticed Joel Steinberg, whose household was the very epitome of the emerging family, freed from coercive institutions, bound only by desire. Joel and Hedda lived together without the legal mumbo-jumbo of marriage; Lisa and her father were not bound by biology or a piece of paper signed by a judge. Exactly what made Lisa a member of the Steinberg family? Just this: Joel Steinberg *chose* to have children.

The worship of choice makes it impossible for us to see the needs of abused children. We keep pursuing the fantasy that more abortion, more contraception, better clinics in schools, more federal funding for abortions, will cure child abuse. It is on the face of it an odd way to think of helping children: by making sure they are never born. But the confusion runs deeper.

We believe that as we reduce the number of "unwanted" children through abortion and contraception, children will be happier, healthier, better adjusted. They will be more loved. Oh, it makes just so much sense to the sexual liberal. It is so hard not to believe that making children products of choice won't make them happier. But erotic love is not that simple; it appears to have very little to do with choice, contract, or control.

Many babies that are unplanned burdens end up being loved and wanted. And many babies that are consciously conceived and desperately desired end up abused and abandoned.[1] In fact, perverse though it may sound, planned children may be prime targets for child abuse. A 1973 study by Dr. E. F. Lenoski, a professor of pediatrics at the University of Southern California found that 91 percent of battered and abused children are the result of planned pregnancies—a rate much higher than the 63 percent of planned children in a matched control group of unabused children. Battered children were also much more likely to be born to mothers who said they were pleased by their pregnancies. Fully 24 percent of battered children were named after one of their parents, a mark of parental pride, compared to only 4 percent of the control group.[2]

The child most likely to be abused is not the unplanned, but unlucky: born to parents who were themselves abused as children. Men and women abused as children often passionately choose to have children, only to visit the sins of their father upon their own child. They consciously choose to have kids hoping to transcend their own unhappy childhoods. All their careful planning though may not keep them from perpetuating the cycle. Men who are sexually abused as children are prime candidates to become child molesters themselves. Women who were sexually abused do not generally tend to sexually abuse their children: instead they marry men who do.

Dr. Phillip Ney, a Canadian psychologist who works with abused children, believes that elective abortion may be an important cause of child abuse. Ney believes that many women who have abortions become depressed only many years later, when they carry a planned baby to term, and this depression frequently interferes with mother-child bonding. Abortion, he says, may also inhibit bonding by providing an escape hatch from pregnancy. In a society that allows abortion, a baby does not become a certainty until birth. This reduces the mother's prenatal adjustment period. It is not lack of planning but lack of bonding which puts parents at risk of battering their children.[3]

Abortion may also have a more direct effect on living children's well being. Today more than 40 percent of women undergoing abortions have living children as well.[4] Evidence shows a mother's abortion may also harm these surviving children. One study of eighty-seven children whose mothers had abortions uncovered both immediate and delayed reactions ranging from ''anxiety attacks, nightmares, increased aggressiveness, stuttering, running away, death phobias, increased separation anxiety, sudden outbursts of fear or hatred of the mother, and even suicide attempts.''[5]

Most women who have abortions do not batter their living children as a result. But nonetheless the ethic of the child-batterer *is* the abortion ethic. Child abusers, like abortion activists, believe in adults' right to be in control of their lives. Child abusers, like abortionists, believe that only children who gratify parental desires have a right to exist. It is hard to believe that the cultural message contained in abortion, the insistent eulogies to control, and the references to parenting as a right and a pleasure have not contributed to the explosion in child abuse and neglect.

Most harmful of all is the culture's attempt to replace the family with a smorgasbord of individual options from which adults can choose. Americans are intent on seeing that no adult is oppressed by a social norm. In shielding adults, we guarantee that more and more children will be poor, physically abused, sexually used, and abandoned.

The sexual revolution, by pooh-poohing sexual taboos, apparently sparked a strong increase in extra-familial sexual abuse of children. And as more children move into institutional settings, pedophiles have more avenues of contact with young children. At any given moment, the California Department of Social Services has about one out of thirty day care centers under investigation, mostly for allegations of sexual abuse.[6]

But the single greatest cause for the apparent rise in sexual abuse is the divorce explosion. A study by two Canadian psychologists published in the *Journal of Ethology and Sociobiology* reports that a preschool age child living with a stepparent is *forty times* more likely to be abused than a child living with his or her biological father.[7] Diana Russell's study of 930 San Francisco women reports that one out of six women raised by a stepfather was sexually abused by him, compared to one out of forty-three women living with their biological father. Biological fathers are also more likely to stop after one incident and much less likely to abuse their daughters repeatedly over a period of years.[8]

Families are no longer for children. They are places for

adults to make choices, foster intimacy, pursue personal growth, find life satisfaction. They are in fact structured around the needs of those adults who are desperately afraid of pain and unwilling to make actual choices. For in America today, it is the perpetual freedom to choose that we celebrate, and not the ability actually to make a choice and live by it. And children pay for our adolescent yearnings.

Intellectuals talk about the continued existence of the family as if there were any choice in the matter. As if we could, if we chose, replace the family with some other network of social institutions. The family, writes another academic, "is a package of roles related to the function of caring for and rearing children. . . The family is not the only social and legal structure that might evolve or be designed to execute this function. . . imagine by way of contrast a society in which the child rearing function is executed in an institution fully as public as courts, legislatures, and prisons. In this society. . . the legal and social responsibility for the care and rearing of all children, the 'parental' role, is assigned to professional caretakers who represent, and are in the service of, the community at large."[9]

Such a society would cut off sex from Eros and in doing so cut off children from what they desperately need. In such a society, children would be dead.

The family is not merely, as intellectuals theorize, an institution in which children *get* what they need, the family *is* what they need. And an important component of children's sense of family is that it is not arbitrary. Being chosen to live when others die is a burden no human being carries easily, least of all a child. Even the ties of affection are no replacement for Eros. For a child, "You are mine, because I love you" is no replacement for "I love you because you are mine." A warm, affectionate family is a delight and an asset to a child. But what he must have from at least one of his parents is something else: an erotic commitment, beyond affection, beyond reason, far beyond contract; he must know the bond is unbreakable.

When children are denied family, as orphaned babies living in institutions, they wither and die at appalling rates. Children, it appears, acquire something much more important from their parents than tooth-brushing, bottle-washing, clean clothing, and hot nutritious lunches. These, indeed could be (and often are) provided by expert professionals in public institutions. What a small child desperately needs is a tie that binds, a tie to life, an erotic tie. Who can watch a baby struggling to master all the confusing details of socialization, facing the harsh world of playmates, mastering one's bodily functions, learning to talk first and later to read, without sensing his desperate need for someone whose approval can reward his vast, painful never-ending effort to become civilized? The task is immense and the lure must be correspondingly strong. And a child knows he cannot accomplish this transformation on his own. Helpless, he must trust absolutely. Professional ties or bonds of contract are of no use to him. A child, deprived of family, makes one up.

Kelly, who has a warm relationship with her stepfather, always understands when her father does not come around to see her. "You see, he didn't have time to come and see me a lot, and he didn't have a lot of money to send child support either, but I know he wanted to. He worked all day and all night and only got three hours sleep," she says urgently explaining how hard it was for her father to spend time with her. It isn't true, but that doesn't matter to Kelly. "Once, a couple of years ago, after he got divorced again, he invited me to spend a weekend. I had the best time of my life, because I love him more than anyone in the world." This was the first time Kelly had seen her father in two years.[10]

In parenting you see two kinds of attachment at work. One makes sense. It is the slow, steady bond of affection, love as it is understood in the drawing room and among marriage counselors. The other is the child's wild longing for his parents, for a real, true, unbreakable connection which is outside of and beyond affection. This love is not tame, it is not steady, it makes no sense and it is the bane of divorced mothers everywhere who watch their children adore faithless Daddies and dependable Mommies with equal intensity.

Even youngsters like Kelly who establish warm and loving relationships with stepfathers continue to long for their biological fathers, to make excuses for them, to create in fantasy the kind of devoted fathers they need to replace the cruelly-absent fathers they are stuck with. In Wallerstein's study, only one child (who was a baby at the time of divorce and whose mother soon remarried) fully substituted her stepfather for her father, and even she as an adolescent, began to talk about wanting to know her real father. "Most children do not give up on their biological fathers, even if they are ne'er-do-wells who have abandoned them without a backward glance..." writes Wallerstein, "...children turn around and construct a credible image of the father they never knew from any scraps of information that they can collect and tend to idealize him in the process."[11]

There is no reason in the behavior of these children, only Eros, making inescapable demands for union, demands so strong they must be satisfied. A child does not reason, face facts, or demand truths if these will separate him from his parents. He will do injury to himself, rather than cast aspersions on that which ties him to life.

Biology is not necessarily destiny. Through adoption, new families can be created that are not biologically related. In successful adopted families, the act of arbitrary choice that began the relationship quickly dwindles in importance. Choice is an accident of history not the moral source of the connection. Successful adopted families become connected *as if* they were biological families, not the other way around. The mistake is to believe that biological families are formed as adopted families are, through choice, and the "assignment of social roles." In a culture where people have a strong sense of family, they may extend that sense to those who are not biologically related, through marriage or adoption. But as the notion of family becomes weakened, our ability to make lifelong commitments to biological strangers atrophies.

Biological connections are under attack from all sides. From anthropologists who view the family as a collection of social roles "assigned" to genetic parents. From social workers who see damaged children and don't want to admit we have nothing better to offer them—no substitute in dry institutions and foster families for the loving family that has been denied them. From psychologists living in a world of father figures who focus on the "psychological parent" and miss the role biology—the inevitability of connection—plays in turning sperm donors and egg carriers into fathers and mothers.

We are ashamed of biology because we want unlimited choices. So, rather than strengthening the institutions which help men and women create loving families, Americans turn to cheap solutions. Abused children are ripped from the only family they have and offered food, shelter, and physical safety in exchange. We are just too cheerful to admit that money cannot buy what these children need, and too enamored of our adult freedoms to consider building our world around what children need. And in the same way,cheerfully, hopefully, full of compassion and social justice, Americans rush to kill off unwanted children, to nip them in the bud so to speak.

Abortion is contract ideology misapplied to children. Choice is no substitute for inalienable connections or inalienable rights. For children, it fails to satisfy the aching hunger to belong; for adults, it constitutes an invitation to abuse. For what does that choice to have children, made so long ago and in such ignorance, really have to do with my burdens now or my pleasure either? The leap is too far, the heart refuses to make it. Choice makes no man a better father, nor does the felt absence of choice turn loving men and women into child molesters and abusers.

Abortion is not a solution to child abuse, it is a temptation and a diversion. We are choking our children with choice, the born as assuredly as the unborn. In America, adults get choices and children get screwed. Or beaten, or burned with cigarettes, or neglected, or starved or strangled in the slow claustrophobic grip of poverty. The abortion ethic feeds a cycle of abuse which tortures ever more children suffering that adults may feel ever more free.

The well being of children, like that of women, depends on a sense of family that is rapidly being rooted out from the law, from our textbooks, from the culture at large and from our hearts. America's traditional concern for children cannot really coexist with an ethic which makes choice the source of parental obligation, and being chosen the source of the child's value. Someday and soon, we shall be forced to choose between our worship of choice and our love for our children. Then, perhaps, we will understand what Joan Andrews wrote from her prison cell while serving two years in solitary confinement for unplugging an abortion machine:

"The simplest solution to the problem of unwanted children is to *want* them."

Endnotes—Chapter 13

1. A study of 220 Czechoslovakian children whose mothers were refused abortions found that although the "unwanted" children fell behind in some measures compared to a carefully matched control group, most of the differences between the groups were too slight to be statistically significant, while on some scales the "unwanted" children rank higher. The differences between the children who were originally "unwanted" and the "wanted" children were, the researchers acknowledged "not very pronounced and not very dramatic." Claims that children of mothers who are denied abortion fare badly rest on a study in Sweden by Forssman and Thuwe which failed to control for marital status of the mother. (Children of single mothers do tend to perform poorly compared to children in intact families.) Legal abortion has not, however, lowered the number of children raised outside of marriage and may in complicated ways tend to increase it. James Tunstead Burchatell, "An Unwanted Child is Not a Reason For an Abortion," *Abortion: Opposing Viewpoints, op. cit.,* pp. 129–30.

2. David C. Reardon, *Aborted Women: Silent No More* (Chicago: Loyola University Press, 1987), p. 224.

3. Philip G. Ney, "Infant Abortion and Child Abuse: Cause and Effect," *The Psychological Aspects of Abortion* (Washington, DC: University Publications of America, 1979), pp. 25+, and also Ney, "Relationship Between Abortion and Child Abuse," *Canadian Journal of Psychiatry*, vol 24 (7) (November 1979), pp. 610–20; Ney, "A Consideration of Abortion Survivors," *Child Psychiatry and Human Development*, vol 13, no 3 (Spring 1983), pp. 169–79. Ney's hypothesis is supported by a study conducted by researchers at John Hopkins University School of Hygiene and Public Health which found that mothers in maltreating families were significantly more likely to have had a stillbirth or reported abortion or a prior child death. See Mary Benedict, Roger White,

Donald Cornely, "Maternal Perinatal Risk Factors and Child Abuse," *Child Abuse and Neglect*, vol 9, no 2, 1985, pp. 217–24.

4. National Center for Health Statistics, *Village Voice*, April 11, 1989.

5. Reardon, *op. cit.*, p. 228. There has been surprisingly little research in this area. But for other studies indicating stress in children who are abortion survivors, see Regina Furlong and Rita Black "Pregnancy Termination for Genetic Indications: The Impact on Families," *Social Work in Health Care* (Fall 1984), pp. 17–34; Vincent Rue, "Death by Design of Handicapped Newborns: The Family's Role and Response," *Issues in Law and Medicine*, vol 1, no 3, (November 1985), pp. 201–225. Other studies indicating that mothers are more likely than aborting women without children to exhibit signs of psychological distress after an abortion tend to support the hypothesis that abortion is potentially harmful to surviving children. See, Raili Peltenen *et. al.*, "Psychopathological Dynamics After Procured Abortion or the Modern Niobe-Syndrome," *Praxis der Kinderpsychologic un Kinderpsychiatric*, vol 43, no 4 (May-June 1983), pp. 125–28 and Amy Hittner, "Feelings of Well-being Before and After an Abortion," *American Mental Health Counselors Association Journal*, vol 9, no 2 (April 1987), pp. 98–104.

6. John Crewdson, *By Silence Betrayed: Sexual Abuse of Children in America* (Boston: Little, Brown, 1988), p. 118.

7. Martin Daly and Margo Wilson, "Child Abuse and Other Risks of Not Living with both Parents," *Journal of Ethology and Sociobiology*, vol 6, 1985, pp. 197–206.

8. 48% of sexually abusive biological fathers in this study victimized their daughters only once, compared to 19% of abusive stepfathers. By contrast 12% of abusive biological fathers sexually abused their daughters 20 times or more compared to a 41% plurality of abusive stepfathers. Diana Russell, *The Secret Trauma: Incest in the Lives of Girls and Women* (New York: Basic Books, 1986), pp. 234–35.

9. O'Driscoll, "Toward a New Theory of the Family," *op. cit.*, p. 84.

10. Wallerstein and Blakeslee, *Second Chances*, *op. cit.*, pp. 241–42.

11. *Ibid.*, p. 234.

Section 3

JUST SEX

14

The Closing of the American Heart

In 1842, John Humphrey Noyes had a problem. His wife endured five pregnancies in six years and produced but one living son. How could his pleasure produce so much pain? It was wasteful, spendthrift, contrary to nature. *Coitus interruptus* he disapproved of on biblical grounds and he considered contraceptives too luxuriously indulgent, indicative of a lack of manly self-control.

What to do? What to do?

For two years he abstained from intercourse with his wife and pondered the difficult problem of perfecting sex. Then, in the summer of 1844, inspiration struck: "I conceive the idea that the sexual organs have a social function which is distinct from the propagative function, and that these functions may be separated practically. I experimented...and found that the self-control which it required was not difficult; also that my enjoyment was increased; also that my wife's experience was very satisfactory, as it had never been before."

He had discovered the manly art of continence, sex without ejaculation and he considered its practice a fine art that would one day excel music, painting, and sculpture in the public esteem. One elated disciple maintained Noyes' discovery "surpassed that of the steam engine and the electric telegraph."[1]

It's amazing how old-fashioned our modern ideas about sex are. At Oneida, the utopian religious community Noyes founded, male restraint was considered a form of worship and female orgasm was the great object of every sexual encounter, which Havelock Ellis (writing fifty years later) maintained could go on for as long as an hour without need for ejaculation. One hundred years ago, Noyes conceived and created a society built on female sexual enjoyment, strict population control, and the abolition of sex roles in work and family life. Men sewed and women hoed. Little girls who showed too great an interest in dolls were made to throw them in the fire, mothers were rarely allowed to see their children and were constantly warned against the selfish maternal bond. Monogamous marriage was outlawed; couples who fell in love were forbidden to see each other, and disobedient couples were forcibly separated. Sex was divorced from reproduction, practically and theoretically. The community closely regulated all personal relationships to ensure no "selfish" bonds developed.

You could, I suppose, find in Oneida an object lesson of the degree of personal freedom that must be surrendered in order to create and maintain an androgynous society.

You could, but why bother?

No, I like to think of those hundreds of perfectionist men, faithfully performing their religious duty, day in, day out, desperately trying for thirty years to avoid that which everyone knows is the *sine qua non* of sex. Sex without the big O; what's the point? The sexual liberal, much as he might approve, could never understand the men of Oneida.

Today's sexual revolutionaries are in hot pursuit of orgasm. It is the light at the end of the tunnel, Nirvana on the half-shell, the explanation and the justification of sexual desire. We want sex and now we get it, but what is it that we want? The death of our desire, the sexual revolutionaries answer. Release. Pleasure. The sexual revolution made sex into a kind of nouvelle cuisine, stripped down but prettied up, visually enticing and verifiably healthy.

Sexual revolutionaries promised an end to sexual repression. Instead they succeeded in imposing a particularly sterile conception of sex on the general culture. Sex was remade in the image of Hugh Hefner; Eros demoted from a god to a buffoon. Over the last thirty years, America transformed itself into a pornographic culture.

"What is pornography?" the Supreme Court once asked and then washed its hands of the matter. The best answer I have found is Angela Carter's, "Pornography is basically propaganda for fucking." Pornography claims that sex is good, all the time and however you want it. The more you want it, the better it is and the better *you* are. It is sex abstracted from of all its complexity, stripped of both its grandeur and its squalor. "[I]t usually describes the sexual act not in explicit terms—for that might make it seem frightening—but in purely inviting terms."[2]

A pornographic culture promises sex will be released from the restraining bonds of civilization. But liberation has a price: nothing is to be forbidden, because sex is nothing; a purely private act—isolated, fleeting, impotent.

Opposing the pornographic culture means defending good sex, and defining good sex in ways that do not include abuse of women. This hidden battle over what sex is, what it means, what it does, is much more critical than the legal debate over which dirty books may be published and which may be banned. For a pornographic culture is not one in which pornographic materials are published and distributed. A pornographic culture is one which accepts the ideas about sex on which pornography is based.

These ideas about sex are not liberating. They are highly restrictive. A pornographic culture demands we ignore our sexual nature and deny fundamental sexual realities. Sexual revolutionaries structured the experience of sex into narrowly tailored categories: uninhibited: good; hung-up: bad. These impoverished constructions form a new kind of repression, banishing politically-incorrect thoughts and rendering us unable to recognize as a problem the sexual use and abuse of women. In a pornographic culture, all forms of consensual sex are wholesome by definition. So that, anything which is sex cannot also be savage, exploitative, or repressive.

Pieces of sex have been spun off, given other names, repressed from awareness so that our virginal image of sexuality can be maintained in its pastoral, Edenic form: two people exchanging pleasure. A friendly act, a humane intercourse, a sensual experience—of the body, the pleasure principle incarnate. My generation, the generation raised on the belief that the only sexual sin is inhibition, is just beginning to recover from the effects of the pornographic ideal, to relearn bit-by-bit as experience overwhelms ideology that, as radical feminist Andrea Dworkin writes, "Sexual intercourse is not intrinsically banal."[3]

American culture protects the simple country innocence of sex by a straightforward denial: Anything which is not pleasure is not sex.

Rape is a sin, we are told, but not a *sexual* sin. A rapist desires to conquer, humiliate, and degrade his victim, and through her all women. Rape is the ultimate one-night stand. He does not need her, or her consent either. He can possess and remain free, sovereign, self-sufficient, in control. Rape is about power, and so according to modern etiquette it cannot be about sex.

Babies have nothing to do with lust. Babies are excrement, and blood, and pain, and death—the new generation whose existence usurps youth, and foretells our slow disintegration. They are small badges of adulthood, omens of continuity and of the grave. Babies are work, meaningful work, even joyful work, but sex is something else. Sex is pleasure, babies are not always that.

And so the procreative dimension of sexuality is repressed from consciousness until eventually we experience pregnancy as something separate from sexual intercourse—not only practically, in the sense that we may want to avoid it, but conceptually. Men and women come to feel we have a right—a *natural* right—to sex without pregnancy. We feel our bodies are betraying us when sex leads to babies. Unless, of course, the pregnancy is chosen, then it is the rational act of the mind, rather than the mere, despised, mindless mechanisms of the body, which is the true author of the miracle of birth.

The trivialization of sex was not a historic inevitability, though we like to say it was. It was the Pill that did it. Or abortion, or the increasingly late marriage age, or any of a hundred other sexual phenomena which are much less new than we suppose. Take late marriage for example. At twenty-three the median age of marriage for white women born in 1960 is actually slightly lower than for women born in 1880.[4] Nor was contraception unknown to our great-grandmothers, though until the latter half of the 19th century it was generally practiced only by unmarried or adulterous couples. Premarital sex is hardly a modern invention. In late 18th century New England, as many as one-third of all brides was pregnant.[5] Nor were our founding fathers necessarily slouches when it came to pursuing sexual pleasure. William Byrd, a wealthy Virginia planter often quarreled with his wife Lucy and made up in the traditional way: "I gave my wife a powerful flourish and gave her great ecstasy and refreshment," he wrote in 1711. (On another occasion, history records husband and wife reconciled on top of the billiard table.)[6]

Sex has been around for quite some time. But the pornographic culture, which simultaneously reduces sex to a set of sensations and proclaims those sensations to the pinnacle of human experience, is a modern invention, born of the thoroughly modern desire to maim Eros.

The reason for our massive sexual denial is simple: reducing sex to pleasure reinforces our illusion of absolute control. Sex is a choice we make to achieve pleasure, or else sex is a mere urgent appetite of the body whose satisfaction has no more affect on our spiritual nature—our personhood—than eating and drinking or defecating. These are contradictory views of sex, but the pornographic culture employs both stratagems, sometimes one, sometimes the other, sometimes both at once, to bolster our illusion of perfectly rational control.

I am in control of my body. I am in control of my body.

Said often enough, indignantly enough, it can be swallowed as a moral truth and a political right. I cannot help it. I keep seeing that Star Trek episode with Spock sobbing on the bridge of the Enterprise: "I am in control of my emotions," *sob sob,* he says, "In control" *sob sob* "of my" *sob* "emotions."

I have the right to control of my body, we say, as it goes on, indifferently, with a life of its own, breathing, bleeding, digesting, getting sick, conceiving life and, despite our desperate efforts to stay fit and young, getting old, ugly, bald, weak, flabby, stupid, wrinkled, and finally dying—all entirely outside the realm of volition, beyond our rational control. Every day we are taught, and yet deny, that we do not control our bodies, we *are* our bodies.

Like an animal gnawing off its leg in a trap, the sexual revolutionary mutilates sex in a desperate attempt to preserve his self image as sole master of his destiny, freely-choosing and, above all, in control. This is what the modern sexual liberal shares with the Victorian prude: he represses sex to salvage his pride.

Andrea Dworkin is no liberal. "In Amerika, there is the nearly universal conviction—or so it appears—that sex . . . is good and that liking it is right; morally right; a sign of human health; nearly a standard for citizenship. Even those who believe in original sin and have a theology of hellfire and damnation express the Amerikan creed, an optimism that glows in the dark: sex is good, healthy, wholesome, pleasant, fun; we like it, we enjoy it, we want it, we are cheerful about it; it is as simple as we are, the citizens of this strange country with no memory and no mind."[7]

Intercourse is rape, says Andrea, and puts her finger on the pulse of a problem that has no name. In sex, persons become male and female, archetypically, exaggeratedly, painfully so. And to us, corsetted in modern sexual views, femininity appears incompatible with the personhood of women. This gendering effect of sex is true even among homosexuals and lesbians. Homosexual culture, as George Gilder points out, offers a whole-bodied acceptance of male sexuality, which a man will generally never receive from a woman.

In sex, men enjoy subordinating women, and often women enjoy their own submission, says Dworkin. In intercourse, a woman's femaleness is driven home to her, in her, over and over again without mercy, until sex transforms her into what sex tells her that she is.

Dworkin was derided by sexual liberals because the sexual power she glimpses cannot be accounted for in their view of sex. What Dworkin observes is essentially true. Sex is not an act which takes place merely between bodies and out of which afterwards, individuals emerge with their personhood intact.

Sex is an act which defines, alters, imposes on the personhood of those who engage in it. It's not an accident that the word for intercourse and the word for gender are one and the same. Dworkin is right. Sex reifies gender. Our disembodied minds enter gendered bodies. We wander through the ordinary course of days as persons, desexed, androgynous, and it is in the sexual act which we receive reassurance that we are not persons, after all, but men and women.

Indeed much of the *sexiness* of sex, comes from this primal reality. Sex satisfies our lust for gender. What we desperately want and most reliably get from sex is not pleasure, but sexual identity.

We have not always been so woefully dependent on the sexual act itself. Two hundred years ago, for example, homosexuality did not exist. There was sodomy, of course, and buggery, and fornication and adultery and other sexual sins, but none of these forbidden acts fundamentally altered the sexual landscape. A man who committed sodomy may have lost his soul, but he did not lose his gender. He did not become a homosexual, a third sex. That was the invention of the 19th century imagination. As social supports for gender collapsed, men were increasingly forced to rely on the primal sexual act in order to feel like men. It is because sex roles are collapsing, because we offer men fewer and fewer civilized routes to a sense of manhood, that sex now carries almost the whole burden of sexual identity.

Stubbornly, intransigently, courageously, Dworkin insists that sex is dangerous. That is true for all of us, men and women. But it is a truth which men fear more than women because they are afraid of becoming like women. To men, constitutionally plagued with gender anxiety, to admit vulnerability is to become feminine. As Dworkin points out, the essential female acts—being penetrated and getting pregnant—are acts of violation, testimony to the limits of rational control, to the futility of the great Cartesian lie, *I think therefore I am*. But unfortunately she fails to see how suffocatingly androcentric her vision of human dignity is.

Dworkin is appalled by femininity foe the same reason men are appalled by it. Men fear penetration. Men fear violation. Men fear vulnerability, which is to say they fear being alive. They are terrified of admitting to submission, though it is an inevitable part of life, of daily life, of the ordinary experience of the successful corporate executive, the law-abiding citizen. Mythically, they suffer from visions of being swallowed up by the womb or castrated by the vagina. Physically, men are impregnable, and childlessness is a form of virginity to which they are permanently condemned.

Dworkin fears sex because she is afraid of gender. Her frail vision of human dignity denies to women the integrity of our bodies. Further, it denies to all people the dignity she passionately seeks for women. If freedom is just another word for never having to submit, then no one is free except those who find the freedom of the grave. She uses the language of life to reject the fundamental conditions of existence: we live as bodies not of our choosing, and move toward an end we cannot escape.

To say that sex is dangerous is not to say, of course, that it is evil. Without risk, there is no romance, no high ambition, no intense love, no high achievement. Sex is dangerous because sex is *powerful,* a power which can be used or abused for many purposes. The more we pretend that sex is mere pleasure, the more likely we are to use and abuse those we love, body and soul.

"The sexual relationship," Karol Wojtyla, writing before he became John Paul II, understatedly remarks, "presents more opportunities than most other activities for treating a person—sometimes without even realizing it—as an object of use."[8] Wojtyla uses unisex language (it is true women can sexually exploit men, but it is harder), but he is talking about the quintessentially male experience stretching back through the centuries to the moment when St. Augustine, "sunk in death" experienced revulsion against monotonously scratching the itching sore of lust, of using a woman's body over and over to relieve tension, induce pleasure, gratify the ego, as if it were a thing, a plaything, a toy; stoically enduring the inconvenience of children and the necessity to care for the woman herself as part of the "bargain struck for lust."

Sexual liberals cannot for the life of them see what either Dworkin or John Paul II is talking about. For sexual liberals, sex is pleasure and pleasure is good. They believe in the morality of contract, each sovereign being trading pleasure given for pleasure received. They endorse consensual sex and strive for orgasm equity. For them, sexual freedom does not mean that a woman will be free to have sex knowing that she will not be abandoned if her body betrays its femaleness. Sexual freedom means men won't have to worry about any of the mess, the pain, the *money* of childbearing. As Barbara Ehrenreich et al., put it in *The Re-Making of Love*, the sexual revolution transformed sex into "a potentially orgasmic activity in which everyone had equal rights."[9] And the great hope, dream, glory, of the sexual revolutionaries is that some day women will be free to use men as thoughtlessly and thoroughly as they use us. This is the sexual ideal of a pornographic culture.

Sex has other, more obvious dangers, which we ignore with equal stubbornness. Educated young women believe, as we have been taught, that today sex and reproduction are no longer related; pregnancy is unlikely, as long as we faithfully swallow or insert our contraceptives. That is what we've been promised, by our teachers, by our doctors, by the magazines we read and the sexperts we look up to. Unfortunately for us, that is a lie. Sex is still risky business. This is true in many ways, but the most obvious and most often denied risk of sex is babies.

In the way contraceptive companies use statistics, a 95 percent theoretical effectiveness rate (about that claimed for the diaphragm and foam), means that five out of one hundred women who use this method for one year will get pregnant.[10] Women have a one out of twenty chance of getting screwed. Seems pretty high to me. But wait, it gets worse. One out of twenty is only the probability of getting pregnant *in one year.* Over time, the odds of getting pregnant at least once increase greatly.[11]

Assuming the diaphragm is 95 percent effective, if a woman starts having sex at eighteen and marries at twenty-eight, and uses her diaphragm correctly and without fail, her odds of getting pregnant at least once over this ten year period are not one in twenty but 40 percent. Studies of contraceptives have found effectiveness rates vary enormously depending on the age, skill, motivation, sexual capacity, and luck of the user. In practice contraceptives are much less effective than advertised, at least in part because in the heat of passion, men and women often throw caution and condoms to the wind.

If one calculates the odds using contraceptives' actual reported effectiveness rates of around 80 percent (and since to err is human this makes the most sense), a woman's likelihood of getting pregnant at least once over a ten year period soars to *89 percent.* Women who use contraceptives are apparently far more likely to get pregnant than not.[12] When I first worked the math out for myself, I was astonished. I had had five years of sex education in school, but this had never occurred to me. Occasionally, when I want to liven up a party, I mention these odds to other young, college educated professional women. I get The Look. Pure panic. They never thought of it like that either. Even in this modern day and age, sex leads to babies. *Often.* Remarkable. Dr. Ruth call your office.

Young men and women today are taught everything about sex except this: It is possible, easy even, for sex to be both consensual and exploitative. A man exploits a woman every time he uses her body for sexual pleasure while he is unwilling to accept the full burden of paternity which arises, not with the frequency of lust, but tolerably regularly all the same. That is to say, single men (and frequently married men) exploit women almost every time they make love. His lover may consent, fully, knowledgeably, enthusiastically to her exploitation. That does not change the nature of the transaction. Her willingness to be used does not license his use of her; she cannot contract away, in exchange for pleasure or counterfeit love, the dignity that is her birthright, or birth doom, the inalienable condition of being human, any more than a woman's willingness to be sold into slavery would excuse a slave owner's willingness to buy.

I am not arguing that any attempt to "lose the fruit of the labor," as one ancient sex manual put it, is immoral. What I ask is very small, really: only that we admit publicly and to ourselves that sex, even studiously contracepted sex, can (and regularly does) make babies. This bargain in which both partners exchange pleasure while she alone accepts the risks of pregnancy, the effort of child bearing or the mutilation of abortion, is unequal, unconscionable, and degrading. It is an intolerable affront that we tolerate quite insouciantly every day.

This is basic sexual ethics. But the facts ask further questions. They tantalize and lure us to contemplate: Why *are* Americans so lousy at contraceptives, anyway? Perhaps it's because sex that leads to babies is *sexier* than sterile sex.

Pregnancy allures in part because it offers the only concrete, enduring, incontrovertible proof of gender. Pregnancy separates the boys from the girls and gives both the illusion of adulthood. But even for adults, the sexual lure of pregnancy is stronger than we admit. Babies are erotic, especially as an idea. They are an actual union of flesh for which intercourse is only a symbol.

Only once we recover a fuller understanding of what a sexual act is, what sex means, and what our sexual natures are can we expect to promote useful sexual ethics, benevolent sexual institutions, or resolve sexual problems from wolf-packs in Central Park, to the explosion in unwed teenage pregnancies. We will never make a dent in our sexual problems as a society until we recognize for ourselves and also for our children that sex makes babies; until transcending the mechanics of biology, we recognize that getting pregnant is a sexual act. If sex is what satisfies our lust for gender, then getting pregnant is perhaps *the* sexual act. Having a baby is not a side effect of sex it *is* sex.[13]

Americans are a practical people. We just cannot understand why here in the land of the free and the home of the condom, girls keep going out and getting themselves knocked up. Expert opinion is that it's a matter of bad conscience. Contraception makes sex "premeditated" and therefore wrong, or at least yucky. But even licit lovers complain that contraception is "unsexy." That is why ads for contraceptives from the Pill to the sponge emphasize how much "spontaneity" they allow; how the sex act won't have to be interrupted by unlusty thoughts about the need for contraception. The suspicion creeps up that perhaps the thing itself is anti-erotic.

Contraception is a form of "protection." But what is it that you're protecting yourself from? The sperm of your lover. Don't let any of that yucky stuff up *here*. The extent to which having a baby would be a disaster is the extent to which the sense of union produced by sex is proved illusory. Too frequently, contraception reveals the act of love for what it is: a temporary and conditional attachment, the mutual use of each other for certain limited and defined purposes, from momentary physical pleasure to emotional intimacy to personal growth. The more noble the purpose for which you are using another, the more easy it is to forget the baseness of the essential act: not sex itself, but turning another human being into an instrument for your purposes.

If sex were only physical appetite, then it would be safe. It could be contained, in the way Oscar Wilde recommended: the best way to get rid of temptation is to give in to it. Then, all sex would be masturbatory. Indeed masturbation is the logical end of the sexual revolution; completely severing sex from Eros, desire from any possibility of the union for which it longs.

"An Erotic Concept Whose Time Has Come" blares the banner headline in an ad for *Sex for One: the Joy of Selfloving* (a new book by the publishers of *The Joy of Sex)*, which comes complete with a sexuality quiz and this endorsement by Phil Donahue: "In the age of AIDS more people are having sex with themselves. It's a lot safer!" The author, noted sex authority Betty Dodson, affirms "Universal acceptance of masturbation is the next step in civilization's sexual evolution." Oh, how right she is. Not only the next step, but the final step, the *telos,* the rousing climax of the sexual revolution.

Reducing sex to pleasure tends towards "sex for one" because it focuses on internal sensations, which can never be shared, only traded. For the Marquis de Sade, the greatest of all pornographers, "Sexual pleasure is not experienced as experience; it does not modify the subject... its sensation is absolutely personal, just as it does not hurt the knife if you cut yourself with it," writes Angela Carter.[14]

Sex for pleasure's sake is sex in the final stage of impotence. Pornography is onanistic; it arouses desire for impossible unions and leaves the consumer to satisfy himself with solitary pleasure. For de Sade, like all pornographers, "Sexual pleasure is nothing but a private and individual shock of the nerves." But pleasure, transformed from an experience into a goal, must always be experienced in this way. This is the epicure's dilemma. He transforms himself from a person into a sensory receiving device, fundamentally solipsistic, condemned by his own shortsightedness to eternal imprisonment between the walls of his own skull.

Sometime between 1960 and 1989, the pornographic view of sex was transformed from a private vice into a national imperative. Sex is pleasure, we agreed, and obediently, diligently, we have attempted to slake our desire with pleasure. At first it was orgasms that were missing and orgasms that were diligently hunted out and achieved. But it's like peanuts, one is never enough. So we tracked down bigger orgasms, better orgasms, multiple orgasms, "Ah but that really hit the old G spot," we tried to say. But it didn't.

What's wrong with sexual pleasure? Nothing at all. Pleasure is a pleasant thing. But how could we be so foolish as to imagine it could assuage or explain sexual desire? There is an unbridgeable gap between desire, which is intense and all-consuming and urgently asserts its importance, and pleasure, which is finite and limited and unable to satisfy. Sexual desire is not a desire for pleasure.

The sexual revolution represents the closing of the American heart. Those who subscribe to its dictates cut themselves off from erotic possibilities, practicing safe sex as best as they can. This is the goal of those educators at Nassau Community College in Long Island who sponsored a course called Family Life and Human Sexuality that three thousand students take each year. Ray Kerrison of the *New York Post* reports that on their first day of class, students are asked to get the signatures of anyone who has had sex with a prostitute, used a condom, seen their parents naked, or gone to a porno flick. The textbook treats adultery, group sex, wife-swapping much as Alex Comfort does in the *Joy of Sex*, merely delicious dishes on the menu of a movable feast of pleasure. The course, says Prof. Joseph Dondero, ''describes various behaviors, but does not endorse any of them,'' as if pornography were not in its nature propaganda. For dessert, students are treated to sex films showing couples copulating in every imaginable place and location. ''It is unquestionably one of the most popular courses on campus, and rarely do we get a complaint'' says Professor Dondero.

What is it that Professor Dondero teaches? Not just that sex is fun (which practically everyone suspects by now), but that sex is *trivial*.

Western civilization once had a very different view of the role of sex in education. Eros was the school of virtue. As Plato put it in Phaedrus's speech in the *Symposium,* ''For that which should guide human beings who are going to live fairly throughout their lives can be implanted neither by blood ties, nor honors, nor wealth, nor anything else as beautifully as by love.... there is no one so bad that, once the god Eros had entered him, he would not be directed toward virtue.'' If Eros is the driving of behind civilization, then managing Eros is the key to peace, liberty, and social order—to our very survival. Behind the legal constitution is the erotic constitution, making even of us Americans, a conglomeration of different races, tribes, and ethnic groups, a mysterious union: one people, under God, indivisible.

The hidden sexual constitution was what George Gilder had in mind when he wrote, "The health of a society, its collective vitality, ultimately resides in its concern for the future, its sense of a connection with generations to come...Women control not the economy of the marketplace but the economy of eros: the life force in our society and our lives."[15]

Men and women who believe what Professor Dondero teaches sequester themselves from Eros, and from their own sexual experience. People who trivialize sex, trivialize their own lives. People who have been taught that sex is pleasure experience intense, shattering intimacy and afterwards hastily retract, "Hey, just kidding." They remain ignorant of the sexual forces shaping their own lives and that of their community.

It seems unkind to pick on one poor professor pursued by a pack of unenlightened parents and outraged taxpayers, who is only carrying out the dominant sexual ethic while hiding behind the fig leaf of academic freedom. He is pursuing the good, within the limits of his insight, offering his students the best he knows: Sexual pleasure for all, the more the merrier.

The word on the street is that the sexual revolution is over, but you can see by what killed it, that it's not. AIDS merely altered the calculus of pain and pleasure, the utilitarian standard which determines when sex is socially acceptable. With AIDS, sex acquired socially-recognizable victims—and so once again entered the realm of morality. Monogamy suddenly looked good. But the basic, stunted perception of the nature of sex and our sexual nature remains. Sex is still a drive, an appetite, which cannot be denied—only sublimated or repressed, whose purpose is pleasure. It's just that, since Herpes and AIDS made the news, we fear pain and death more than we lust for pleasure.

I cannot deny that AIDS has had the effect of mimicking sexual morality, but I am amazed. Sex *is* dangerous, but not because of AIDS. On June 27, 1989, the Center for Disease Control reported that heterosexual transmission of AIDS currently accounts for 4.4 percent or 4,305 of the total AIDS cases in the U.S., a decline from 5.2 percent in 1983. AIDS has produced a social panic that all the routine suffering of women did not.

Teenage promiscuity? Women escaping from the double standard. Twenty million abortions? Women escaping from the tyranny of biology. Unmarried mothers sinking into poverty? Women bravely forging a new definition of family in the face of obsolete Ozzie-and-Harriet stereotypes. We have blinded ourselves to far more obvious dangers than those of disease.

"There is nothing to be afraid of and never was," concluded Alex Comfort in *More Joy of Sex*. But he is wrong. In sex as in life, the only safety is in the grave. Safe sex is dead sex, sex stripped of its power, meaning, and possibilities. And dead sex kills love. It is the trivialization of Eros, the porning of America. Ah, but they are wrong, these prophets of sexual liberation. Sex isn't trivial, and in the end it will triumph over sexual ideology.

In one of the most lyrical passages in philosophy, Plato attempts to describe the cornucopia of love, the bounty of Eros in our everyday lives: "He empties us of estrangement, he fills us with attachment; he arranges in all such gathering as this our coming together with one another; in festivals, in dances, in sacrifices, he proves himself a guide . . .father of luxury, splendor, glory, graces, yearning, and longing. . .''

What has been driven out of sex in America is precisely this Eros. I remember sitting in a large lecture hall at Yale listening to an introductory lecture in philosophy where the professor was explaining the erotic nature of the attachment between student and teacher in the Greek view. I was thoroughly confused. I knew what erotic meant: dirty books, basically, plus half-naked love scenes, a long and tender goodnight kiss. Erotic things were things which aroused a desire for sex. What was my professor talking about? Did teachers in Ancient Greece mean to have sex with their students? (Sometimes of course that's exactly what they meant.) My confusion sprang from the culture in which I was raised, which reduces sexual longing to a desire for sex: "What you really need is to get laid."

Earlier and more intensely than any other nation, America took Freud to its bosom. And the comedy of erotic error we are acting out today is Freud's error. Sensing the intense eroticism of familial relations, especially the mother-child relationship, he saw all platonic affection as a lie. A child's longing for his mother was not only a sexual longing, it was a longing for sex. Freud insisted the elaborate forms Eros takes in civilized society are only a kind of subterfuge, masking its real, insistent aim: the Id's unconscious and unconscionable desire for sexual intercourse with the object of its desire: especially the mother.

But Freud observed that intercourse, though infinitely desirable, is not always obtainable. And where obtainable, it is not a dependable source of gratification. The beloved may cease to love, or may die. And so the ego, out of self-preservation, builds castles in the air to contain desire. Of all the ways of sublimating sexual desire, says Freud, none is more effective than art, science, or philosophy. All of man's highest achievements begin with the twitching of the groin and provide a pale, anemic, sublimated satisfaction of the original, blood-hot desire.

Freud was right in one sense. Civilization is sublimated Eros. But then *so is sex*. Sexual intercourse is but one way of attempting to satisfy, and frequently a poor one at that, the longing for union which Eros inspires. This is the emptiness which so many women feel after casual sex; the act which ought to express union instead highlights in Day Glo yellow our indissoluble separateness; our alienation from our bodies which have gone through a pantomime of union while our hearts remain unbearably naked and untouched; our alienation from our "lovers," who in the act of physical union partake of a female body with the same lusty pleasure they would attack a fine steak. (That we are using male bodies in the same way makes it worse not better.)

To retrace the links between the fumbling in the sheets, the cradle, community, law, art, science, and philosophy was Freud's greatest achievement. His greatest error was to believe that the fleeting, fumbling, unsatisfying satisfaction of physical desire is the primal human act. His faith was that of a man raised in sexually-repressive times, the faith of the prude: that lust is more real than love.

But I have been hiding behind a figleaf of my own. I have been hiding behind Eros, for lack of better word, a more articulate phrase to tell you what I mean. I am trying to cover the nakedness of my belief. It is simpler to say what sex is not than what it is. To say the emperor has no clothes is easy but how embarrassing to describe in any detail the hidden glory of his body.

How to describe sex? Sex is paradoxical, it establishes sex differences in order to create the possibility of union. Sex creates gender so that we may overcome it in desire.

269

Sex creates people who need each other, erotically; a perpetual adult act of joining which replaces the perpetually adolescent act of breaking free.

Sex is dangerous, which is another way of saying sex is powerful. Sex leads to babies and having a baby is a sexual act. Sex binds. It reconnects the soul to the body, the man to his lover, the woman to her child, children to their parents, parents to other parents and to the future. Not inevitably, but unevenly. It is possible—easy—to close oneself off from Eros, so that sex is not experienced as an experience but purely as an internal sensation. This is sexual repression for our times.

America today is a nation full of ironies. People running around having sex without knowing what it is. A female elite more fiercely committed to the good name of feminism than to the welfare of women. Self-described libertarians who want to permit judges to do to family life what they have already done to our business environment. Sexual revolutionaries bravely touting as new and progressive ideas about sex that were old when our grandparents were young.

And all the while women are getting poorer, more exposed, more often beaten and abused, as the fabric of our family life which restrains the untutored aggression of men and binds them to us unravels. Our children are fewer in number, too few now even to replace the population. Those that remain are more often battered, beaten, neglected, isolated, sexually-used, or simply ignored. More girls, seeking love, end up pregnant and abandoned. More boys (seeking gender) end up as thugs and beasts, or as accident and suicide statistics. Brutalized by divorce and paternal abandonment, children long for stable family life, for erotic attachment, but are unable to achieve it. The cycle repeats, spiralling progressively downward, all because of our determined ignorance of a few basic facts of life.

The family is about children and the future. Marriage is about children and the future. Sex is, ultimately, about children and the future. A society which tries to reduce sex to its pleasures, to cut off gender from sex, sex from Eros, Eros from children, cuts itself and its people off from the resources we need to survive and to triumph. For these are the bonds by which our fathers and mothers bequeathed our present pleasures to us. These are the only bonds strong enough to build a future which our children may enjoy.

How to describe sex? The desire of one's body for the soul of another human being. The longing to break the boundaries of the flesh altogether, to incarnate love. A couple's desire for a baby in whom two are made one flesh. A baby longing for its mother. A mother's longing for her baby. The surrender to fertility, the desire to give birth, both of the body and as Socrates said so long ago, of the soul, "to generate and give birth in beauty."

These are words and they sound like metaphors, but I am not talking metaphorically, any more than Socrates was. Sex is a living pathway of connection, an intricate web of desire that begins with lust and ends not with orgasm but with children, families, communities, and nations. That ends, in fact, with love.

Endnotes—Chapter 14

1. Muncy, *Sex and Marriage in Utopian Communities*, *op. cit.*, pp. 182–83.

2. Angela Carter, *The Sadeian Woman And the Ideology of Pornography*, (New York: Pantheon Books, 1978), pp. 14–15.

3. Dworkin, *Intercourse, op. cit.*, p. 21.

4. Sweet and Bumpass, *American Families and Households, op. cit.*, p. 13.

5. D'Emilio and Freedman, *Intimate Matters, op. cit.*, p. 43.

6. *Ibid.*, p. 24.

7. Dworkin, *op. cit.*, p. 47.

8. Karol Wojtyla, *Love and Responsibility*, translated by H.T. Willetts (New York: Farrar, Straus, Giroux, 1981), p. 30.

9. Barbara Ehrenreich, Elizabeth Hess, Gloria Jacobs, *Re-Making Love: The Feminization of Sex* (Garden City, New York: Anchor Press/Doubleday, 1986), p. 98.

10. Reported rates of effectiveness of contraceptive methods vary greatly. According to Dr. Howard Shapiro, in *The Birth Control Book: A Complete Guide for Men and Women* (New York: Discus/Avon, 1978), pregnancy rates for diaphragm users have varied from 6 to 29 pregnancies per 100 woman-years, depending on the studies. The Pill's effectiveness ranges from 97% to 99%, while in three large surveys of condom users (the contraceptive of choice in the age of STD's), pregnancy rates ranged from a low of 3 to a high of 36 per 100 woman-years. The figures I have chosen were those given to me by a local birth control clinic.

11. If this doesn't seem intuitively obvious to you think about the chances that a penny will come up heads at least once. If you have five chances to get a coin to turn up heads at least once, you're more likely to succeed than if you have only one chance. There is a simple statistical formula for determining the probability over time, $1-X^N$, where X represents the odds of an event not happening in any given year (expressed as a decimal) and N is total number of years. So that if there is a 5% (.05) chance of an event happening in any one year, the formula for determining how likely it is that it will happen at least once in ten years is $1-.95^{10}$.

12. If a woman starts having sex at 18 and marries at 23 (the current median age for marriage for white women) her chances of getting pregnant at least once are theoretically 23% (using a 95% theoretical effectiveness rate), and 62% (using the 80% actual effectiveness rate).

13. One study by Irma Hilton, a psychologist at the Ferkauf Graduate School of Psychology found that teenage fathers were generally happy about their girlfriend's pregnancy, whether or not they planned to take any responsibility for the child. They felt it affirmed their masculinity. And many teenage girls feel similarly pleased. Gerard Kitzi, director of the Adolescent Resources Corporation which runs three school-based clinics in Kansas City, Missouri, agrees that many teen pregnancies are on some level deliberate. Many girls who come for pregnancy tests "are disappointed when the test is negative." See Elizabeth Stark, "Young, Innocent and Pregnant," *Psychology Today*, (Oc-

tober 1986), p. 30. Another study of black teens found that 86% who became pregnant knew about contraceptives at the time they became pregnant, and almost 75% also knew where to obtain contraceptives. See Evelyn Landry, Jane Bertrand, Flora Cherry, Jane Rice, "Teen Pregnancy in New Orleans: Factors that Differentiate Teens Who Deliver, Abort, and Successfully Contracept," *Journal of Youth and Adolescence*, vol 15, no 3 (June 1986), pp. 259–74.

14. Carter, *op. cit.*, p. 144.
15. Gilder, *Men and Marriage, op. cit.*, pp. 16–18.

Index

Abandonment, 51, 197
  of child, 88–90, 113
  paternal, 111
Abortion
  effect on surviving children, 246
  general issues concerning, 10,
    218–34, 238–39, 244, 245
  rate, 76
Abortion Hotline, 221
Abortion: Law, Choice and Morality,
    228
Abramson, Jill, 64
Adolescent Resources Corporation, 272
Adoption, 180–81, 243
Adult children, 202
Adultery, 23–26, 34–35
Adulthood, 188–89
*Advances in Developmental and
    Behavioral Pediatrics,* 98
Affairs, extramarital, 23–26, 34–35
Age of Innocence, 10
Aggression, 153
AIDS, 266–67
Almost Husband, 31–32
Ambivalence of Abortion, 230
American Academy of Pediatrics, 95
American Couples, 25, 125
Andrews, Joan, 245
Androgyny, illusion of, 8, 12, 14,
    27–29, 37, 49, 58, 61–62, 69,
    131, 147, 150–52, 206, 250

Antifeminism, 135
Antinatalism, 68, 81–82
Aristotle, 136
Artificial insemination, 167–68, 179,
    183, 188
Associated Press, 73

Baby
  boys, 127
  lust, 43–53
  M, 170–71, 182, 206
  violence toward, 89–90
Bank Street College of Education
  Work and Family Life Studies, 104
Behavior, of women, 65
Belsky, Jay, 98
Bernard, Jessie, 51–52, 57–59, 81–82,
    87–88
Best interests of the child rule, 205–6
Better parent rule, 207
Biological connections, 243–44
Biologically-based behavior, 136
Birth Dearth, 82
Birth rate, illegitimate, 76
Black, Barbara, 69
Blumstein, Phillip, 25–26, 122
Boyce, Neith, 130–31
Brain waves, fetal, 233–34
Breadwinner anxiety, 122
Breier, Dr. Alan, 198–99

Brom, David, 73
Brothers, Dr. Joyce, 27
Brownmiller, Susan, 140
Burrelle, Betty, 204
Burrelle, Dale, 204–5
Bush, George, 94
Byrd, William, 254

Callahan, Daniel, 228
Carter, Angela, 251, 263
Census Bureau, 34, 107, 111, 196
Center for Disease Control, 95, 267
Center for the Family in Transition, 78
Center for Research on Women, 59
Chambers, Robert, 74
Chancer, Lynn, 230
Cher, 140
Chesler, Phyllis, 206
Child abuse, 235–40
Child care, 85–105
  arrangements, 127
  per Census Bureau, 107
  and drugs, 106
  paternal, 109
  by relatives, 100–1
  tax credits for, 94
Child Development, 98
Child rearing, 85–88, 91–92
Children, 73–83
  abandonment of, 88–90
  devaluation of, 80–82
  and divorce, 78–80, 198–200, 202,
    208–9, 216
  in high-conflict divorced families,
    200–1, 216–17
  in high-conflict intact families, 200–1,
    216–17
  importance of family to, 240–42
  in low-conflict divorced families,
    200–1, 216–17
  in low-conflict intact families, 200–1,
    216–17
  planned, 237

  status of, 76–78, 80–81
  unwanted, 235–37
Child Trend, Inc., 113
Chodorow, Nancy, 25, 57
Choice
  and child abuse, 235–36
  children of, 218–20
  in general, 14–16, 20, 49–50, 58, 61,
    149–50, 159–60, 163–64, 194,
    227, 235, 244
Christensen, Dr. Bryce, 94
Cognitive dissonance, 29
Cohabitation, 32
College students, spousal selection by,
  53
Columbia Law School, 69
Comfort, Alex, 265, 267
Commercial transactions, 179–80
Commitment, 30
Communication, 26–27
Concubine, 212–13
Consciousness, 74–75
Continence, 250
Contraception, 219, 259–60, 262–63,
  272–73
Contract, 19–21, 157–64, 209–10
  family, 174–75, 189
  marriage, 210–11, 214
  model, 162–64
  surrogate mother, 170–78, 181, 184–86
Coparenting, 110
Coran, Thomas, 90
Corleone, Don, 211
Cultural conditioning, 12
Cultural mores, 27–28, 39–40
Custody
  laws, 205–7
  maternal, 207
Czechoslovakian children study, 245

Darwin, 133
Day care, 13–14, 71–72, 78, 85–105
  and aggression, 97–98, 106–7

diseases found in, 95–96
effects of, 98–99
federal subsidy of, 101
for ghetto children, 96–97
de Beauvoir, Simone, 58, 92, 132–33, 144–48
de Chastellux, Marquis, 90–91
DeJong, Daphne, 232
DeMause, Lloyd, 88
Democratic Party, 6
Department of Labor
National Longitudinal Survey, 99
Dependency, 30
de Sade, Marquis, 263–64
de Tocqueville, Alexis, 91
Dinnerstein, Dorothy, 56–57
Dinosaur's Divorce, 113
Divorce
and children, 200, 202, 208–9, 216
and child support, 113
economic consequences of, 196–97
and fatherhood, 113–15
fault-based, 195
in general, 12–13, 15, 33–34, 50–51, |78–80,| 112–15, 191–209
no-fault, 191–93
psychological results of, 197–200
public burden of, 209
as social remedy, 79–80
unilateral, 193, 195–96, 205, 212, 214–15
Divorce Decision, 207
Dodson, Betty, 263
Domestic violence, 14
See also specific forms
Donahue, Phil, 263, 266
Dondero, Joseph, 265
Downey Jr., Morton, 3
Dukakis, Michael, 109
Dworkin, Andrea, 183, 253, 255–59

Education, 75–76
Eggebeen, David, 75

Ehrenreich, Barbara, 259
Eichenbaum, Luise, 119
Einstein (Albert) College of Medicine, 60
Ellis, Havelock, 130, 250
Emotion, 176
Enterprise, 255
Eros, 209–10, 214–15, 218–19, 240, 242, 251, 254, 265–71
Existentialism, 144–45, 149
Expectant fathers, 122

Fallows, Deborah, 99
Family
v. career, 58–59
-centered woman, 63
concept of, 158–59
contract, 174–75, 187–89
day care, 104, 107
defection from, 116–17
in general, 16, 160, 174–75, 211–13, 239–41, 271
importance to children, 240–42
and individual, 161–64
law, 171
male role in, 115–18, 124–25
new ideal of, 236
outline of, 213
relationships, 67
and sex, 20–21
Family in America, 94
Farran, Dale, 97–98
Farrell, Dr. Warren, 36, 47
Father
absence of, 114–15, 199
-child attachment, 107
and housework, 127
role of, 109, 174, 178–79
Female
elite, 9–10
roles, 147–48
Feminism
elitism and, 147

liberal, 147, 148
mainstream, 9–10, 13, 80, 135
orthodox, 39, 43, 56, 81, 146–47, 149–50
Ferkauf Graduate School of Psychology, 272
Fetal transplants, 224–25
Fetus
  farms, 225–26
  in general, 220
  human dignity of, 224
  value of, 225
Firestone, Shulameth, 188
Fleischer, Belton, 98–99
Forehand, Dr. Rex, 200–1
Francke, Linda Bird, 230
Franklin, Barbara, 64
Frank Porter Graham Development Center, 97–98
Franks, Marlene, 160
Free will, 134. See also Choice
Freud, 68, 131, 268–69
Friedan, Betty, 10, 17, 57, 147, 150, 220
Friendship, 36
Frost, Robert, 174
Future of Motherhood, 51, 59

Galinsky, Ellen, 104
Gellius, Aulus, 90
Gender
  behavior, 135
  debate, 133–37
  differences, 12
  justice, 158
  liberationists, 132, 135
  lust, 140–42
  neutrality, 126
  revolution, 109–11, 119, 122–25, 132
  roles, 9
  stereotypes, 141–42, 159
Gender Justice, 160

General Motors, 148
Genetic tests, 179
Genevie, Louis, 60
Gilded Age, 7–8
Gilder, George, 119, 121, 178, 256, 265–66
Gilligan, Carol, 25, 48
Girls and Boys, the Limits of Non-Sexist Childrearing, 140
Glamour, 93, 97
Glendon, Mary Ann, 194–95, 211
Glick, Paul, 111
Godiva's, 136
Goldberg, Stephen, 135
Grobstein, Clifford, 223, 228–29
Grundy, Mrs., 4

Hagestad, Gunhild, 202
Hall, Annie, 140
Handel, William, 186
Hapgood, Fred, 37
Hapgood, Hutchins, 130–31
Happiness, 59
Harris poll (1980), 62
Harvard University
  Law School, 64, 194
  Medical School, 209
Hefner, Hugh, 251
Herman, PeeWee, 223
Hewlett, Sylvia Ann, 64
High school graduates, 75–76
Hilton, Irma, 272
Hitler, Adolf, 223
Hoffman, Dustin, 109
Homosexuality, 256–57
House of Representatives, 94
Housewife, 47, 55–70, 129
Housework, 110–11, 127
Human dignity, 224
Human identity, 233–34
Human Life Review, 230

Idol, Billy, 74
Ignorance, 10–11, 30, 34, 39
Illegitimate birth rate, 76
Independence, 29
In a Different Voice, 48
Individualism, 161–64
Industrial Revolution, 39, 91
Inevitability of Patriarchy, 135
Infidelity, 38
Institute of Psychohistory, 88
Intercourse, 255–256
Intercourse, 183

Jacklin, Carol Nagy, 137
Jackson, Michael, 74
Japanese relationships, 27
Johns Hopkins University School of
    Hygiene and Public Health, 245
Journal of Ethology and Sociobiology,
    239
Joy of Sex, 263, 265
Juvenile delinquency, 76

Kansas State University, 36
Kaye, Peggy, 78
Kerrison, Ray, 264
King, Florence, 47
Kirkpatrick, Jeanne, 69, 150
Kirp, David, 160
Kitzi, Gerard, 272
Kramer v. Kramer, 127
Krauthammer, Charles, 178, 324–35

Ladies Home Journal, 61
Lassie, 221
Laudanum, 106
Learned behavior, 28, 136
Lenoski, Dr. E.F., 237
Letter of intent, 177
Lourdes High School, 73

Love, 20
    maternal, 43–53
Lust
    for baby, 43–53
    gendered nature of, 5–10

Maccoby, Eleanor Emmons, 137
MacIntyre, Alasdair, 144
Mackinnon, Catharine, 28
Mademoiselle, 31–32
Madison Square Garden, 7
Maine, Sir Henry, 160
Male
    behavior, 112
    -female equality, 70
    -female interaction, 27, 35–37, 119
    role, 121–23
Mann, Judy, 118
Man and Superman, 210
Margolis, Maxine, 86–87, 110–11
Marolies, Eva, 60
Marriage
    buying happiness, 41
    contract, 19–21, 210–11
    and divorce, 207–8, 191–209
    egalitarian, 129
    in general, 32–33, 48, 190, 209–15
    median age of, 254
    partners, 14, 26
Married men, 120
Marshner, Connie, 96
Masculinity, 123
Mason, Mary Ann, 12–13, 17, 29
Maternal
    bonding, 68–69, 85–87, 89, 92, 176,
        184, 238
    custody rule, 207
    desires, 51
    instability, 52
    love, 232
    role, devaluation of, 207
    See also Mother

McDonnell, Kathleen, 230
Mead, Margaret, 117
Medical University of South Carolina, 95
Men, capricious nature of, 16
Men and Marriage, 178
Midlife crisis, 48
Missouri v. Webster, 226
Monogamy, 34, 213
Moore, Terrence, 98
Moral rules, 39
More Joy of Sex, 267
Mother
  absence of, 128
  -child bonding, 68–69, 85–87, 89, 92, 176, 184, 238
  gratifications of, 59
  at home, 13
  and intimacy, 65–66
  in maltreating family, 245
  parenting, value of, 66
  role status of, 51–53, 57–70, 80–83
  single, 13
  spouse's attitude toward, 60
  as unwed teen, 128
  working, 71
Motherhood Report, 141
Mothers and Such, 86
Mothers on Trial, 206
Mother's Work, 99
My Little Ponies, 12
Myths of Gender, 135

Nannies, 103
Nassau Community College
  Family Life and Human Sexuality, 264
The Nation, 183
National Association of Surrogate Mothers, 169
National Center for Health Statistics, 33
National Enquirer, 166

National Review, 173, 186
Nazis, 70
Neely, Richard, 206–7
Negative Population Growth, Inc., 82
Neutral spouses, 41
New Age Doctrines, 152
New England Journal of Medicine, 95
New Man, 108–11, 126, 137, 207
New Other Woman, 35
New Republic, 224
Newsweek poll (1986), 62
New Woman, 62
New York Mercury, 90
New York Post, 4, 127, 264–65
New York Times, 33, 56, 82, 104, 127, 167, 198
Ney, Dr. Phillip, 238
Nicholi, Armand M., 128, 209
Nietzsche, Friedrich, 144–45, 148
No-fault divorce, 191–93
North, Oliver, 40
Not an Easy Choice, 230
Not possessive spouses, 41
Noyes, John Humphrey, 249–50
Null self, 153
Nurturing, 47

Oedipus complex, 68
Old Man, 109
Oneida commune, 179, 250
Oral contraceptives. *See* Contraception
Orbach, Susie, 119
Orgasm, 20
Other woman, 34–35
Over-population panic, 80–81

Parent
  -child relations, 90
  loss of, 198
  poor, 198–99
  rights of, 13, 184
  role of, 163–64, 171

work leave of, 64–65, 92–93
Parity, 62–63
Paternal role, 119
Pavek, Carol, 168–69
Pennsylvania State University College
    of Human Development, 202
Personal relationships, 158
Personhood, 220–22, 226, 229
Phaedrus, 265
Philosophy, 143
Plato, 265, 267
Polikoff, Nancy D., 207
Pollit, Katha, 183
Pope John Paul II, 258–59
Population police, 80
Pornography, 251–52, 254, 264
Possessive spouses, 25–26, 41
Potentiality, 230
Poverty, feminization of, 197
Pregnancy, 253, 261–62, 272
Premarital sex, 254
Pro-choice, 230
Probability formula, 272
Professional women, childless, 50
Prostitution, 182–83
Public policy, on sex, 21
Publishing guidelines, 8–9

Quality time, 127

Rand, Ayn, 221
Rape, 217, 253, 255–56
Raphael, Sally Jesse, 3
Rawls, John, 143
Reagan, Ronald, 181
Real self, 136
Red Cross, 172
Rejection, 42
Rekers, Dr. George, 114, 199–200
Relationship, 48–49
Re-Making of Love, 259
Reproduction of Mothering, 25, 57

Richardson, Laurel, 35, 37
Rivera, Geraldo, 165
River's Edge, 74
Rockford Institute, 94
Roe v. Wade, 220, 226
Roper poll, 68, 99
Rothenber, Dr. Michael, 104
Rousseau, 131
Russell, Diana, 217, 239
Rutgers University, 127

Saal, Frank, 36
Safe sex, 267
Saint Augustine, 258
Saint-Gaudens, Augustus, 7
Sanger M.D., Sirgay, 93
Sartre, 144–45
Schoolroom, 8–9
Schroeder, Pat, 57
Schuman, Dr. Stanley, 95–96
Schwartz, Pepper, 25–26, 122
Science and the Unborn, 223
Second Chances, 78–80
Second Sex, 92
Second Stage, 17
Secret Self, 130–52
Self-consciousness, 222–23
Selfhood, 153, 187
Self-respect, 30
Separate spheres, 7
Sex
    as appetite, 19, 21
    economics of, 139
    in general, 256, 269–71
    prevalence of, 4–8
    roles, 138–40, 142, 144, 151, 206,
        250
    uncommitted, 26
Sexual
    abuse, 238–39, 246
    difference, 40
    equality, 5, 9, 27
    etiquette, 8
    freedom, 16, 259

identity, 124
information, 10–11, 20
innuendo, 36–39
repression, 3–8, 10–11, 29–30, 131, 150–51, 252
revolution, 16–21, 40, 80, 130–31, 239, 251, 259, 264, 266–67
stereotypes, 141–42
Sex for One: the Joy of Selfloving, 263
Shalev, Carmel, 172
Shapiro, Jerold Lee, 122
Sharpton, Al, 223
Shaw, George Bernard, 210
Sills, Judith, 45
Single, 33
man, 120, 125
parent, 52, 78, 109, 111–12, 118, 162
women, 39
Skoloff, Gary, 167, 171
Smart Women/Foolish Choices, 16
Social
conditioning, 140
decay, 112
justice, 157–58
problems, 112
Social Justice, 143
Socio-biology, 134
Socrates, 271
Sodomy, 257
Sophisticated woman, 37–38
Sorkow, Judge, 166, 170, 182
Sovereign individual, 161
Sowell, Thomas, 173
Spock, Dr., 199, 255
Spock's (Dr.) Baby and Child Care, 104
Sports Illustrated, 4
Stalin, Joseph, 223
Star Trek, 255
Stein, Sara Bonnett, 140
Steinberg, Lawrence D., 98
Steinem, Gloria, 147
Sterling, Ann Fausto, 135
Stern, Betsy, 182
Stern, Melissa, 182

Stern, William, 165–67, 170, 182–83
Stillbirth, 245
Stole, Leo, 120
Stowe, Harriet Beecher, 101–2
Submissiveness, 30
Substitute caregivers, 102–3
Suicide rate, 76
Supreme Court, 207, 219–20
Surrogate mother
and Baby M case, 165–67
and Catholic church, 167
contract, 170–78, 181, 184–86
opposition to, 167–68
role of, 43, 162, 172–73, 184
Surrogate Parenting Associates, Inc., 177, 185
Surrogate Parenting Associates, Inc. v. Commonwealth of Kentucky, 177
Sutton, Jan, 169, 185
Swaddling, 89
Swaggart, Jimmy, 223
Sweden's parental leave policy, 64–65
Symposium, 265

Taboos, 9–10
Teen pregnancy, 128, 272–73
Terms, forbidden, 9
Tile Club, 7
Time budget studies, 110–11
Tolstoy, 183
Total woman, 70
Tower, John, 221
Traditional woman, 153

Uhlenberg, Peter, 75
Unilateral divorce, 193, 195–96, 205, 212, 214–15
University of Arizona, 94
University of Georgia, 200
University of Michigan Institute for Social Research, 127
University of Pennsylvania, 114

University of Santa Clara, 122
University of South Carolina School of
    Medicine, 114
University of Southern California, 237
Unwanted children, 245

Values, 145
Vatican, 173, 224–25
Victorian America, 7
Victorian in the Modern World, 131
Village Voice, 230
Violent death rate, 76
Vitz, Paul, 8

Wallerstein, Judith S., 78–80, 197,
    199–200, 202–5, 242
Washington Post, 4–5, 8, 46, 118, 178
    Magazine, 100
Wattenberg, Ben, 82–83
Wauk, John, 230
Weitzman, Lenore, 196
Wellesley College, 43, 59
Westheimer, Dr. Ruth, 40, 260
West Virginia Supreme Court of
    Appeals, 206–7
Wharton, Edith, 10–11
White, Sanford, 7
Whitehead, Mary Beth, 165–67, 171,
    175–76, 182
Whitehead, Rick, 182
Why Males Exist, 37

Wilde, Oscar, 263
Wilson, Edmund O., 133
Wojtyla, Karol, 258. *See also* Pope John
    Paul II
*The Woman Who Works, the Parent
    Who Cares*, 93
Women
    abandoned, 14
    without children, 13
    issues of, 13
    and work, 64, 105
Women's Legal Defense Fund
    Child Custody and Child Support
        Project, 207
Women's Ways of Knowing, 24
Women Who Love Too Much, 16
Working mothers
    cultural pressures on, 58
    and day care, 99–100
    in general, 9, 13, 44, 59, 61–62, 127
    spousal encouragement of, 45–46
Working wives, 121–23, 129
Wright, Robert, 133

Yale University, 226
    Law Journal, 171
Youth culture, 74
Yudof, Mark, 160

Zill, Nicholas, 113–14